THE BRITISH RIGHT

The British Right

Conservative and right wing politics in Britain

Edited by
NEILL NUGENT
Senior Lecturer in Politics
Manchester Polytechnic

ROGER KING
Principal Lecturer in Sociology
Huddersfield Polytechnic

 SAXON HOUSE

Published by
SAXON HOUSE, Teakfield Limited
Westmead, Farnborough, Hants., England

ISBN 0 566 00156 X
Library of Congress Catalog Card Number 76–58615

Printed in Great Britain by Biddles Ltd, Guildford, Surrey

Contents

Preface

It should be stated at the outset that it is not our claim to be presenting here a completely comprehensive account of right wing political activity in Britain. Even if it was supposed that the boundaries of 'the Right' could be accurately identified, such a task would involve a far weightier volume, or number of volumes, than ours.

What we do present are eight essays which not only give a flavour of the breadth of the British Right but also a focus on some of the central problems concerning its nature. The three parts have thus been deliberately constructed so as to direct the attention of the reader towards different aspects of the question: theoretical problems, contemporary mainstream 'rightism', and extremism.

The essays themselves have two sources. Some, notably those in the third section, arose out of long term research interests of the authors. Others were specifically written for the book. Overall we believe they result in a balance, not only in terms of the subject material, but also in terms of the perspectives taken.

Acknowledgements, where appropriate, appear in the individual chapters. We would however like to thank here Maureen Nugent who, despite frequent changes in deadlines, still typed most of the manuscript.

Neill Nugent
Roger King
January 1977

PART I

PROBLEMS OF IDENTIFICATION AND DEFINITION

1 Introduction: the concept of 'the Right'

R. BENNETT, R. KING, N. NUGENT

Any book or collection of essays that purports to cover a field of study or a set of associated themes denoted by a single generic term such as 'right wing', must try to justify, or at least explain, the use of the term. This is particularly necessary when the label is used to describe the number of diverse and wide-ranging essays included in this book. However, the task is by no means simple and perhaps only barely possible. As commonly used, the term is even more chameleon-like than most social science concepts, often blanketing more than it reveals. When used in conjunction with ill-defined prefixes such as 'radical' or 'extreme', clarity becomes highly problematical.

Not that the analysis of political ideologies and movements in terms of Left and Right is new. It is true that they were not commonly used in Britain until the early years of the twentieth century but their roots can be traced back to the early days of the French Revolution when deputies in the Assembly established the European custom of seating themselves from left to right, as seen from the president's chair, with the more radical and egalitarian to the left, and the more reactionary to the right. Nowadays the terms have become an essential part of the language of politics: for political analysts a simple shorthand method of scene-setting, for political participants labels that are sought or alternatively avoided at all costs.

With the language of politics plagued by vague catchwords and indeterminate phrases such as 'the common good', 'justice', 'equality', 'democracy', etc., and with virtually all political movements appealing, at a formal level, to such notions, it is extremely difficult to formulate criteria which clearly and unambiguously identify the Right. Problems arise precisely because people have differing conceptions of what constitutes 'justice', 'equality' or 'democracy'.

As a consequence of this conceptual confusion, some commentators have advocated that the terms Right and Left should be jettisoned altogether. Schapiro has asserted: 'There are probably no two terms in the language of politics which are more imprecise and subjective in the meanings which are attached to them than 'Left' and 'Right', and which are more misleading in their common usage . . . there is no illumination to be derived from the misleading 'Left–Right' classification'.[1] Brittan has devoted a whole book to the subject and argues strongly that the whole idea of a Left–Right spectrum is positively harmful, obscuring far more than it illuminates: 'It leads . . . to the muffling of important issues, to a bias in favour of certain viewpoints against others, and to the erection of unnecessary barriers between those who should be natural allies'.[2]

These writers, and others, thus maintain that the term 'right wing' is almost impossible to specify with any degree of exactitude, and that it has become so fleeting and elusive as to be virtually useless for analytical purposes. It is of interest that many of these writers also stress that they have become convinced of this view the more they have studied individuals, groups and ideas generally thought to be on the Right. As E. Weber states in his introduction to *The European Right*, '. . . the more we have inspected the image of the Right, the less sure we have become of what it is'.[3]

Perhaps the two greatest difficulties we face in our attempt to identify and classify the Right are: (a) distinguishing the differences in both ideology and social support that lie between groups, movements, or individuals generally regarded as being right wing, while at the same time finding a connecting principle that justifies placing them in this common category; and (b) justifying the frequent discrimination made between right wingers *per se* and *radical* rightists or right wing *extremists*.

In taking our first problem, a glance at the recent political history of right wing politics in most major Western societies reveals the criteria for labelling groups and movements 'rightist' to be vague indeed.

France, the country in which the terms originated and have been in common usage longest, illustrates some of the problems. Broadly speaking, Left and Right, until well into the nineteenth century, were identified by their differing attitudes towards the Revolution of 1789: the Left believing it to have heralded the dawn of a new and more enlightened era, the Right deploring the attack on monarchy, Church and nobility. Under these two banners, however, all shades of opinion and all manners of division were to be found. For the Right two questions in particular became sources of deep friction: could *certain* principles of 1789 be accepted?; was monarchism absolutely sacrosanct or could it be discarded if privilege and the Church remained unmolested under an alternative system? Because of disagreement on these questions there was firmly established in France not one Right but three when liberal democracy was launched in the 1870s: legitimism/traditionalism; Orleanism/liberalism; Bonapartism/authoritarianism.

The picture was further complicated as the republican system established itself in the last quarter of the nineteenth century, for the whole political

4

spectrum naturally moved leftwards. Many who had been on the Left had now achieved their aim and wished for no further reforms. At the same time many on the Right made their peace with republicanism and increasingly turned their attentions to resisting the emerging forces of socialism. Had it not been for the Dreyfus Affair, which saw all republicans, socialist or not, unite to resist the threat of Church and army, a major re-alignment might have taken place resulting in Left–Right politics being conducted primarily in terms of a socialist–capitalist debate. But that was not to be. The Affair inflamed dying issues and arguably was the major reason why the Left–Right spectrum in France continued, until after the Second World War, to be based on political and clerical questions as much as economic ones. Left and Right thus became increasingly elusive terms, as is exemplified by the behaviour of the Radical Party, a cornerstone of the Third and Fourth Republics. Left as regards the Republic, and Left on the clerical issue, it was also the most ardent proponent of limited government and non-State intervention in the social and economic life of the nation. Accordingly, on a number of occasions Radicals allied themselves with the socialist parties in general electoral agreements designed to defend the Republic, control the Church, or fight fascism. However when social and economic problems were raised unity vanished and they quickly moved towards the orthodox bourgeois parties – the so-called moderates. In the now time-honoured phrase, the Radicals had their hearts on the Left but their pocketbooks on the Right.

It is really only in the 1970s that the terms Left and Right have again come to have in France some use as tools of analysis and methods of description. As the main political and clerical questions have been solved, so again has the Left–Right spectrum become uni-dimensional. To be sure, there are still many shades of opinion and indeed a multi-party system but there is clearly one fundamental line of division. This is primarily economic in character and expresses itself, on the one hand, in the socialist and communist demands for greater collectivism and socialism, and, on the other, in the aim of the parties of the presidential majority to defend the status quo.

Similarly, in Britain the problems of identifying the Right are many, for there is no one monolithic block which is united on all or even most issues. Rather, there are diverse right wing groups and if the Right exists at all, then it is a house with many windows – ranging from the National Front, through 'Powellism', the Monday Club, and into traditional Toryism which has its boundaries located in the centre of British politics. Whilst all right wing theorists and politicians have deprecated the ideas and policies of the Left, they have done so for different reasons, and while they would all reject the grandiose claims made upon human reason and political activity as means of changing man and society, they would disagree as to just how far the government should intervene in the individual's life, and upon what basis. Thus, although all right wing groups agree on the need for drawing a line between the respective claims of State and citizen, they differ as to where it should be drawn, and upon the criteria to be employed. So, on one of the key questions of politics – the nature, grounds an1 extent of the citizen's obligation – there is no unified right wing response. Again, in the economic field those ideas traditionally classified as being Right range from the old style paternalism and *noblesse oblige* of Toryism, through present day corporatism, to the laissez faire neo-liberalism of various exponents of unfettered capitalism. Similarly, in the social sphere there is a spectrum which covers the self-professed moderation and humanitarianism of conservatism to the racially-imbued doctrines of the National Front. On constitutional matters too the Right embraces a range of opinion: from those who adhere rigidly to Parliament to those who consider it an outmoded institution. Indeed, the task of unity is exemplified by considering the very different ideas of Mosley and Powell, for while both have been classified as right wing their economic and constitutional theories are mutually exclusive – Powell advocating an abrasive capitalism unimpeded by government intervention, while being deeply committed to the basic procedures of parliamentary government, whereas Mosley's recipes have involved an inversion of Powell's prescriptions: large scale central direction of the economy, and a deep suspicion of parliamentary institutions.

The conceptual confusion has been compounded by the fact that the largest element of the British Right, the Conservative Party, cannot necessarily be considered as the political embodiment or expression of the philosophy of conservatism. The present day Conservative Party is a curious hybrid of liberalism and Toryism and contains many diverse and possibly conflicting groups, encompassing views barely distinguishable from the National Front at one end of the spectrum and views little different from the right wing of the Labour Party at the other.

Nor, as Lipset and Raab[4] have shown in the American context, is a right wing ideology the prerogative of any one social class. Whilst Runciman's statement that Left and Right is 'basically nothing other than the perennial argument between the poor and the rich' remains generally true, [5] Lipset and Raab suggest that the groups and movements on the radical Right are characterised as much by different types of social support as they are by their distinct ideologies. Wallace's appeal to the 'ordinary common man' in the 1968 Presidential campaign, which stressed the material and welfare rights of the working class, earned him support in areas and groups that was denied in 1964 to Goldwater, whose advocacy of economic conservatism and vigorous capitalism did not appeal to the 'pocketbook interests' of blue-collar workers, despite the similarity of both candidates' moral, 'nativistic', ideology.[6]

Ideological and sociological differences of this kind are similarly the essence of the second problem referred to above – distinguishing between the Right and the extreme Right. It is clear, for example, that whilst few would dissent from the placing of, say, the John Birch Society or the National Front on the far Right of the political spectrum in their respective countries, there would be no such consensus on figures such as Wallace, Goldwater, Powell or even Mosley. Thus Lipset and Raab appear to place Wallace but not Goldwater in the 'extreme' category, despite the fact that the former is closely identified with the more liberal Democratic Party, and the latter has long been regarded as a leading champion of the right wing Republicans.

The criterion taken by Lipset and Raab for prefixes such as radical and extremist is a procedural one. The Republican Party, for example, whilst committed to 'preservatism' – 'maintaining or narrowing lines of power and privilege' – nonetheless acts in accordance with pluralist rules. Radical or extreme Rightists, however, whilst still preservatist in ideological outlook in ways not dissimilar to those of the Republican Party, seek to impose a moral dogmatism by advocating 'the repression of differences and dissent', the closing down of the 'market place of ideas'. In Lipset and Raab's terminology, they are 'monist' or 'antipluralist'.[7] It boils down to a refusal to accept differences of interest and opinion, different centres of power, and the tendency to treat cleavage and ambivalence as illegitimate.

The problem with this formulation is that many on the so-called extreme Right, such as Wallace, the Populists, and possibly Powell, who is a strict upholder of parliamentary sovereignty, are quite happy to co-operate within democratic procedures. Conversely, the major parties are not averse at times to using extremist methods, viz. Watergate, or, indeed, to co-opting extremist policies if this means attracting more votes. This suggests that it may not just be an ideological criterion that determines the radical label, but also an organisational one. Views expressed within the membership of a major party may not damn a politician to the 'politics of unreason', whilst similar views promoted outside conventional electoral politics may well do so.

To come back now to the general problem, perhaps the greatest difficulty in contemporary usage of the term 'the Right' has been presented by the development of the modern twentieth century State and the concomitant responses and attitudes invoked amongst groups to the increasing encroachment of state planning in all aspects of society, especially the economy. With the associated problems of economic crises, international market competition, and the need for large scale investment and planning, many members of the Right have been faced with an ideological crisis. Whilst classical nineteenth-century Rightism could equate the national cause with economic laissez faire (and Bennett's contribution to the present work suggests a unique and identifiable British conservative tradition of thought with just this emphasis – see chapter 2), the development of the State together with a recurring pattern of crisis and poor performance in the international market, which appeared to necessitate centralised action by all nation states, has seen a reappraisal of the role of government by many on the Right. With its taint of socialism and regulation, this has by no means been easy. But some have seen in corporate state management of the economy the means for resurrecting a truly national partnership of estates and interests.

Increasingly, therefore, the Right has come to be defined in cultural terms, in the moral gloss and rhetoric with which it interprets the need for the economic decisions and social reforms that are frequently little different to those of the Left. Nationalism and partnership, not class or conflict, often become the distinguishing facets between Left and Right. Social reform and defence of Commonwealth or Empire become harnessed to perceived needs for tariff barriers and government intervention. As a result, a fervent nationalism may be matched by an almost 'socialist' economic programme, whether this be tariff reform, income policy, or state aid to industry. This strand, as Wilson and Phillips make clear in Part II, may be termed 'collectivism' and it is to be contrasted with the 'libertarian' response of reduced government expenditure and state interference that has long been seen by many on the Right as a central tenet of their political philosophy.

Consequently, when the narrowing of economic attitudes and alternatives is combined with the familiar problems of rhetoric – the common appeals to 'freedom', 'liberty' and 'sovereignty' by both Left and Right – it becomes increasingly difficult to distinguish a coherent and unambiguous set of right wing attitudes.

The term 'right wing' is possibly best accepted as an orientating concept that may provide in certain contexts a sensitising guide to a number of ideological attitudes. Generally, it is possible to isolate a cluster of inter-related concepts by which we can identify the Right. These are descriptive criteria, and a case can be made for their retention. Thus:

(1) The Left believes that classes and class struggles are the prime force of history, whereas the Right usually sees the nation, or possibly cultural or geographical phenomena, as the basic unit. This often implies a *strong nationalism or patriotism*, together with a concomitant propensity to dislike foreigners or immigrants and all perceived enemies of the nation. In its most extreme expression, the theme running through all the European fascist movements of the inter-war years was the almost Darwinian notion of the

organic unity of the nation, whether it was the rather romantic–nostalgic variety of the agrarian Eastern European societies or the more virulent biological racism and anti-semitism of German Nazism. In British and Italian fascism, the community ideology based on race was not as strong as that based on the concept of the State. But in all of these, class co-operation, harmony and *Gemeinschaft* were the overarching ideals.

(2) The Left is egalitarian, the Right is elitist. We tend to find not only *anti-egalitarianism* on the Right, but also the associated ideas of hierarchy, leadership, elitism, and often militarism. Perhaps one of the essential differences between fascists and conservatives is to be found in the source or the basis of anti-egalitarianism and hierarchy. For while such notions are of long standing, to be found in many conservative traditions, the essence of fascist versions is the establishment of *new* elites, based not on Church and Throne, or ownership of land or capital, but on service to party.

Some have argued that the fascist assertion of the hierarchical principle has resulted in the distinction between fascism and conservatism, between radical and reactionary rightism, becoming blurred, thus enhancing its fatal attraction to many conservatives in the years between the wars. Whether this is true or not, and despite the common advocacy of nationalism, hierarchy, leadership and elite, the two doctrines must be carefully distinguished. Conservatism prefers the status quo, looking to traditional regimes for its models. It is frequently patrician, discouraging activism and radicalism and the mobilisation of the masses. Fascism on the other hand positively seeks a mass base, it presents a radical ideology, and through a society mobilised by the fascist party it aims for fundamental political change involving the abolition of the institutional arrangements of the liberal democratic state – openly elected parliaments, political parties, pressure groups, trade unions etc.[8]

(3) The Left appeals to reason and man's rationality, whilst the Right sees man as a creature of passion. According to the Left, man is fundamentally good but corrupted and alienated by bad social, political, or economic institutions. Man is malleable, and mankind can be remade by a change in environment and education. In principle, man is perfectible. For the Right, however, man has a *fixed, constant human nature*: one cannot scrub the slate clean and start again because of inherent imperfections in mankind. The Left's argument is seen to be essentially contradictory, for unless the educators are singularly exempt from the corrupting influence of the old society, they are themselves tainted with its defects. Who educates the educators?

A case can be made out then for the retention of the Left–Right distinction as an ultimate philosophical difference. These considerations do not however lead in the direction of any one specific policy or common programme for the Right. Crucial differences of doctrine remain over practical political issues. The Right is more united in what it opposes than in what it proposes. All right wing theorists for example may be anti-egalitarian, but merely to state this can blur important differences in the type of elite advocated.

Again, although all right wing theorists reject the claims made on behalf of reason by left wing writers, they differ on the grounds offered for this rejection. For instance, Hume and Burke plot the limitations of reason by pointing to the fallibility of the human mind, and, with Taine, they stress the largely non-rational processes of thought. In contrast, however, fascism and national socialism make a cult of the irrational.

Consequently, whilst terms like Left and Right may be unavoidable and too deeply embedded in political language to ignore, their usage must be treated with the greatest care and be seen as frequently revealing more about the emotions and the prejudices of the writer than the combatants.

Notes

[1] L. Schapiro, *Totalitarianism*, Papermac, London 1972, p. 84.
[2] S. Brittan, *Left or Right The Bogus Dilemma*, Secker and Warburg, London 1968, p. 11.
[3] H. Rogger and E. Weber, *The European Right*, Weidenfeld and Nicolson, London 1965, p. 5.
[4] S. Lipset and E. Raab, *The Politics of Unreason; Right Wing Extremism in America 1790–1970*, Heinemann, London 1971.
[5] W. G. Runciman, *Social Science and Political Theory*, Cambridge University Press, Cambridge 1963, p. 149.
[6] Lipset and Raab, op. cit., chs. 9–10.
[7] Ibid., p. 6.
[8] These points are well made in P. Hayes, *Fascism*, Allen and Unwin, London 1973.

2 The Conservative tradition of thought: a right wing phenomenon?

R. J. BENNETT

A Tory philosopher cannot be wholly a Tory, but must often be a better Liberal than Liberals themselves; while he is the natural means of rescuing from oblivion truths which Tories have forgotten, and which the prevailing schools of Liberalism never knew.

J. S. Mill[1]

In a work which is primarily concerned with right wing movements, it is necessary at the outset to sound a note of caution. For, in the vocabulary of politics we deal with no fixed entities, and the dichotomy of 'Left' and 'Right' is built upon vagueness and imprecision. Specifically in the context of British history and politics the boundaries between 'Left' and 'Right' have been blurred, and the terms themselves have often been a substitute for, rather than a supplement to, clear analysis.

It is a basic contention of this chapter that there is a clearly discernible mainstream of British politics which derives in large measure from the nature of British conservatism.[2] It will be argued furthermore that British conservatism must be sharply distinguished from extreme right wing movements that draw upon fascist, racialist or nationalist theories. This might seem obvious, but it is a point worth making in connection with that growing form of student manicheism in which the political world is divided into goodies and baddies, and the term 'fascist' is applied indiscriminately to any political views with which one disagrees. In order to rectify this devaluation of the political currency it must be stated that the modes of thought employed by conservatives – their views on the nature of man, society and politics – place them in an entirely different category of political thought.

There is a curious uniqueness and insularity which permeates British conservatism, and in a sense it is essentially an 'English' phenomenon, with all the connotations of moderation, compromise and muddling through that the term implies and which makes it quite distinct from the rigidly authoritarian parties of the European Right.

The aim here is to trace some of the main reasons for this development. Before embarking on that theme, however, it should be observed that from a theoretical angle conservatism presents an immediate problem: whether there is such a thing as a conservative philosophy of politics. Conservatives themselves have often tried to place their ideas and beliefs on a different plane from communism, socialism, liberalism, fascism, etc. on the grounds that conservatism is not an ideology. Usually this takes the weak form of ascribing to politics a purely secondary or subordinate role in human affairs. In its stronger form this exhibits itself in what is virtually an apolitical stance. In the eyes of its exponents, conservatism differs from the other 'isms' precisely because of its anti-ideological nature, and this is underwritten by an abhorrence of the rationalism of ideological styles of thought. On this account, conservatism is a set of attitudes and dispositions rather than a fully-fledged political programme, and this serves to emphasise the basic problem of dealing with conservatism as a theory of politics. For by its very nature it appears elusive and amorphous. The more one tries to track down its hard core, the more insubstantial and shapeless it becomes. Thus as White observes:

> To put up Conservatism in a bottle with a label is like trying to liquify the atmosphere . . . the difficulty arises from the nature of the thing. For Conservatism is less a political doctrine than a habit of mind, a mode of feeling, a way of living [3]

The overarching difficulty, then, is that it seems impossible to isolate a set of basic, unambiguous, unchanging ideas which are adhered to in any consistent fashion. And it has been argued that conservatism is qualitatively different from all the other 'isms' precisely because it has no set body of doctrine, no fixed creed. As a consequence of this, it is difficult to state just what conservatism is, or what constitutes the 'essence' of conservatism. Indeed, in a historical perspective, one of the most notable features is the remarkable elasticity of conservative thought. This is probably the single most important factor to bear in mind when approaching conservatism: there appears to be no one thoroughgoing or uniform doctrine that all conservative theorists have unequivocally adopted.

In a recent article Greenleaf pushes this approach to its logical conclusion and argues that there is 'no single set of key concepts that must be called the core of the doctrine'.[4] In particular, Greenleaf attacks the standard textbook form of itemisation and rejects any attempt to single out *the* conservative view of religion, the nature of society etc., on the grounds that this whole procedure is too contrived and mechanical. He argues that there is no agreed shopping list of articles which can be ticked off in this way. Thus he writes

12

that 'it is too simple and artificial to say that conservatism above all can be reduced to a set of basic ideas because it is essentially static.[5]

The rationale behind this critique of the traditional style of classification is that such lists do not do justice to the diversity of reasons why different theorists and politicians have counted themselves conservatives. Moreover, according to Greenleaf, it would be possible to subscribe to such a list of vague generalities and not be a conservative at all. Historically, there is much *prima facie* evidence to support this interpretation. Various conservatives have described the 'essence' of conservatism, although they have often come up with different items and meant diverse things by it, e.g. the reversal of policy over Catholic emancipation, the Repeal of the Corn Laws, Tory hostility towards democracy in the nineteenth century contrasted with its self-professed present role as defender of democracy.

At face values these examples constitute strong supporting evidence for Greenleaf's assertion that there is no 'essence' of conservatism. It is also true that the alleged key concepts of conservative thought are vague and have to be 'programmatically cashed'. There is no single or simple relationship between political philosophy and political practice. Nevertheless, Greenleaf's approach is rather too cavalier in jettisoning such organising principles altogether, since it is possible to select four main elements in a distinctively conservative approach to politics and society, namely:

(1) A particular attitude towards political and social change,
(2) A dislike of abstract rationalism;
(3) A qualified pessimism as regards human nature; and
(4) The view that government is a limited, and primarily remedial, institution.

Of course, these features are still vague, but they are not totally vacuous. These four recurring themes in conservative thought do not, it is true, constitute clear, precise grounds for the adoption of any one policy in any given political situation. But they do delimit the kinds of considerations that conservatives will think appropriate in coming to a decision. At the very least they will act as general guidelines, and at best they will rule out certain proposals as being inherently un-conservative.

Greenleaf is correct in stressing that there is no monolithic unity to conservatism, and, in the most obvious sense, it cannot be reduced to one single pattern. But this is true of all the main ideologies such as communism, socialism and liberalism. They all have internal variations. What for instance, unites such diverse figures as Fox, Cobden, Mill, Lowe, Hobhouse and Lloyd George? Or Morris, Marx, Fourier, Lenin, Mao, Castro or Bevan?

Of course, then, there is a need to guard against flabby generalisations about conservatism, and for that matter about any system of political beliefs.

13

But equally one must guard against the opposite tendency: of qualifying the subject matter out of existence. Thus, while it is true to say that there are diverse strands of conservative thought, it is possible to disentangle a mainstream of conservatism. The basic elements of a distinctively conservative approach to politics, man and society can be found in a particular set of attitudes toward change – and this is intimately bound up with a particular conception of human nature, the role that reason and theory play in political matters, and the role of government.

It is true that this does not add up to an 'essence' of conservatism. But one of the most fundamental points to grasp is that conservatism does not consist of a set of substantive proposals that must be defended come what may, or a specific group of policies that must be implemented in order to bring about the conservative 'good society'. For, ultimately, conservatism is more concerned with the form or method of change than with the concrete objects of change. This is a constantly reiterated theme in the works of conservative theorists.

This attitude towards change – and those aspects internally related to it – can be seen especially in the writings of Edmund Burke, generally regarded by conservatives to be the father of their tradition of thought. The lack of a detailed consideration of Burke constitutes a major failing of Greenleaf's analysis, and yet it is no exaggeration (if one may paraphase Whitehead) to say that all accounts of conservatism have hitherto consisted of footnotes on Burke. Any adequate account of conservatism as a political theory must start with, and largely consist of, Burke's thought. This mitigates the rather nominalist account of conservatism that emerges in Greenleaf's article. For conservatism was forged in the furnace of the French Revolution and its aftermath, and it was this cataclysmic series of events which crystallised and brought to self-consciousness, in the writings of Burke, many disparate and inarticulate strands of past British experience. The rest of this chapter will therefore refer mainly to the late eighteenth century and the nineteenth century; it makes no pretence to cover all the significant figures up to the present day.

Burke

In him is contained all that is necessary to political salvation. 'Back to Burke' ought still to be our motto. Read and re-read the *Reflections on the Revolution in France*: this is an exercise that should be performed at least once a year.

T. E. Utley[6]

Burke's attitude to the specific issues of his day is underpinned by certain fundamental beliefs about human nature, change, and the role of theory in political questions. Conservatives, while conceding that change might often be necessary, argue that it must be gradual, evolutionary. Wholesale or revolutionary change is an impossibility because in politics men can never wipe the slate clean and start from scratch. The basis of this theory is that slow, but continual, change is a necessary ingredient of conservation. Burke saw no contradiction in his commitment to preservation and improvement; the one implied the other.

> We must all obey the great law of change. It is the most powerful law of nature, and the means perhaps of its conservation. All we can do, and that human wisdom can do, is to provide that the change shall proceed by insensible degrees. This has all the benefits which may be in change, without any of the inconveniences of mutation.[7]

Closely related to this attitude towards change we find Burke's reasons for rejecting abstract rationalism in politics. Change, when necessary, must be in accordance with the historical growth and development of institutions, customs and practices, and not based on *a priori* principles. Here Burke invoked a distinction between two different forms of reasoning: speculative and practical. As he saw it, practical political life could not be run by an abstract ideology or a set of premeditated ideas, or any blueprint of the ideal State. For political activity had to be grounded in, and derived from, experience and not generated by axioms or shreds or paper emanating from any would-be Newton of the political world. The whole bent of his mind was inductive, and he loathed the deductive political models devised by the philosophers of the Enlightenment and theorists of the French Revolution.

The cornerstone of Burke's whole attack upon the abstract rationalism of the Enlightenment was that politics is an art, not a science. The Englightenment philosophers had based their attempted reformation of society upon a method wholly inappropriate to social affairs. They were, according to Burke, applying the criteria and techniques that were appropriate to the exact sciences, and in particular the methods of geometry and mathematics, to the study of society and the result was inevitable confusion.

Politics for Burke can never be reduced to exact quantities and precise formulae because it involves qualitative factors and differences of time, place and circumstance.

Therefore one line of attack upon rationalist theories was that they were founded on an initial category mistake: a confusion between the abstract and the practical modes of reasoning. Burke proceeded to argue that such systems were built upon human vanity, and that in the long run they would be proven to be inexpedient, leading to anarchy and destruction.

Abstract blueprints of the good society are never practicable, according to Burke, because they necessitate a *tabula rasa*, destroying the inheritance of the past. Against this, Burke argued that politics can never be a blank sheet of infinite possibilities. Instead of destruction as a precondition for regeneration, Burke thought that the only sound way of changing society was to build upon the past. This point of contrast between conservatism and radical or revolutionary theories is expressed as follows:

> ... a true politician always considers how he shall make the most of the existing materials of his country. A disposition to preserve, and an ability to improve, taken together, would be my standard of a statesman.[8]

It is important to note that reason plays a dual role in Burke's philosophy. He denies the validity of the unchecked power of human reason in the speculative sense employed by the Enlightenment theorists, but he pits against it the notion of respect or reverence for the past, and especially the amassed wisdom of previous generations. This constitutes another basic and recurring theme in conservative thought – the contrast between the frailty of reason residing in the individual and the accumulated reason which is embodied in longstanding customs and institutions. This polarisation between rationalist theories, which emphasise the rational capacities of the individual, and conservative theories, which stress that such ideas are based upon a complete overestimation of man's rational faculties, has been a key criterion in helping to locate different political thinkers. Burke expresses the conservative view as follows:

> We are afraid to put men to live and trade each on his own private stock of reason; because we suspect that this stock in each man is small, and that the individuals would do better to avail themselves of the general bank and capital of nations and of ages.[9]

This view of the limited, partial nature of human reason forms the basis of Burke's approach to radical reform, and constitutes another fundamental facet of conservative thought. The theory he advances is that society is a very complex, interrelated system, there being no single key to unlock this complexity, no one solution for all political problems. Consequently, there are many dangers in tampering with the structure of society, or in attempting to bring about wholesale change, because such actions would lead inexorably to unforeseen consequences. Radical or revolutionary change is extremely precarious because it leads men into uncharted waters. Such change as is necessary must be pursued along the lines of conformity with the historical development of a society, and not by invoking abstract, absolute and untested theories. On Burke's analysis, change is necessary when it both preserves and extends the slowly accumulated character, spirit and tradition of a society, thus in particular, Burke argued that the French Revolution was doomed to failure. It constituted a direct break with the past in its attempt to re-model the social and political structure of French life on the basis of an abstract philosophy grounded in the 'rights of man'.

Burke thought there was a flaw or defect in the psychological make-up of revolutionaries and in a number of writings he offered an analysis of what he considered to be the tensions and paradoxes in the mentality of revolutionaries, pouring scorn upon their high-sounding yet hollow rhetoric. In particular, Burke contrasted their protestations of love for humanity in the abstract with a hatred of human beings in the flesh. They were concerned with Humanity, not human beings, Man, not men; and they would throw existing society into turmoil for the sake of uncertain future benefits. With more than a tinge of irony, Burke pinpoints the ambivalence in the revolutionaries' attitudes towards man thus:

> This sort of people are so taken up with their theories about the rights of man, that they have totally forgot his nature.[10]

Moreover, after the period of revolutionary optimism has subsided, and the era of humanity has not been ushered in, the present generation will be sacrificed in order to eradicate the imperfections of man. As Burke writes: 'Their humanity is at their horizon – and like the horizon, it always flies before them.'[11] Revolutionary theories, in their preoccupation with an ideal humanity, eventually come full circle: 'By hating vices too much, they come to love men too little.'[12] This critique of radicalism is crucial in the development of conservative thought.

In contrast with the delusive optimism of radicals and revolutionaries, Burke's attitude, like that of most other conservatives, is grounded in the Christian concept of human nature, with its emphasis upon Original Sin – man's inherent fallibility, frailty and infirmity. Human perfectibility cannot be attained in this world: 'That man thinks too highly, and therefore he thinks weakly and delusively, of any contrivance of human wisdom, who believes that it can make any sort of approach to perfection.'[13] This pessimism acts as a counterweight to optimistic radicalism, and Burke argues that the authors of such theories commit the sin of pride which, 'when full grown . . . is the worst of vices.'[14] The presumption of a perfect humanity in this life is an act of impiety: 'He censures God who quarrels with the imperfections of man.'[15]

In contrast with premeditated schemes for human perfection that leave actual human beings out of their calculation, Burke thinks that at best we can only aim for limited human improvement. All substantive proposals for political good are tempered by considerations of time, place and circumstance. There is no one correct form of government, derived from *a priori* foundations. Questions concerning human affairs 'cannot be settled upon abstract rule; and nothing is so foolish as to discuss them upon that principle.'[16] It is worth stressing that while Burke has no truck with any golden age of the future, neither does he seek refuge in some illusory golden past. Nothing is fixed, static, absolute. Even Burke's abhorrence of democracy is hedged with qualifications and he concedes that there may be circumstances in which democracy is legitimate.

Now Burke's ideas can be seen as the highest articulation of distinctively conservative principles. Conservatism, in the sense of an explicit, self-conscious, philosophy of politics, emerged as a counter-movement to the optimistic rationalism of the Englightenment and French Revolution. As Sabine asserted:

> The point is not, of course, that before Burke there was no conservatism, but it is almost true to say that there was no conservative philosophy.[17]

This belief in gradual, evolutionary change, based upon a rejection of abstract rationalism, a recognition of human imperfection, and the consequent need for improvement rather than innovation, forms the groundwork of all subsequent conservative theory, clearly demarcates conservatism from radical right wing ideologies, and forms the cornerstone of conservative attacks upon various forms of rationalism – Benthamite utilitarianism, socialism, communism, etc.

Nineteenth century conservative thought

Nineteenth century conservative thought is conditioned by the Enlightenment and the French Revolution. Writers such as Coleridge, Wordsworth and Southey who first supported the French Revolution subsequently became disenchanted with the movement. Coleridge rejected the Jacobin–radical view that man is basically good and the fault lies with imperfect institutions. Like Burke, he saw the Jacobins as being concerned with Humanity rather than human beings, though he recognised the need for continuous adaptation, change and reform. He expressed it as the need to balance the two great paramount interests of society, the forces of 'permanence' and 'progression'.[18] The overriding aim of this reconciliation was:

> to preserve the stores, to guard the treasures of past civilization, and

thus to bind the present with the past; to perfect and add to the same, and thus to connect the present with the future.[19]

This sense of tradition, of continuity between past and future is basic to conservative thought. Thomas Carlyle saw it as a major constituent of the English temperament:

> In our wildest periods of reform . . . you notice always the invincible instinct to hold fast by the Old; to admit the minimum of New; to expand, if it be possible, some old habit or method, already found fruitful, into new growth for the new need . . . The Future hereby is not disserved from the Past, but based continuously on it; grows with all the vitalities of the Past, and is rooted down deep into the beginnings of us.[20]

This fundamentally Burkean belief in ordered change, based on the principle of historical growth, is given its best expression by Disraeli in a speech at Edinburgh, October 1897:

> In a progressive country change is constant and the great question is not whether you should resist change which is inevitable, but whether that change should be carried out in deference to the manners, the customs, the laws and the traditions of a people or whether it should be carried out in deference to abstract principles and arbitrary and general doctrines.[21]

This quotation illustrates the threads of continuity in conservative thought. Further elucidation of this theme is unnecessary, as the substance of this position has merely been repeated by later conservative thinkers. Whether this attitude towards change, and those features of belief allied to it, constitutes a hard core of conservatism is more problematic. Greenleaf, for instance, points out that conservatism has a 'dual inheritance'[22] of 'two opposing tendencies',[23] libertarianism and collectivism. It is important though to emphasise the fact that the collectivist strand is older and that conservatism has primarily upheld the authority of the State. As Cecil expressed it, 'the tradition of authority is naturally a Tory tradition.'[24]

Conservative collectivism

> It has been regularly the conservatives who have compromised with socialism and stolen its thunder.
>
> F. A. Hayek[25]

19

The mainstream of conservatism has always been collectivist and paternalistic in basis, and again this has had a profound impact upon the course of British history in the nineteenth and twentieth centuries. Moreover, it helps us to distinguish conservatism as a political philosophy from extreme right wing ideologies such as fascism, nationalism or racialism. For, as Levin observes, 'it was the conservatives who first provided a comprehensive critique of capitalism'.[26]

In recent years a number of conservatives have attacked the 'unacceptable face of capitalism'. In 1947 Anthony Eden stated that:

> We are not a Party of unbridled, brutal capitalism, and never have been . . . We are not the political children of the 'laissez-faire' school. We opposed them decade after decade.[27]

Similarly, Harold Macmillan stated in 1936 that 'toryism has always been a form of paternal socialism'.[28] Again, R. A. Butler and other 'progressive' conservatives have been accused of 'pink' or 'creeping' or 'milk and water' socialism. But as Butler puts it: 'if my brand of Conservatism was unorthodox, I was committing heresy in remarkably good company'.[29] Indeed, in a historical perspective, Butler is quite correct in making this assertion, and he cites Bolingbroke, Burke and Disraeli as examples of this political ancestry.

This further pinpoints the notion of balance at the core of the Tory philosophy. In the nineteenth century conservatives attacked the doctrine of laissez faire whilst defending individual freedom; in the twentieth century they attack what they consider the excesses of socialism whilst admitting the principle of state intervention. In both cases their primary target is a doctrinaire abstract theory which erroneously purports to be universal in application. Yet they reconcile this distrust of all-embracing formulae with the extraction of valuable elements from both doctrines. In Baldwin's pointed phrase, 'Socialism and *laissez faire* are like the north and south poles. They don't really exist.'[30]

This theory of balance was employed against the abstract Liberal philosophy of freedom in the nineteenth century, and some of the most vociferous critics of the growth of unrestrained capitalism were Tory humanitarians – Lord Shaftesbury, Richard Oastler, John Wood, Coleridge, Disraeli, and members of the Young England movement. These figures instigated the campaigns for the abolition of the slave trade, factory and colliery legislation, the abolition of child labour, and so on. Shaftesbury considered his chief opponent on the question of collectivist legislation to be the radical laissez faire Liberal, John Bright, for even in the late 1880s Bright rejected the principle of legal restriction of working hours. Disraeli enunciated the principle that 'labour also has its rights as well as its duties'[31] in a speech to his constituents in 1843. He announced in 1848 that 'our study will be constantly to promote the welfare of the people of this country.'[32] The best expressions of this commitment to social reform are found in Disraeli's famous speeches at Manchester and Crystal Palace in 1872, in which he re-asserted that one of the great objects of conservatism was 'the elevation of the people . . . the time has arrived when social, and not political improvement is the object.'[33]

Recent commentators have called into question Disraeli's motives for the legislative programme of the 1874–80 administration, which included a Public Health Act, the Artisans' Dwelling Act, the Sale of Food and Drugs Act, the Rivers' Pollution Act, the Plimsoll Line Act, trade union legislation, etc. Disraeli himself claimed of his actions with regard to the 1867 Reform Act that 'I had to prepare the mind of the country and . . . to educate our party'.[34] Harris describes this as 'colourful rhetoric',[35] and Blake and Smith have both argued that Disraeli did not implement some far-seeing Tory philosophy which stretches back to the days of the Young England movement in the 1830s, but merely responded to the situation facing him with a series of *ad hoc* measures.[36]

Whatever the relative merits of this debate, the fact remains that conservatism was sufficiently pliable (whether on principle or for considerations of pure pragmatism) to move with changing circumstances and to act as a bridge between the agrarian past and an increasingly industrialised future. Moreover, it is interesting to observe the differences between Tories and 'libertarians' on the vexed issue of collectivist legislation. For their conflicting attitudes towards the proper role of the State are grounded in different conceptions of liberty. Libertarians (Whigs?) postulate a sharp, clear distinction between individualism and collectivism, as if they were mutually exclusive whereas this is considered a false dichotomy in the perspective of traditional Tories who see state intervention as being not only consistent with liberty, but an essential prerequisite of it. Indeed, collectivist legislation has been justified as a means of redressing a loss of liberty on the part of one section of the community, or as a precondition for any meaningful freedom. This was clearly the way in which Lord Shaftesbury construed the question of collectivism, and he regarded such laws as an enlargement rather than an abridgment of liberty.

As Shaftesbury saw it, the 'freedom' which was the catchphrase of Liberals and Whigs of his own time was a mock, hollow, or purely formal freedom: freedom for the pike to devour the minnows.

Thus Greenleaf's whole categorisation of two distinct strands of conservatism is question-begging, for what he describes as the libertarian strand is, in fact, neo-liberalism masquerading as conservatism. This issue of

21

collectivist legislation (whether in the social sphere, as in the nineteenth century, or as more recently in terms of government intervention in the running of the economy) is one of the key criteria for distinguishing between conservatives proper, and the political offspring of the Manchester School – Herbert Spencer, Ernest Benn, Peregrine Worsthorne, Enoch Powell, and various contemporary advocates of a free market economy. Tory thinkers have never had any objections *in principle* to the notion of intervention, whereas freedom from governmental interference has been a cardinal point in the libertarian creed. And whilst many libertarians seek refuge within the confines of the Conservative Party (and Greenleaf is quite correct in noting the tensions and ambivalence within the Party), one can legitimately ask whether this can be counted as 'tory' at all in the philosophical sense. For it carries all the hallmarks of Manchester liberalism rather than the pedigree of toryism in the traditional mould. Howell writes of the need 'to keep business attitudes and business folklore – the *laissez-faire* Whiggery in the modern Conservative Party – in a proper subordinate relationship to Tory national policy',[37] and he refers to this kind of thinking as 'Manchesterismus, the very antithesis of Toryism'.[38] To put this another way: the definition of conservatism employed in this article (as a manner of thinking, a philosophy of politics) possibly excludes some members of the Conservative Party, and probably includes many who are not members of that organisation. Conservatism is neither co-terminous nor synonymous with the Conservative Party, and the failure to disentangle the two has been a constant source of confusion.

Conclusion: a philosophy of balance

While at first sight conservatism might appear to be amorphous or diffuse, on closer inspection it is possible to extricate a mainstream of conservative thought. This posits a coherent philosophy of politics, man and society which reaches its apotheosis in the writings of Burke and is reiterated in the works of such figures as Coleridge and Disraeli. Conservatism revolves around a distinctive conception of reason and human nature. It implies a suspicion and rejection of abstract theory; a belief that politics is the realm of experience, not experimentation. It emphasises the concrete, the historical, the inductive as opposed to the deductive. Political theories have to be accommodated to existing humanity and not vice versa. Its theory of human nature is pessimistic and sceptical in tone, although not cynical. Man is seen as a frail, fallible creature. Whether or not this theory is underpinned by religious or theological considerations, it implies that a perfect, unalienated humanity is a myth which cannot be attained by tinkering with external social arrangements. According to the conservative, the radical worldview which attributes social evils solely to forms of government and faulty institutions is a facile view of man. Hence there are no blueprints for the conservative 'good society' because conservatives have no conception of an ideal society, no all-embracing panaceas. As Oakeshott puts it, they prefer 'present laughter to utopian bliss'.[39] Trouble arises when men try to implement their ideals and dreams at the societal level: 'What has always made the state a hell on earth has been precisely that man has tried to make it his heaven.'[40]

Thus, although it might be difficult to assert just what the conservative attitude might be in any specific situation, nevertheless we can exclude certain political stances, given the basic assumptions and presuppositions that are made by conservatives. We can state what is not conservatism: conservatism is anti-radical and anti-utopian, and any attempt to bring heaven down to earth is rejected as being illusory. This de-limits the type of criteria that conservatives will bring to bear on any concrete issue, although it does not state in advance exactly what their policy would be.

Conservatism, in the eyes of its exponents, is a disposition, not a doctrine. Much less is it a dogma. It is a philosophy based upon a series of tensions: a dialectic of authority and freedom; collectivism and individualism; permanence and progress; past and present; continuity and change. It is synthetic in nature; a philosophy of eclecticism, a theory of balance. In its negative form it stresses the need to avoid excesses and extremes; absolutism and anarchy. In short, it is a philosophy of equipoise, gradualism, or, as Burke puts it, 'the two principles of conservation and correction.'[41]

Notes

[1] 'Essay on Coleridge', in *Mill on Bentham and Coleridge*, edited by F. R. Leavis, Chatto and Windus, London 1967, p. 167.
[2] It should be noted that this chapter is concerned with conservatism as a political theory and not primarily as political practice. The extent to which the rhetoric corresponds to the reality lies outside its scope, although a certain degree of congruence is noted in passing. Moreover, although reference will be made to the Conservative Party, conservatism as a way of thinking about politics is not confined to that party; 'conservatism' and the 'Conservative Party' are therefore not treated as synonymous, for conservatism transcends party boundaries and embraces a number of figures who might not accept the specific policies or the political programme of the Conservative Party.

[3] R. J. White, *The Conservative Tradition*, Black, London 1950, p. 1.

[4] W. H. Greenleaf, 'Modern British Conservatism', in R. Benewick, R. N. Berki, B. Parekh (eds), *Knowledge and Belief in Politics*, Allen and Unwin, London 1973, p. 173.

[5] Ibid.

[6] T. E. Utley, 'The State and the Individual', in *The Good Society*, Conservative Political Centre, London 1953, p. 41.

[7] Edmund Burke, *Works of Burke*, Oxford University Press, London 1906, vol. 5, pp. 206–7.

[8] Burke, *Reflections on the Revolution in France*, Pelican Classics, London 1968, pp. 266–7.

[9] Ibid., p. 183.

[10] Ibid., p. 156.

[11] Burke, 'Letter to a Noble Lord' (1796), *Works*, vol. 6, pp. 70–1.

[12] Burke, *Reflections*, p. 283.

[13] Burke, 'Speech on a Bill for Shortening the Duration of Parliaments', *Works*, vol. 3, p. 338.

[14] Burke, *Works*, vol. 4, p. 298.

[15] Burke, 'Speech at Bristol Previous to the Election' (1780), *Works*, vol. 3, p. 4.

[16] Burke, *Reflections*, p. 151.

[17] G. H. Sabine, *History of Political Theory*, Methuen, London 1937, p. 317.

[18] Coleridge, *On the Constitutions of Church and State* (1830), Everyman ed., London 1972, p. 6.

[19] Ibid., p. 34.

[20] T. Carlyle, *Past and Present* (1843), Everyman ed., London 1970, p. 258.

[21] Cited in T. E. Kebbel (ed.), *Speeches of the Earl of Beaconsfield*, Longmans, London 1881, vol. 2, p. 487.

[22] Greenleaf, op. cit., p. 184.

[23] Ibid., p. 181.

[24] H. Cecil, *Conservatism*, Home University Library, London 1912, p. 247.

[25] F. A. Hayek, *The Constitution of Liberty*, Routledge and Kegan Paul, London 1960, pp. 398–9.

[26] M. Levin (ed.), 'Marxism and Romanticism: Marx's Debt to German Conservatism', in *Political Studies*, vol. 22, no. 4, December 1974, p. 413.

[27] A. Eden, in *The New Conservatism*, Conservative Political Centre, London 1955, pp. 11–12.

[28] Quoted in A. Sampson, *Macmillan*, Pelican, London 1967, p. 36. Indeed N. Harris, in *Beliefs and Society*, Watts, London 1967, p. 117,

argues that Macmillan's proposals in *The Middle Way* (1938) were more radical than the 1945 Labour government's plans.

[29]   R. A. Butler, *The Art of the Possible*, Penguin, London 1971, p. 136.

[30]   Quoted in K. Middlemas and J. Barnes, *Baldwin: A Biography*, Weidenfeld and Nicholson, London 1969, p. 208.

[31]   Kebbel, op. cit., vol. 1, p. 52.

[32]   Ibid., vol. 2, p. 468.

[33]   E. Boyle (ed.), *Tory Democrat: Two Famous Disraeli Speeches*, Conservative Political Centre, London 1960, p. 46 and p. 48.

[34]   Kebbel, op. cit., vol. 2, p. 479.

[35]   N. Harris, *Competition and the Corporate Society*, University Paperback, London 1973, p. 286.

[36]   R. Blake, *Disraeli*, Eyre and Spottiswoode, London 1966; and P. Smith, *Disraelian Conservatism and Social Reform*, Routledge and Kegan Paul, London 1968.

[37]   D. Howell, 'Modern conservatism in search of its principles', *Crossbow*, July–September 1963, p. 22.

[38]   Ibid., p. 25.

[39]   See M. Oakeshott, 'On being conservative', in *Rationalism in Politics*, University Paperback, London 1967, p. 169. Unfortunately, there is not space here to examine Oakeshott's relationship with conservative thought. Readers are referred to *Rationalism in Politics* and also *Oakeshott's philosophical politics*, Longmans, London 1966.

[40]   Hölderlin, quoted in F. A. Hayek, *The Road to Serfdom*, Routledge and Kegan Paul, London 1962, p. 18.

[41]   Burke, *Reflections*, p. 106.

PART II

MODERN CONSERVATISM

3 The Conservative Party: from Macmillan to Thatcher*

KEN PHILLIPS and MIKE WILSON

After many years of relative neglect, the Conservative Party has, of late, attracted renewed interest among students of contemporary British politics. This is in part a reflection of a number of significant developments within the Party and it is with those that have occurred during the period from the start of Macmillan's leadership in 1957 to the present day that this chapter is principally concerned.

Central to these developments has been the change in the Party's electoral position. Its claim to be 'the party of government' has been undermined by recent electoral performances and doubts have arisen concerning its future electoral prospects. Accompanying this decline the Party has suffered a significant fall in its membership, but attempts to boost this and to improve its social representativeness have met with little success. While the traditionally elitist background of the Party's parliamentary leadership continues to be gradually eroded, more dramatic developments have occurred with regard to the selection and social background of the Party Leader.

Of the various elements of the Party under examination here, it is the organisation that has remained most clearly unaltered, although considerable effort has been expended to make it more efficient. This stability is highlighted by the failure of attempts to make it more democratic.

In examining the policies of the Conservative Party from Macmillan to Thatcher an obvious scenario suggests itself. The first element of this is the camouflaged retreat from world power status in the policies adopted in the post-Suez situation, the retreat from Empire, and entry into the European Economic Community as the new role for a post-imperial Britain. The second element is the Party's attempts to present itself as the successful manager of the economy. In the first instance this took the form of continuing expenditure within the social democratic consensus together with physical planning when this consensus began to get into difficulties at the start of the 1960s. However, when these approaches, whether by Conservative or Labour governments, seemed to be having little effect on Britain's economic performance, or on the rapidly rising inflation rate, the Conservative Party increasingly turned away

* We are grateful to Michael Moran for his comments on an early draft of this chapter.

29

from such consensus and moved to the right. This initially involved state disengagement, a philosophy of less government, and attacks on the trade unions as economic monopolies. After the aberration of 1972–74 this progress towards the right has continued apace. The only major alteration in this policy is that the solution to Britain's economic ills is now seen to lie not in the cul-de-sac of confrontation with the trade unions[1] but in the reduction of public expenditure – the main source of domestic inflation. A development and examination of this brief scenario is the central concern of this chapter.

Two years after his selection as Party Leader and Prime Minister in 1957, Harold Macmillan led his Party to an overwhelming general election victory. With the Labour Party divided, the Conservative Party's third successive election victory seemed to hold out the possibility of an undefeated Conservative government leading Britain into the twenty-first century.[2] From the contemporary perspective such prognostications seem particularly unfortunate. Table 3.1 makes clear that since 1959 the Conservative Party has suffered a

Table 3.1

The performance of the Conservative Party in general elections,
1950 to October 1974

	1950	1951	1955	1959	1964	1966	1970	Feb. 1974	Oct. 1974
% of votes cast for Party	43·5	48·0	49·7	49·4	43·4	41·9	46·4	37·9	35·8
No. of seats gained in House of Commons	298	321	344	365	304	253	330	297	277
% of seats in House of Commons	47·7	51·4	54·8	57·9	48·3	40·2	52·4	46·8	43·6

Source: D. Butler and A. Sloman, *British Political Facts 1900–75*, Macmillan, London, 1975, pp. 184–5.

dramatic change in its electoral fortunes. Of the five elections since the post-war peak of 1959, the Conservatives have won only one. Comparing electoral strengths in 1959 and October 1974, the Party has seen its percentage of the poll fall from nearly 50 per cent to 35·8 per cent,[3] and its share of seats in the House of Commons decline from 57·9 per cent to 43·6 per cent, despite the advantages of the electoral system to the major parties.

While in 1959 the Party saw itself, and perhaps was seen by the electorate, as the natural party of government, such a claim would attract little credibility today. In the twenty years from 1957 to 1977 the Conservatives were in power for almost twelve, but of the six general elections of the period they won only two. Electorally, the two major parties are now much more closely matched.

Behind these broad electoral statistics lies a mass of data and competing analyses which are beyond the scope of this chapter. But there are two particular facets of voting behaviour that are of importance in describing the present position of the Conservative Party. The first concerns the identification of the voters with one or other of the political parties. While not an accurate guide to electoral behaviour, the strength of identification is relevant to the longer term nature of the party system. What has become evident in recent times is that the proportion of the electorate that identifies strongly with the two major parties has dramatically declined. In 1964 opinion poll surveys indicated that around 40 per cent of the electorate were very strong Labour or Conservative partisans. By 1974 the proportion had dropped to 24 per cent, and after the referendum on the Common Market it had fallen even lower, to a mere 17 per cent. The Conservative Party, alongside the Labour Party, appears to be losing its battle to win the hearts and minds of the electorate and needs to look with increasing trepidation to future general elections.

The other aspect of voting behaviour that is of relevance to the present study concerns the decline in the class alignment of voters to the two major parties. Studies of voting behaviour have shown the Conservative Party to have a much wider class-based electorate than the Labour Party and this has supported the Tories' long-held claim to be a 'One Nation' party. During the 1950s and early 1960s the Conservative Party attracted about one-third of the working-class vote together with three-quarters of the middle-class vote. And, as Table 3.2 indicates, the 1970 general election demonstrated a similar pattern with the Conservatives attracting about 79 per cent of the middle-class vote (IPA classifications AB); 59 per cent of the lower middle-class (C1); 35 per cent of skilled working-class (C2); and 33 per cent of the unskilled and welfare dependants (DE). The two elections of 1974, and particularly that of February, however, indicate an important change in the traditional pattern: the Conservative Party is losing its hold of the middle-class vote. Table 3.2 clearly shows that there was a disproportionate swing against the Tories from among the middle-class voters. Between the 1970 and February 1974 elections the Conservatives suffered a decline of 16.1 per cent amongst these voters, compared to declines of 8·2 per cent, 8·6 per cent and 11·2 per cent from the other social groups. While the data in Table 3.2 might be taken as demonstrating a general weakening of class alignment in voting, it also shows that it is changes in the class basis of the Conservative vote that largely account for this. The declining vote of the different classes for the Labour Party is much more evenly spread. And it is of particular significance that the Conservative Party suffered its greatest defection from the ranks of the middle-class in an

Table 3.2

Voting allegiance and social class,
general elections 1964 to October 1974 (%)

		Social class		
	Middle class (AB)	Lower-middle (C1)	Skilled working (C2)	Unskilled and 'very poor' (DE)
October 1974:				
Conservative	38·7	67·3	51·4	30·1	24·6
Labour	38·0	10·4	21·3	47·2	53·7
Difference	+0·7	+56·9	+30·1	−17·1	−29·1
February 1974:				
Conservative	36·0	63·0	51·0	26·0	22·0
Labour	39·0	12·0	24·0	49·0	57·0
Difference	−3·0	+51·0	+27·0	−23·0	−35·0
1970				
Conservative	46·2	79·1	59·2	34·6	33·2
Labour	43·8	10·4	30·5	55·4	57·3
Difference	+2·4	+68·7	+28·7	−20·8	−24·1
1966:				
Conservative	41·4	72·2	58·8	32·4	26·3
Labour	48·7	15.5	29·9	58·5	65·2
Difference	−7·3	+56·7	+28·9	−26·1	−38·9
1964:				
Conservative	43·0	74·7	60·7	33·9	30·9
Labour	44·8	8·9	24·8	54·4	59·1
Difference	−1·8	+65·8	+35·9	−20·5	−28·2

Source: Based on Nuffield General Election Studies.

election in which there was a clear appeal from the Conservative Government to class politics.

At the same time as experiencing these changes in its electoral performance and appeal, other marked changes occurred in the *membership* of the Conservative Party both outside and within Parliament.

The most apparent development concerning the membership of the Conservative Party's mass organisation, the National Union, has been the dramatic fall in its size – a fate which has been shared by the Labour Party. Statistics on party membership are virtually non-existent but figures for membership in the period 1953–54 and 1969–70 appear to be accepted as fairly authoritative. In 1953 the Conservative Party publicly announced a national membership of 2,805,832 – the highest figure ever recorded. This figure, however, was somewhat inflated because it followed a year-long membership campaign, and a private investigation the following year suggested that membership had settled at $2\frac{1}{4}$ million. As part of their research for the 1970 general election study, the Nuffield team surveyed a sample of Conservative Associations and their findings suggest that membership in the year 1969–70 had fallen to between $1\frac{1}{4}$ and $1\frac{1}{2}$ million. There is nothing to suggest that the figure has since risen, and in all probability it has fallen even further.

It is even more difficult to discover the social background of party members, but local studies on the topic have consistently found that Conservative Associations consist predominantly of businessmen, professional and managerial workers. In a private poll of March 1966, Central Office also found that members of the Conservative Party were most commonly self-employed, and that the bulk of these self-employed members were small traders. Furthermore, in terms of sex, women members were more numerous than men, whilst the elderly, too, were well over-represented. That these findings caused concern among party leaders is evident by the implementation of two special campaigns in 1967. The first, 'Project '67', was designed to encourage constituency associations to make their membership more socially representative, with particular regard to the composition of committees. But the scheme appears to have met with little success, not least because of the resistance of many constituency leaders. The reticence of the latter to widen the net of active Conservative members is also demonstrated by the failure of Central Office to establish successful working-class organisations within the Party either at national or local level. In the early 1960s attempts were made to improve trade union organisation within the Party, but these met with little success and, in the view of some of those involved, this failure was marked by the decision in 1967 to wind up the post of trade union organiser at the area level. One observer of this aspect of the Conservative Party's organisation has summed the situation up as follows:

If the working class Conservative has retained his voting allegiance, this success has not been achieved in any real sense as a result of the contribution made by the Party's working class organisations, but rather in spite of their failure to develop a meaningful level of activity. In the long run it is constituency resistence to working class integration which has triumphed. Years of opposition in the face of Central Office pressure weakened the organisation, and finally left it too weak to resist once Central Office itself decided to discontinue the fight.[4]

The Party has also seemed unable to attract the number of young people that it enjoyed at the end of the 1940s. Membership of the Young Conservatives has been put at 157,000 in 1949. Ten years later it had declined to 80,000 and by 1968 was as low as 50,000. The latest figure given is significant because in 1966 the Conservative Conference adopted a parallel campaign to 'Project '67' called 'Action '67' which was designed to boost membership of the Young Conservatives. The project, which ran until spring 1967, had been given the target of achieving a membership of $\frac{1}{4}$ million by Edward Du Cann, the Party Chairman. But it achieved only the limited success of raising membership to 62,000 by the end of 1967 and, as we have seen from the membership figure for 1968, its impact was shortlived.

A similar kind of concern regarding the social composition of the Party is evident in the matter of selection of parliamentary candidates. Following the election defeat of 1964, the Party Chairman instituted a review of the Central Office roster of candidates. But he let it be understood that this would be more than the customary exercise. His aim was to achieve a much more fundamental redrawing of the list in order to achieve 'a younger, more broadly based and more widely representative list of candidates'. But this exercise, too, appears to have been thwarted by the resistance of local associations and in the 1970 election there was little perceivable difference in the age, education and occupation of candidates compared to other post-war elections. This conclusion is supported by an examination of the social background of Conservative MPs.

Table 3.3, based on the Nuffield General Election Studies research, outlines the changing social structure of the Conservative Party in the House of Commons from 1959 to October 1974. The only significant trend shown in the table is the gradual increase in the proportion of Conservative MPs with a university education. But it has been argued that the numbers of representatives of some of the older professions – notably law and the armed forces – have declined at the expense of the newer professions of teaching and journalism.[5]

The Conservative Party has been likened to a pyramid in which each level from Party membership to the Party leadership becomes more and more socially unrepresentative of the Conservative electorate. Towards the apex of this pyramid the marked difference between Conservative Party MPs and

Table 3.3

Changing social structure of the Conservative Party in the House of Commons, 1959 to October 1974

	1959	1964	1966	1970	Feb. 1974	Oct. 1974
Public school education (%)	72	75	80	74	74	75
University education (%)	60	63	67	69	67	69
Professional or business background (%)	76	74	75	76	77	78
Working-class occupational background (%)	1	1	1	1	1	1
Median age (years)	48	45	48	48	48	47
Women (no.)	12	11	7	15	9	7

Source: Based on Nuffield General Election Studies.

Conservative Cabinet ministers has been frequently noted.[6] Table 3.4 provides a detailed analysis of the social background of Conservative Cabinet ministers from 1957 onwards, including the 1975 Shadow Cabinet of Margaret Thatcher. The latter contrasts in interesting ways with earlier Conservative Cabinets. In certain respects it conforms to general trends: there is little difference in the mean age of its members; it represents a continuation of the declining proportion of Conservative Cabinet members with an aristocratic background; and, rather dramatically, it continues the trend for an increasing proportion to have had an occupational background in law. In other ways, however, it departs from earlier patterns: the Thatcher Shadow Cabinet has reversed the trend towards a decreasing proportion of members with an elite public school educational background, and Cambridge graduates have finally overtaken their Oxford colleagues. Perhaps more significantly, the present Shadow Cabinet has the smallest proportion of members with an occupational background in business.

All these various statistics, however, hide one very important detail concerning the relationship between backbenchers and their parliamentary leaders: the social background of the leader. Both Macmillan and Douglas Home embodied the elite tradition in the leadership of the Party – a tradition which has been seen as even creating a social gap within the Cabinet itself.[7] But to some extent that has all changed. The two latest leaders of the Conservative Party since 1965 can claim to have come from relatively humble origins and to have had only a grammar school education.

Table 3.4

Social structure of Conservative Cabinets January 1957 to February 1974
and the 1975 Shadow Cabinet of Mrs Thatcher

	Macmillan Jan. 1957	Home Oct. 1963	Heath June 1970	Heath Feb. 1974	Thatcher 1975
Total no.	19	23	18	23	20
Mean age	50	56	52	53	52
School (%):					
Eton	36·8	47·8	22·2	26·1	35·0
Other Clarendon public schools	21·1	13·1	22·2	17·4	20·0
Other public, grammar	42·1	39·1	55·6	56·5	45·0
University (%):					
Oxford	42·1	56·5	55·6	52·2	40·0
Cambridge	36·8	13·1	27·7	28·6	45·0
None	15·8	30·4	16·7	21·7	15·0
Occupation (%):					
Barrister	26·3	39·1	38·9	39·1	50·0
Lecturer	5·3	4·3	–	–	–
Journalist	5·3	–	5·6	–	10·0
Medical	5·3	–	–	–	–
Civil Service	10·5	13·1	16·7	8·7	–
Business	31·6	21·7	16·7	30·4	10·0
Farmer, landowner	10·5	4·3	16·7	13·0	10·0
Military	–	13·1	5·6	8·7	20·0
Engineering	–	4·3	–	–	–
Not known	5·3	–	–	–	–
Aristrocratic* (%)	31·6	30·4	33·3	26·1	20·0

* Aristocratic background is distinguished here on the basis of parents' possession of an hereditary title.
Source: Data obtained from various editions of *Who's Who*.

One obvious, but by no means sole, explanation for this dramatic change in the social background of the leader lies in changes in the method of selection. Considerable disquiet followed the selection of Sir Alec Douglas Home in 1963 by the traditional method of 'emergence' following private soundings by the leadership – selection by the 'magic circle' as it was dubbed. In its place Home introduced, in February 1965, a new procedure by which the leader would be elected on the basis of balloting members of the Party in the House of Commons. The new procedure allowed for the possibility of three ballots. To win on the first ballot a candidate is required not only to gain an overall majority but also a lead of 15 per cent over his nearest rival. If no candidate is successful in the first ballot, a second is held for which new candidates can be nominated and in which the winning candidate is merely required to gain an overall majority. If a third ballot is necessary, it is restricted to the three leading candidates and the gaining of an overall majority is ensured by a system of transferable voting. When Home retired in 1965, the first use of the new election procedure resulted in the election of Heath.

Two deficiencies in this procedure were later discovered. Following considerable disillusionment with Heath's leadership after the two election defeats of 1974, it became very apparent that the procedure allowed no formal challenge to a leader who refused to resign. The procedure also allowed for no formal participation by the mass membership. Accordingly, and under pressure from the Party, Heath, in November 1974, appointed Home, the architect of the original scheme, to head a commission of Party leaders to suggest changes. Their recommendations were accepted by Heath and although they embody no major changes in the election method they do allow for annual re-elections of the leader and for soundings of the mass membership to be reported to Conservative MPs through the 1922 Committee. Heath therefore subjected himself to re-election in February 1975 and in the first ballot could gain only 119 votes to Margaret Thatcher's 130. He decided not to stand in the second ballot but four further nominations were received – those of Whitelaw, Howe, Prior and Peyton. The new candidates, however, could only gain 79, 19, 19 and 11 votes respectively which was insufficient to stop Mrs Thatcher, with 146 votes, easily gaining an overall victory to become the first woman leader of a major British party.

The election procedure adopted in 1965 and revised ten years later was by far the most important organisational change in the Party during the period under examination. (It will be argued later that it was one of the few factors that have had a fundamental effect on the nature of the Party itself.) Other organisational changes have occurred but with only limited impact.

There was indeed little interest or stimulus during the thirteen years in office from 1951 to 1964. The Party, or at least its leaders, were preoccupied with the problems of government and in any case extensive modernisation had recently taken place. This had followed the report of a committee of inquiry into party organisation under the chairmanship of Sir David Maxwell-Fyfe, which had been set up by the National Union after the 1945 election defeat.

One result of the relative stagnation of the organisation from 1951 was that by 1964 it was commonly felt that a serious gulf had opened up between the different segments of the Party: between the leadership and backbenchers; and between the parliamentary Party, the administrative machine of Central Office and the constituency associations. But the factor that made this gulf particularly disturbing and in need of serious attention was its threat to the Party when it found itself in opposition. Electoral defeat is invariably the occasion for political parties to re-examine themselves and this is especially true of the Tories. The Maxwell-Fyfe inquiry has already been mentioned. The election defeat of 1964 was followed by an equally far-reaching attempt at reform but without the fanfare of a full-scale commission of inquiry.[8] There were three main areas of concern: the social representativeness of Party members in and out of Parliament; the structure of the organisation; and the Party's policy-making process. The various schemes designed to make the Party more socially representative, and their very limited impact, have already been discussed. Concentrating now on the other two aspects of organisational change, it will be seen that they demonstrate the at times opposing forces of integration, economy, centralisation and democratisation.

Changes in the top personnel of Central Office have been amongst the most important structural changes that have occurred since 1964. Home was responsible for the appointment of one of the Party's principal fulltime professionals – Sir Michael Fraser – to a new post of Deputy Party Chairman. His general task was to act as the lynchpin between the Chairman of the Party and the fulltime bureaucracy and to co-ordinate policy and organisation. In the latter respect his specific task was the integration of research and publicity, which had become increasingly isolated from each other. One way in which this was achieved was by bringing the Conservative Political Centre more fully into Central Office. Heath carried this process of rationalisation through by abolishing, in 1966, the two posts of General Director and Chief Organisation Officer and thus gave equal status to the four major branches of Central Office – research, political education, publicity and finance.

These personnel changes at the top levels of Central Office were to remain largely intact until the electoral defeat in February 1974 led to their re-appraisal. In March of that year, Heath recreated the post of Director-General which he had abolished in 1965 and gave it to one of his most trusted political servants, Michael Wolff, as Heath's earlier changes had not achieved the desired degree of integration within the Party bureaucracy. Wolff was not to have long to accomplish his task because when Mrs Thatcher assumed the leadership she embarked upon a clean sweep of the major offices of the Party. In what was seen by many as a 'purge' of Heathites, Thatcher replaced Wolff with William Clark MP who, though relatively unknown, had played an important part in her leadership campaign.

The need for economy, which was evidenced by a successful special appeal to raise £2 million under the guidance of Lord Carrington between 1967 and 1969, also led to some pruning of officers in Central Office following a review by a management consultancy team. More importantly, in 1967, it led to a reduction of staff in the area offices of the Central Union. This was accomplished by amalgamating the three separate area posts of publicity officer, trade union organiser and CPC officer into a new post of deputy area agent.

The intention of this reform was also to encourage greater integration of these essentially connected responsibilities.

The need for economy also encouraged the development of new budgetary procedures in 1966. Mrs Thatcher's appointment of Lord Thorneycroft as Party Chairman in 1975 is likely to lead to further developments in this area and further cuts in personnel at Central Office have followed the renewed financial plight of the Party following the expense of the two elections fought in 1974.

The efforts made by Central Office to revise their list of parliamentary candidates, discussed earlier, can be seen as an attempt to exert greater pressure on constituency associations. So too were efforts to integrate the city associations into the area structure of the Party. These previously all-powerful and prestigious bodies became particularly tarnished after the election defeats of 1964 and 1966, not least because of their disastrous electoral performance and their increasingly embarrassing financial position. The Party Chairman, following the 1966 election, established a committee under Lord Brooke of Cumnor to examine the position of these associations. The recommendations of this committee to integrate the city associations into the area structure of the Party was strongly resented by the city associations. That they were able to resist the proposal until their own financial and organisational difficulties forced them one by one (with the exception of Manchester) to concede is evidence of the limited influence of Central Office on the constituencies.

More recently a working party under Reginald Eyre MP, set up by the new Party Chairman Lord Thorneycroft, has recommended that five new Central Office areas be created for the conurbations. That the problems of the Conservative Party in these areas have by no means been solved is indicated in a confidential report from the North West Area suggesting that if recent electoral trends in Greater Manchester continue, the Party 'could be virtually wiped off the political map so far as parliamentary representation is concerned.'[9]

Two further moves to reform the structure of the Party were initiated following the general election victory in 1970. The first concerned the recruitment of constituency agents. An inquiry by a committee chaired by Lord Chelmer in 1965 had led to an improvement in the pay and status of constituency agents, but the 1970 establishment of 386 fulltime agents was considerably less than the 421 that were employed in 1966. The solution adopted to stem the increasing number of resignations among experienced agents has been the gradual introduction of a scheme for the central employment of agents. This has been described as 'the major organisational change in the Conservative Party during 1970–3'.[10] It can also be seen as another step towards centralisation since it provides for greater leverage on constituency associations from the central and area offices.

While the major changes in the structure of the Party since 1964 examined so far have been primarily concerned with such things as economy, integration and centralisation, the most far-reaching inquiry into Party organisation has been concerned, at least in its origins, with democratisation.[11] Motions submitted to the Party's annual conference during the years of opposition consistently included a number calling for the reform of the Party structure. Particularly vocal in calling for such reforms have been the Young Conservatives, and especially a group from the Greater London branch. Reform of the procedures for candidate selection has included a number of major demands: the introduction of primaries, the establishment of permanent selection committees at the constituency level, and the accountability of the Standing Advisory Committee on Candidates to the National Union. Other suggested reforms have been for a greater emphasis on political affairs in the National Union and constituency associations, the election of shadow cabinets by the Parliamentary Party, and the election of Party officials by the National Union.

These pressures culminated in a successful resolution at the October 1969 meeting of the Central Council which led directly to the National Union Executive Committee establishing, in June 1970, a committee under Lord Chelmer 'to carry out an investigation into the extent, if any, to which the Conservative Party in all its aspects outside Parliament might be made more democratic'.

In carrying out its terms of reference the committee gave precedence to the question of candidate selection. In an interim report in 1971 it proposed that only candidates on the SACC approved list could be considered for selection and that this list should be reviewed constantly. While it rejected the idea of primaries, the committee did support the idea of permanent constituency selection committees. It also reasserted the right of constituency associations to consider alternative candidates to their sitting MP.

The response of MPs and constituency associations was hostile to those aspects of the recommendations that served to weaken their traditional positions and as a result each of the committee's proposals were so diluted that little effective change resulted.

In its final report, the committee made important recommendations designed to strengthen the political activities of the National Union and constituency associations (with regard to the latter by the introduction of constituency political committees to replace trade union advisory committees). Virtually nothing, however, was recommended about making the officers of the Party more accountable to annual conferences. But even these limited recommendations were eventually thwarted by internal division within the National Union. Seyd has summed the whole exercise up in the following way:

The committee produced a set of proposals, radical in the context of Conservative politics, which were successfully opposed by an alliance of people committed to the belief that the Party activist should play little part in policy deliberations . . . in its internal affairs [the Party] maintained the hierarchical and elitist structure established in the days of its aristocratic composition.[12]

It should be remembered, however, that the Chelmer Committee sat during a period in which the Party was in government. It is likely that fresh voices will be added to the cry for democratisation now that the Party is again in opposition. An early indication of this, again from the Young Conservatives, was strongly voiced criticism of the new procedures for electing the Party leader which were seen as giving an insignificant role to the constituency members. During the February leadership election they called for the establishment of an electoral college to include representatives of the voluntary side of the Party.

Another area in which demands for democratisation are likely to continue is with regard to the policy-making process within the Party. A number of important developments have already occurred in this field. On the one hand there have been changes in the official machinery of policy-making, on the other a significant alteration in the informal influences on Party policy-making.

From the election defeat of 1964 onwards, extensive machinery was built up to feed into the policy-making process within the Party the views of the electorate, grass roots membership, experts and backbenchers. Concerning the electorate, it was accepted in 1964 that the Conservative Party had made far less use of survey research than the Labour Party. In addition to their previous use of National Opinion Poll data, the Party in early 1965 commissioned a wellknown private polling organisation – ORC – to provide them with greater knowledge of how they were viewed by the electorate and to identify those voters crucial for a Conservative electoral victory.

An attempt to canvas membership opinion was undertaken by the Conservative Political Centre which encouraged the formation of constituency discussion groups who were regularly sent topics on which they were asked to report back. Their reports were amassed and passed on to the Party leadership by Central Office. In the opinion of Butler and Pinto-Duschinsky, the CPC's Contact Programme, as it was called, 'scarcely made a great impact'.[13] Nevertheless between 300 and 400 discussion groups regularly reported back to Central Office between 1966 and 1970.

Party conferences also played some part in the formal policy-making process but, as already indicated, there was a feeling within the Party that there was room for considerable improvements in this respect. There are signs, however, that the annual conference has become more vociferous during the years following 1964. Perhaps in anticipation of such a development, Heath on attaining the leadership broke with tradition and regularly appeared throughout conference. Another indication of this change in the nature of the conference is the number of motions put to a ballot. A ballot may be requested by the members of conference – standing order 11 states that a ballot shall be called if 100 members stand to request one – or alternatively it may be instigated from the platform where a show of hands indicates a close vote. In both instances the calling of a ballot suggests that a significant proportion of the conference is out of accord with the views of the platform who seek to gain as great a unanimity of voting as possible. Between 1950 and 1966 no ballot was held, although Lord Salisbury attempted unsuccessfully to have one taken on a motion concerning Rhodesia in 1965. Subsequently they have been more common. In 1967 a ballot was held on a motion opposing Rhodesian sanctions. In 1969 three ballots were held – on law and order, immigration and the EEC. No ballot was taken in 1970 but one was held in each of the next three years on the EEC, immigration and capital punishment respectively. There was no conference in 1974 and in the 1975 conference no ballots were called. By far the most comprehensive development in the formal policy-making machinery was, however, the extensive use of the Party's Policy Advisory Committee and its various policy committees which were initiated by Home and further developed by Heath.[14].

However, Heath's policy review exercise cannot be claimed as innovative; R. A. Butler, for example, was responsible for a similar exercise after 1945. But what is peculiar to the Heath exercise was the emphasis on detail and attention to the means of implementing agreed policies. And to support this emphasis, the Party's research department, which provided both information and secretarial assistance to the policy committees, was expanded and more fully integrated into Central Office. It has been suggested that Heath's attention to detail and means 'was to enable him to show that, in lieu of fundamental ideological change, he could run the government more efficiently than the Labour Party.'[15]

Following the election defeat of February 1974 a similar exercise was re-instituted by Heath and since then between 60 and 70 groups have been operating. Mrs Thatcher has not abandoned the procedure but has placed her nominee, Sir Keith Joseph, in the vital position of chairman of the PAC, and Angus Maude MP has been appointed chairman of the research department.

Just as the party conference has become more vociferous in its attitude to its part in Party policy-making, so too have members of the Parliamentary Party. One of the main manifestations of this has been changes in the number and nature of unofficial party groups. In a seminal work on this subject Rose concluded that the Conservative Party was a party of tendencies rather than factions – of *ad hoc* issue groups rather than permanent programmatic groups.[16] Events since 1964, however, might be taken as bringing this conclusion into question.

The best known of Conservative unofficial groups is the Monday Club which was established in 1961 to act as a ginger group within the Party, largely on matters concerning the government's African policies. From a small London-based clique, it became transformed after 1964 into a national organisation with a mass membership and broadened its policy platform to a general campaign in favour of libertarian Conservative policies. To this end it has centred its activities on Conservative constituency associations in order to pressurise individual Conservative MPs to support its cause and to support friendly candidates in the selection process.[17] It has also been instrumental in putting its views before conference by organising the submission of resolutions. In conclusion to a detailed study of the Monday Club, Seyd has written that '[It] is a manifestation of something new within the Conservative Party and something which is altering the whole style of conservative intra-party conflict.'[18]

One of the original reasons for the institution of the Monday Club was a desire to counteract an influential group which was considered to be on the 'left' of the Party – the Bow Group. Formed ten years earlier, the Bow Group saw itself not as a pressure group within the Party but as an intellectual channel for discussion and research.[19] It has, however, built up a fairly large membership and in 1975 could boast about 50 MPs amongst its membership of 1,000. Perhaps in reaction to the Monday Club, it has attempted to exert some influence in candidate selection.[20] But, insofar as it is possible to detect change in a body which does not express a corporate view, its traditional place in the spectrum of Conservative Party thinking appears to have shifted significantly since 1974. Certain recent publications suggest that first under the chairmanship of Peter Lilley and now under Patricia Hodgson, the Group has become more stridently right-wing with a greater acceptance of monetary economics, less expression of 'social concern', and appeals for a greater sense of national purpose. The Group has disowned Heath (in earlier days a favourite) and has turned its allegiance towards Powell and Joseph.[21]

But though the Monday Club and the Bow Group are the best known of the 'unofficial' Tory groups, they by no means have the field to themselves. The Selsdon Group, for example, exists to foster the spirit of the 1970 election manifesto and to denounce the abandonment between 1970 and 1974 of so many of its provisions. Perhaps a body that will take up the traditional mantle of the Bow Group will be the Tory Reform Group. Set up in September 1975, it incorporates three smaller groups of earlier years – Pressure for Economic and Social Toryism (PEST), the Social Tory Action Group, and the Macleod Group. From the members of the 1970–74 Heath administration it contains Peter Walker (Patron), Lord Carr (Chairman of Trustees), and Nicholas Scott (President) among its senior members. Another group recently established is the Centre for Policy Studies, a new Conservative research organisation under the control of Sir Keith Joseph, wedded to the cause of 'the social market economy'.

Consequently, there has been a bifurcation of unofficial groups within the Party, each searching for comprehensive programmes of policy embodying their particular brand of Conservative principle. Broadly speaking however, and apart from the Tory Reform Group, they share a similar orientation towards libertarian Conservatism.

One final indicator of unofficial pressure on the Party's policy-making process is the extent of back bench dissension. Earlier studies have found that few Conservative backbenchers are persistently out of accord with Party policy in Parliament. In the 1940s and 1950s only a very small minority of Conservative MPs consistently defied their front bench. In the 1959 parliamentary session, Jackson found that only 5 per cent used dissident action more than five times in the life of that session.[22] But a more recent study by Norton demonstrates that the extent of rebelliousness increased dramatically during the life of the 1970 Conservative government. Following an exhaustive study of the subject of dissension in the House of Commons, Norton draws out the following salient features of Conservative dissension between 1970 and 1974:

(1) *The Government was actually defeated on five occasions as a result of dissenting votes (plus abstentions) cast by its own backbenchers.* This is without precedent in the post-war history of Parliament.

(2) The majority of Government backbenchers proved willing, if necessary, to vote individually against the Government on a whipped vote. In the Session 1970–4, *two-thirds* of Conservative backbenchers actually voted against the whips on at least one occasion, despite the Government's small majority; twelve members each voted against the Government in 50 or more divisions. J. E. Powell voted against the Government in 113 whipped divisions, 10% of the total of all divisions.[23]

His research also led him to see a connection between increased dissension and the role of informal Party groups. In his view, these groups 'were more clearly defined and persistent than had been the case in previous Parliaments.'[24]

It is against this background of electoral, social, and organisational change that we must now assess the development of Party policy. Attention will be directed towards the two areas which have most exercised the minds of Party policy-makers, namely relationships with the outside world and the management of the economy.

To begin with the former, the Suez fiasco together with the decolonisation of the British Empire were, in the words of Hugh Fraser, 'traumatic' for the Conservatives,[25] for they implied a retreat from great power status, although not surprisingly this was not publicly recognised as such by the Party. That this was accompanied with only a relatively mild Party upheaval was due (particularly in the immediate post-Suez period) in no small measure to the skill of Macmillan. He was able to fill what were (for the Conservative Party) potentially dangerous vacuums with new symbolic concepts of Britain's supposed importance in world politics. There was, for example, the introduction of the concept of a British mediating influence on international affairs. Through this Macmillan hoped that Britain – as a medium-sized power, yet with all the diplomatic experience, contacts and prestige of its recent great power status – could exercise an important placatory influence on the tensions between East and West, not to mention those between the 'new' Afro-Asian countries and the older established countries. The means through which he sought to achieve such influence were, firstly, through a very personalised form of foreign policy, as seen in personal contacts and summit conferences between the world's leaders, and secondly, by the pursuit of agreements to limit armaments and stop nuclear testing. The results of these methods were, in the latter case, particularly successful – the test ban treaty of 1963 was widely regarded as one of the greatest of his diplomatic achievements. However, the results of his personalised foreign policy were not always those that he intended, as is illustrated by the collapse of the 1960 summit conference at Vienna and the subsequent Berlin crisis of the following year.

Nevertheless, such a policy was not only popular with the electorate but also with his own party, as can be seen from motions to the party conferences of 1958, 1960 and 1961.[26] Moreover, to a party suffering acutely from the national humiliation of Suez he offered the additional balm of what Sampson has illuminatingly called 'the smokescreen of a mushroom cloud'[27] – an independent nuclear deterrent. This smokescreen was important in a number of respects. Firstly, it convinced the Party that in any disarmament talks Great Britain was negotiating from a 'position of strength'. Secondly, it appeared to secure some form of independence from the USA in the sphere of foreign policy. Finally, and most important, it convinced the Party in the aftermath of Suez (and for many years after) that it was the key to Great Britain remaining a world power.[28]

Macmillan's policy on the dissolution of the Empire was more fraught with difficulty in terms of reaction within the Party. How could it be otherwise when for most Conservatives 'the Empire [was] their most important ideological symbol'.[29] Indeed, Gamble further states that 'some Conservative MPs have barely recognised that a domestic politics existed at all.'[30]

Nevertheless, Macmillan's Commonwealth tour of 1958 and the development of his concept of a looser multiracial commonwealth of equals as the natural successor to the Empire were developments which, with the help of notable lieutenants such as Iain Macleod, helped to smooth the transition. His 'Wind of Change' speech – delivered to the South African Parliament in 1960 – did not, however, have the same effect, at least amongst the newly emergent Commonwealth countries. Indeed, it has been seen as an important factor in encouraging 'some of the new members of the Commonwealth to strike a dramatic pose as the guardians of the rights of man' at the Commonwealth Conference in 1961.[31] The undoubted target of such a posture was the somewhat anomalous (in terms of a Commonwealth devoted to racial equality) State of South Africa. Nevertheless, it is surely attributing too much importance to a single occasion to see in it *the* cause of South Africa's subsequent withdrawal from the Commonwealth in 1961. It is even more melodramatic to attribute, as Kilmuir does, the posture of 'some new members of the Commonwealth' solely to the 'Wind of Change' speech.[32]

Yet although Macmillan was 'distressed' at this development it was not an emotion that deeply permeated the Party during the early 1960s. Party activists, aided by up and coming young MPs such as Peter Walker, continued their practice of submitting to conference motions which called for Britain to foster more unity within the Commonwealth; calls which were occasionally bracketed with pleas for more British investment in the Commonwealth. These demands for more investment should not, however, always be taken at face value, as they occasionally acted as a palliative, to accompany calls for the prevention of coloured immigration into Britain.[33]

Coloured immigration and South Africa were two of the factors which were to play an important part in souring a large section of the Party against the Commonwealth and which were consequently to weaken resistance against attempts by the Conservative leadership to take Britain into the EEC. However, gut reaction to these two issues really awaited the catalysts of Rhodesia and Powell. During the late 1950s and early 1960s they were only visible in the form of the occasional motion deploring the 'humiliating' attacks on British foreign policy in the United Nations by the newly emerging countries. The United Nations has, in fact, never evoked much warmth of feeling either from the Party as a whole or from Conservative overseas spokesmen such as Sir Alec Douglas Home. Nevertheless, the latent hostility towards the organisation, which occasionally erupted during times of 'imperial problems' (e.g. Suez and Rhodesia), was capable of being hypocritically submerged when Britain faced the much more dangerous enemy of the Soviet Union.[34]

During this period the Commonwealth was still viewed favourably. Indeed, in 1961, when Macmillan announced his intention of seeking British membership of the EEC, the number of motions to conference which were suspicious of the EEC and greatly worried about the consequences of entry for the Commonwealth – not to mention the straightforward motions against entry and for a stronger Commonwealth – vastly outnumbered the pro-EEC motions. After a year's mobilisation of opinion by the Party leadership the position was partially reversed at the next Party Conference. Not surprisingly, after de Gaulle's rebuff, the 1963 motions showed a return to a preponderant inclination towards strengthening Commonwealth ties.

The attempt to achieve EEC membership was, of course, the last of the three major foreign policy developments associated with Macmillan's premiership. The three have together been described as Macmillan's 'Grand Design'.[35] The first stage of this Design is held to be Macmillan's intention to retreat from world status, submit to American leadership in the fight against communism, and to reassure the USA that there would be no more independent nuclear moves in return for American nuclear protection and a privileged place in the councils of the Western Alliance. The second stage was to wind up the colonial Empire, in particular in Africa, whose mounting cost now far outran the economic advantages of protected markets for trade and investment. The third stage was to negotiate entry into the EEC, where Britain's trade was growing fast.

This is a neat and powerful case. However, there are several factors which disturb the symmetry of the argument. Firstly, as we have seen, there was a commitment to an independent nuclear deterrent. That it failed, and that Macmillan had to go cap in hand to Kennedy at Nassau in order to secure the American Polaris missile, was hardly a result of strategic planning but rather an *ad hoc* reaction to the setback of the cancellation of Blue Streak due to prohibitive development costs and obsolescent design. Secondly, although the costs of running the Empire were high, Macmillan's government was accepting the logic of the new nationalisms and was running down large conventional forces overseas. Britain would then have been left with only its trading links with the Commonwealth to worry about. These links were still more valuable in 1961 than those with the EEC. Indeed, there is evidence to suggest that if Macmillan had achieved an industrial free trade area agreement with the EEC in 1958 (a move which had been initiated by the Eden government), then a move towards full integration with the EEC might have been avoided.[36]

As it was, French resistance to Britain's determination to protect her Commonwealth agricultural and primary products trade was, according to Macmillan in his memoirs, an important factor in the breakdown of the talks. Thus, although Macmillan's application for fullscale membership of the EEC can be presented as part of a long term economic strategy, one should not neglect the short term political and economic factors behind his decision. Particularly important examples of the latter were the deteriorating diplomatic situation in Europe following the collapse of the 1960 summit; the troubles of the British economy which had begun to appear in the same year; and the domestic political difficulties of an old and tired government losing its momentum and with it a number of important by-elections. Though Macmillan had learnt the lesson of Suez, which was that foreign policy initiatives were impossible without economic strength, most of the evidence of his memoirs suggests that international political considerations of a defensive hue were uppermost in his mind – as they appeared to be with the Americans, who supported British entry.[37]

Macmillan's chief European lieutenant at this time was, of course, Edward Heath. It is interesting that then, as later, similar political considerations of international defence played an important part in Heath's desire to achieve a united Western Europe. But Heath was much more of a European than Macmillan in that he saw Europe as a more complete third force rival power to the USA as well as to the USSR. A good example of this was to be seen not only in his desire before 1970 to revive a British presence east of Suez but also in his plan to develop an Anglo-French nuclear force. However, neither of these plans survived the acid test of power for very long and he was forced to realise, like Pompidou, that the drive for European independence had shifted from nuclear defence to monetary and economic policy.[38]

On achieving power he was not unhappy to do this, particularly in view of his disengagement and competition policy for the British economy. This had first been revealed when he steamrollered the abolition of resale price maintenance through the Commons in 1964. Now he was to be given a much broader stage and he saw in the EEC laws supporting competition and attacking restrictive practices the ideal solvent for sluggish British industry. However, from 1965 to 1970 the Party as a whole was not as enthusiastic about entry into the EEC as their leader, particularly in 1968 and 1969 after the rejection of Britain's second application. 1965 and 1970 were the exceptions – though here there were special political factors obtruding, namely his election to the leadership and his general election victory. However, even in 1970 affirmative motions (twenty-two) were very nearly counterbalanced by those which were suspicious and hostile (seventeen).

Nevertheless, whilst this tepid reaction might have been an obstacle to

Heath in his desire to educate his Party towards a pro-European position, he could take heart from the other developments within the Party. Firstly, there was the surprising fact that, despite the picture of rank and file opinion as displayed through conference motions of the late 1960s, when the EEC question was debated at conference it was always on the basis of a pro-EEC motion. Furthermore, such motions were always carried by a large majority despite the desperate tactics of the opposition. The second development was the increasingly rapid disenchantment of the Party with the traditional counter-attraction of the Commonwealth. The sobering lessons of Commonwealth immigration, Rhodesia, the truculence of former British colonies on the subject of Rhodesia (particularly as expressed in the UN assembly), and the consequent questions raised over the subjects of overseas aid and arms to South Africa were all echoed consistently in motions to the Party conferences after 1965.

Although not all such sentiments were shared by Heath, he did become impatient with the Commonwealth as it was then developing. In contrast with Macmillan's distress at the demands of the newly independent Commonwealth countries during the 1961 Commonwealth Prime Ministers' Conference, Heath asserted – to a similar gathering at Singapore in 1971 – the British government's right to be free to do what it thought advantageous to itself on the matter of South African arms, just as with all external security matters.[39] Although pressure was successfully exerted on him not to implement the South African arms sale proposal, his attitude towards the Commonwealth was now clear.

In the face of such overwhelming odds the traditionalists resorted to increasing the emphasis on the danger posed to national sovereignty by EEC entry. However, it was not on a par in Conservative thinking with the former attraction of the Commonwealth. Moreover, the latter had gradually receded, to be increasingly substituted by vague proposals for a North Atlantic or an English-speaking peoples' free trade area as the major hope of opponents of EEC entry. After the successful completion of negotiation and the signature of the treaty of accession to the EEC the Party settled down to making observations relating to the reform of EEC institutions, particularly on the question of direct elections to a European Parliament.

By contrast, Heath's successor, Mrs Thatcher, has been deprived by these previous events of taking similar initiatives in foreign policy. However, she has made abrasive speeches against the Helsinki agreement and the build-up of Soviet military and naval might throughout the world. Her 'Iron Maiden' approach found an echo in the motions to the 1975 conference. In addition to the hardy old perennials of calls for an independent nuclear deterrent and a presence east of Suez, there were strident calls for a build-up of the defence forces in view of Soviet expansion and frenzied denunciations of Socialist savaging of defence expenditure. Even the plight of the British economy was not held to be an excuse for cutting back on this indispensable part of public expenditure.

Reference to public expenditure and the British economy brings us to what has come to be the dominating issue of British politics since the early 1960s – the performance of the economy. In assessing the development of Conservative Party policy in this most important area the categories of liberal on the one hand and collectivist/corporatist on the other have increasingly been used to describe the tensions which have operated in the Party on the making of economic policy. The exact meaning of these terms is discussed extensively elsewhere.[40] Suffice it to say here that they have increasingly become identified with the right and the left wing of the Party respectively, and in the years after 1964 – a period mainly of opposition – many have described the apparent drift away from Macmillan's 'middle road' as a move towards the liberal right.

At the beginning of our period however, in 1957, it can be safely said that despite the need to voice liberal slogans the Conservative government, together with the solid support of the Party, maintained the social democratic consensus established during the war and the years of the third Labour government. Indeed, such widely divergent writers as Harris and Vander Elst both seem to agree that the so-called liberal 'golden age' only lasted for about four years after the accession of the Conservatives to power in 1951.[41]

The major elements in the maintenance of the 'mixed economy' consensus are well-known. Firstly, acceptance of the rise in public expenditure (especially after the resignation of the monetarist team of Thorneycroft, Birch and Powell in 1958) as a proportion of GNP; particularly important here was the expenditure on welfare services. Secondly, there was the use of short term monetary and budgetary methods to steer the economy (increasingly important after 1955). Allied to this was what has variously been known as a voluntary collectivist or a pluralist corporatist approach to the major organisations of both labour and capital. The not inconsiderable role for the State that such an approach necessitated was only accentuated when the British economy – which had already shown signs of faltering from the effects of 'stop-go' in the late 1950s – began to run into chronic difficulties in 1960. The result was, according to one commentator, a move along the planning spectrum towards full-blown corporatism during the 1960s, involving as it did increasing State control over not only public expenditure but also the determination of wages, the running of nationalised industries, the co-ordination of private enterprise and finally the 'inspiration' of the planning machinery.[42]

However, one should not ignore the important qualitative change that came over British management of the economy in the early 1960s. Indeed, some authors have gone further than Harris in emphasising the fact that there was a radically new departure in such management coinciding with the chancellorship of the unfortunate Selwyn Lloyd: 'Mr. Lloyd's tenure of the Exchequer deserves to be remembered . . . for the changes he inaugurated which transformed the long-term environment in which day-to-day management took place.'[43] Placed alongside the whole series of official and party inquiries instituted by Macmillan with a view to modernising Britain for her entry into the EEC, it is difficult indeed to underestimate the importance of the change in direction.[44] It is all the more interesting therefore to find, in 1961, commentators both inside and outside the Party drawing attention to what they considered to be an increasingly liberal trend within the Party. The most clearcut example of the 'economic model' being much more emphasised than the 'organic model' was in the field of welfare expenditure.[45] However, one should perhaps not make too much of this as, throughout the 1950s, the Conservatives had been feeling their way towards a new selective definition of social services which sought to contain expenditure of this particular section of the state sector. After 1965 the Party became officially fully committed to this approach.[46]

The Conservative Party was, however, unable to develop the new changes in direction which it had initiated in the early 1960s for it was defeated in the 1964 election. Coming suddenly after their long occupation of office, electoral defeat was bound to lead to much introspection. This took place in one obvious sense with the proliferation of the various policy committees reporting to the Policy Advisory Committee. However, even more important than this institutional innovation was what has since come to be seen by certain Conservatives as a fundamental shift in Tory thinking, towards the individualistic, less-state-intervention ideas of liberalism which actually gelled into specific, detailed policy proposals published whilst in opposition and implemented for a heady two years from Heath's assumption of office in June 1970. That this momentum was not sustained is one explanation of why Heath not only blundered into an election in February 1974 but also lost the subsequent October election.[47]

The Conservative Opposition of 1964–70 produced far more detailed policy documents than any previous Conservative Opposition. Moreover, they comprised the heart of some of the most important government legislation and activities after 1970. The changes in direction that those documents embodied reached their apogee in the pre-election Selsdon Park Conference of 1970. However, such detailed preparation was not without its drawbacks. As an example, Peter Jay, commenting on the 1968 manifesto, implicitly criticised

Heath's concentration on 'micro-economic reform such as modernising industry, both management and labour' at the expense of 'macro-economic management, such as fiscal and credit policy . . . incomes policy and the wider environment of world trade and payment.'[48] For Jock Bruce-Gardyne MP, one of the most enthusiastic supporters of Heath's 'Quiet Revolution', such a situation was a major factor in explaining the inability of the incoming Conservative government to deal with the 'inflationary stampede' by means of the 'rather haphazard and last moment attempt' of the 'alternative [economic] strategy' of specific tax reductions and control of public sector prices. That it was defeated by the Treasury is seen as the major explanation for the Conservative government's increasing concentration on the control of prices charged by nationalised industries. This led inevitably to confrontation with the miners.[49]

Thus it would appear that though Heath's policies were radical in their orientation, they were not comprehensive. This judgement is borne out by an examination of some of the most important components of the 'Quiet Revolution'. Reference was made above to the miners: they were just one part of a problem facing the Tories from the mid-1950s onwards – the trade unions.[50] The Conservative attitude towards trade unions was one of the major planks on which the maintenance of the social democratic consensus rested throughout the 1950s. This attitude can be summed up as benign neutrality on the question of wage claims, a conciliatory attitude towards strikes, and non-intervention as regards the internal workings of trade unions.

Nevertheless, such an approach was not without its tensions. For example, in the area of wage determination successive Conservative chancellors urged the unions throughout the 1950s to restrain their wage demands, while Conservative Cabinets, with the Minister of Labour as their agent, normally conceded the unions' case – a farcical situation, according to Macmillan.[51] In 1958, however, Macmillan and Macleod reversed the previously conciliatory attitude of 'Moncktonism' in defeating the London bus strike. Macleod's biographer has undoubtedly overdramatised the significance of what was still at that time an isolated event.[52] Nevertheless, it was part of a development which quickened considerably after the economic difficulties of 1960 and culminated in the abandonment of the laissez faire theory of wage determination with the pay pause of 1961 and the setting up of the National Incomes Commission in 1962.

Parallel with these developments was the Conservative government's increasing retreat from state abstentionism in the other areas of industrial relations. The main catalyst to this change in attitude was the huge increase in strikes starting in 1957. The consequence of the Conservatives' reaction to this phenomenon was the 1963 Contracts of Employment Act. This Act, whilst proffering workers the carrot of additional security, also held over them the stick of forfeiture of such rights if they indulged in unconstitutional industrial action (a fact which also demonstrated the increasing impatience of the Conservative leadership with the inability of the official union leadership to control their members).

Nevertheless, although these developments represented a drift away from abstentionism, they still did not amount to direct legislative intervention in either wage determination, strikes or union organisation. However, under the impact of the worsening economic situation and a deterioration in industrial relations (especially in the area of unofficial strikes), the Conservative Party came to see in the trade unions the major obstacle to the solution of Britain's economic problems. The major part of their drive to 'do something about the unions' was, however, mainly confined to the issue of strikes and union organisation. This was a result of the increasing strength of liberalism on this matter throughout the 1960s. Such liberalism was expressed in two major forms. The first saw the trade unions as economic monopolies in restraint of trade. If the restrictive practices of business could be abolished through legislation, such as the abolition of resale price maintenance in 1964, then why could not the same apply to trade unions? The second form was more moralistic in that it objected to the unions' 'coercive' role – not simply regarding the community but also regarding their own members. Such an attitude is best illustrated by the Conservatives' enduring hostility towards the closed shop.

Concern over the trade unions was not, however, confined to the Conservative Party during the 1960s. Employers, particularly those in the engineering industry, complained of being trapped in a pincer attack. On the one hand there were the interlocking phenomena of a breakdown in national wage agreements with consequent wage drift, accompanied by the rise of the shop steward movement and shop floor control of day-to-day operations. To compound this difficulty of controlling industrial costs there was also the accelerating influx of increasingly competitive foreign goods. However, whilst the employers desired new forms of control over the unions – through devices such as the Registrar and the enforcement of wage agreements – they nevertheless wanted the restoration of national order. To this end they were willing to enlist the power of the national union officials and consequently they were prepared to extend various disciplinary powers to them, the most important of which was the official recognition of the closed shop.

However, although the Party leadership was similarly interested in securing union co-operation in enforcing wage agreements (especially after Robert Carr took over as Shadow Minister of Employment from Sir Keith Joseph), the strength of liberal feeling in the Party prevented the offer of this important *quid pro quo* to the unions. This was not the only important area in which the Conservatives ignored the wishes of the large employers as well as those of the unions. Particularly staggering for the former was the implementation of the enforcement of procedure agreements solely at the level of individual undertakings – an obvious threat to the national system of collective bargaining.

Indeed it would appear that after drawing up 'Fair Deal at Work', independently of the major interest groups, the Conservative Party quickly implemented its major proposals almost to the letter without going through the usual channels of meaningful consultation with interest groups before the implementation of election proposals. Yet although the liberal element was strong in what was essentially the development of a Party policy in the most literal sense, it would be mistaken to regard other viewpoints as having no influence at all within the Party between 1965 and 1970. Thus, for example, the issue of the closed shop – which was clearly offensive to both economic and and moral strands of liberalism – produced a compromise in 'Fair Deal at Work' and in the subsequent Industrial Relations Act. This compromise sprang from the necessity of achieving unions strong enough to enforce national agreements. Thus whilst denying official recognition to the pre-entry closed shop, this was extended to the agency shop. The hope of such a compromise was that whilst it would preserve for management the power to hire and deploy whoever they thought fit, some of the benefits of the stabilising influence of the closed shop would be maintained.

Another example of the influence of voluntary collectivism came with the one important institutional addition to the 'Fair Deal' proposals, namely the Commission on Industrial Relations, whose brief was to be 'primarily concerned to assist employers and unions in the voluntary reform of industrial relations'.[53] Compulsory collectivism in the form of direct intervention by the State was also evident in the post-'Fair Deal' period through the idea of the unfair industrial practice.[54] This increased the likelihood of legal intervention, since affected individuals or organisations could ask the National Industrial Relations Court to issue an order to desist. Not only did this increase the possibility of legal intervention, it also brought the Court more directly into enforcement, since a refusal to desist would constitute contempt. Thus although the Industrial Relations Act was very largely a Party product in which liberal thinking played an important part, it would be wrong to designate it a liberal document. Liberalism, however, can be held to have been more prevalent in the Conservatives' attitude towards the one remaining area of importance for trade unions, that of wage determination. Indeed, the abolition of the Prices and Incomes Board and the refusal of the government to countenance any form of incomes policy were the *quid pro quo*s which the

Conservatives were prepared to offer the trade unions in return for agreeing to legislative interference in their other areas of activity. However, the consequence of such a policy was that the only way open to a Conservative government in combating what it considered to be excessive wage increases was through the marshalling of public opinion behind it in standing firm against such claims. Unfortunately for the Conservatives this policy was breached by important sections of the labour movement – namely the power workers and the miners. Moreover, when this was allied with spiralling inflation the return to an incomes policy became inevitable, with results for the Conservative government which were even more catastrophic than those brought about by the widely disregarded Industrial Relations Act.

Documents did not of course play a role in that other important branch of the supposed Selsdon industrial thinking – that of state disengagement from industry. A recent commentator on the development of Conservative policy on the State's relation to industry between 1964 and 1970 has described it as a *volte face* from 'intervention' to 'disengagement'.[55] A number of comments on such an evaluation immediately spring to mind. Firstly, the extent to which the Conservative government was *fully* committed to 'intervention' in 1964 must at least be queried on observing the passage of the abolition of resale price maintenance as a major impetus to competition. On the other hand, the refusal by the Conservatives to overthrow completely the regulatory structure for industry, and the commitment to Concorde and a fixed exchange rate obviously indicated that they were not prepared to go too far down the laissez faire market economy path. Nevertheless, one can say with certainty that there was definitely a new direction in industrial policy. The question of whether it was fully implemented is another matter. In the period immediately after the June election victory of 1970 the Conservative government moved swiftly to abolish the Prices and Incomes Board, the Industrial Reorganisation Corporation, the Industrial Expansion Act, investment grants and the Regional Employment Premium. However, in other areas of industrial policy the direction was not so straightforward. In connection with the nationalised industries the government had entered office pledged to do three things: to end nationalisation where possible; to return certain parts of nationalised industry to private ownership; and to ensure that the remaining nationalised industries were run more efficiently. Government action to implement the first two of these policies had only marginal effect and barely touched the mainstream of nationalised industries. The one important action – the transfer of lucrative West African air routes from British Airways to British Caledonian – was more an example of positive discrimination towards private industry than of state disengagement.[56] The latter, of course, had a long pedigree within the Conservative Party, as demonstrated in the White Paper of 1961 which committed nationalised industries to behaving like independent commercial ventures. Nevertheless, the Conservative government, as had all governments before them, found that the necessity of using the nationalised industries as part of its broader macro-economic policies led to intervention in their affairs. Thus in March 1971, when the Steel Board announced price increases of 14 per cent, the government reacted by halving the increase. All the nationalised industries were subsequently called on to limit price rises to 5 per cent in line with the CBI price restraint policy. In addition to these developments the detailed monitoring of the performance of nationalised industries ensured that the aims of 'less government' and 'more efficient government' were not merely incompatible but contradictory.

In the sphere of private industry attention has already been drawn to the Party's commitment to 'disengage' through the abolition of certain governmental agencies and government funds. Many of these promises were implemented when the Conservative government took power in 1970. Nevertheless, the Party leadership was not averse to helping competitive industry through devices such as a Small Business Development Bureau and through the more vigorous use of existing governmental regulatory agencies and legislation such as the Monopolies Commission and the Restrictive Trade Practices Act. However, even more important was the commitment, made shortly before the 1970 election, to a policy of special treatment by the State of certain key industries such as aircraft, shipbuilding, electronics and other high technology industries.[57]

Given these facts, it is perhaps not surprising that the Conservative government, faced with successive crises at Rolls Royce, UCS and Harland and Wolff, backed down so quickly on their most extreme commitment to the philosophy of 'disengagement' – the policy of no aid to 'lame ducks'. Additional incentive – if one was needed – was provided by the fact that the collapse of these firms brought with it disastrous consequences to that section of industry which was particularly close to Conservative hearts – small and medium-sized firms. The budget of 1972 and the subsequent Industry Act of the same year only set the seal on the complete abandonment of disengagement. These latter two developments, which committed the government to huge additions to public expenditure, also indicated that the Party leadership had abandoned the attempt – never very successful anyway – to use liberal responses to the problems of economic policy in general. The one aspect of the 'Quiet Revolution' which did survive relatively unscathed was the move to reorganise central government with a view to making it work more efficiently. The only irony was that many of these reforms were the product of developments which had been going on for a long time in the Civil Service itself and which had been adumbrated in the Plowden and Fulton Reports.

It is against this background that Mrs Thatcher's election is seen as marking a radical departure for the Conservative Party from the centrist policies of the later years of Heath's administration. It should be remembered, however, that a time of opposition is also a time for Party introspection during which many calls will be made for the Party to return to its fundamental principles. The Conservative Party has been no exception to this rule. Moreover, Thatcher protested during the leadership elections that her fight against Heath was not one of the Right against the Left.[58] Nevertheless, her wholesale removal of Heathites from the Party organisation, together with her speeches on competitive capitalism, do appear to mark a definite change in course for the Party. Such a view would seem to be reinforced by the appointment to leading positions within the Party of avowed liberals such as Joseph and Biffen.

Certainly such lieutenants have been only too keen to enter the lists against former Heathite policies. Thus they have called for the capturing of the common ground of politics for the Right, believing that it has already been moved too far to the Left by successive Labour and Conservative governments. This is to be achieved by rolling back the juggernaut of collectivism, inflation and high taxation. High government expenditure – the chief cause of inflation – should be cut back and with it the need for higher taxation. This can be achieved not only by Heathite policies of selectivity in the social services but also by 'unHeathite' policies such as a government refusal to give assistance to what it thinks are potentially successful industrial ventures. The market should take its course.[59]

This should also be the case in respect of incomes policy – 'The mistaken quest . . . based on the authoritarian concept that Government should decide the worth of a worker's hire.'[60] Such sentiments illustrate what is for the Conservatives yet another important reason for cutting back on state expenditure and intervention in the economy. This is the need to resist the growing encroachment of the corporate state – that 'communist' threat to parliamentary sovereignty and individual freedom,[61] which might even require a Bill of Rights to forestall further encroachment.[62] Only then would it be possible to achieve those bourgeois values of 'social responsibility: hard work: thrift' etc. which are the products of 'personal and family economic independence based on ownership of property or marketable skills – the family firm, the one-man business, the self-employed craftsman, the free professions . . .'[63]

There is no doubt that these developments have been seen by the Heathite faction as a definite move to swing the Conservative Party towards the doctrinaire Right. This is exemplified by the resurrection of the Tory Reform Group as an attempt to organise resistance to this development. Nevertheless, we should not necessarily conclude from all this that the Party is now polarising the British political spectrum. There are a number of factors which indicate the contrary.

Firstly, the personality issue, which seems to have played a small though (in view of the closeness of the first ballot) significant role in the 1975 leadership election, has undoubtedly played some part in perpetuating the division between Thatcherites and Heathites. This has blurred the extent to which there is still broad agreement on many policies – for example, the level of taxation, opposition to the Capital Transfer Tax and the Community Land Act, and the importance of private enterprise. Moreover, even during her election campaign, Thatcher has sought, through quiet changes in her personnel, to subdue her image as the militant champion of the south-east suburban middle-class. Geoffrey Howe, rather than the more extreme liberal monetarist Joseph, has been appointed Shadow Chancellor, and, of course, many prominent Heathites are in the Shadow Cabinet.

Such developments have led to speeches by the liberals within the Shadow Cabinet which have portrayed some of their uncertainty about their influence in the formation of Conservative policy. Furthermore, and more importantly, there has been the vacillation of the leadership on the crucial questions of the £6 pay limit, the nationalisation of British Leyland and the public expenditure cuts.[64] The question of the £6 pay limit is particularly interesting as Tory abstention in the Commons could hardly be further removed from Joseph's arguments against *all* pay restraint policies, voluntary or otherwise.[65] Indeed, the relatively pragmatic approach towards the unions of most leading Tories is not only exemplified in their attitude towards wages policy but also in their woolly and half-hearted attempts to cope with the areas of union activity. Unlike the dedicated liberal monetarists they seem to think that they might need the unions in the management of the economy, but they are unsure what they want them for. Hence the attempts to publicise lists of 'moderates' in trade union elections, and the emphasis on Tories actually participating in union life. Unions, according to James Prior, are 'the child of capitalism'.[66]

It is unclear whether this pragmatism is due to successful resistance by the Heathite faction within the Shadow Cabinet or to the success of Mrs Thatcher in overcoming her suburban middle-class image. Nevertheless, it would seem that, despite the rhetoric and some press comment, the Party is not really seeking to polarise British politics between Right and Left as Heath seems to believe. Indeed, even if the Party is moving some way towards the right it can hardly be said to be polarising British politics. This is especially the case when one considers that in accepting the fight against inflation as more important than that against unemployment, and in cutting back public expenditure, the

Labour government is in fact implementing Conservative policies. The Conservatives are not unmindful of this and Biffen – not usually noted for his bipartisanship – has gone on record as advocating the need to actually support the Labour government in such policies. Far from the common ground having been captured by the Left, it would appear that it has been captured by the Right. Thus the limit to those right wing policies which any future Conservative government *may* wish to introduce has been lowered by a Labour government's actions, just as it was in 1969 by the publication of 'In Place of Strife.'

In conclusion, then, what can be said about the development of the Party from 1957? The one incontrovertible fact is the change in its electoral fortunes. It is no longer the 'natural party of government'. Furthermore, the number of people voting Conservative has steadily declined, together with the proportion of middle-class Conservatives – the heart of Conservative activists. Whether this development will continue is almost impossible to say, given the new volatility of British electoral opinion.

Nevertheless, despite the experience of opposition and the change to elected leaders, the leadership of the Party as a whole has retained its control over organisation and policy-making within the Party. This has been achieved despite rank and file calls for greater democracy. The abandonment of attempts during the 1960s to achieve a more representative social composition amongst Party members and parliamentary candidates also signalled a defeat for those who sought to democratise internal procedures.

It would be misleading, however, to conclude that Party opinion, whether inside or outside Parliament, has had little effect on the policy of the leadership and only when the Party has been in opposition at that. The elaborate precautions that Macmillan took to disguise Britain's retreat from world power status is indicative of *some* influence. Nevertheless, on the whole, Conservative leaders – even the elected ones – have led the Party where they want it to go, despite the difficulties of opposition and rank and file suspicion. The policy of the Conservative leadership and the reaction of the Party conference on Europe between 1965 and 1970 is a good illustration of this.

What is not so clear are the criteria on which the leadership has based its policies. Thus, in relation to the scenario sketched in the introduction, a number of qualifications must be made. In the field of foreign policy, although there appears to have been a 'Grand Design' in Macmillan's efforts to reduce Britain's world and imperial roles, the short term political factors should not be neglected. Nor were short term considerations entirely absent from Heath's mind when he advocated EEC membership.

In contrast to these short term political factors on the international scene, and despite the rhetoric of the post-1965 period, the Conservative leadership has generally followed interventionist criteria in domestic economic and industrial policy. 1970–72, not 1972–74, was the period of aberration. Moreover, even in the former period the alleged triumphs of the liberal Right – notably state disengagement from industry and the Industrial Relations Act – have been shown up as far less sweeping than might at first have been thought.

Although the post-1974 situation is much more confused and uncertain, it would appear that there is enough evidence to suggest that the same forces are asserting themselves within the present Conservative leadership. The one important qualification to all this is the implementation of policies of the liberal Right by the present Labour government. These appear to be having the undoubted effect of lowering the inhibitions of any future Conservative government with regard to the introduction of at least *some* modified version of measures associated with the liberal Right.

Notes

[1]   A cul-de-sac for Conservatives in at least two senses. Firstly, it was unsuccessful. Secondly, it was, for the liberal monetarists, irrelevant to the solution of the inflation problem.

[2]   S. H. Beer, 'Democratic one-party government for Britain?', *Political Quarterly*, vol. 32, 1961, p. 114.

[3]   Of the total electorate (as opposed to the voters), the Conservative Party support fell from 37·8 per cent to 26·2 per cent over the same period.

[4]   J. Greenwood, 'The Conservative Party and the working class – the organisational response', University of Warwick, Department of Politics Working Paper no. 2, June 1974, p. 66.

[5]   P. G. J. Pulzer, *Political Representation and Elections in Britain*, Allen and Unwin, London 1975, p. 73.

[6]   See, for example, S. H. Beer, *Modern British Politics*, Faber, London 1965, pp. 382–3.

[7]   See A. King, 'The changing Tories', in J. D. Lees and R. Kimber, *Political Parties in Modern Britain*, Routledge and Kegan Paul, London 1972, p. 134.

[8]   Butler and Pinto-Duschinsky, in their Nuffield Study of the 1970 general election, have referred to the changes as the 'quiet revolution at Central Office' and much of the material that follows here is based on their excellent examination of this so-called revolution. See D. Butler and M. Pinto-

Duschinsky, *The British General Election of 1970*, Macmillan, London 1971, especially chs. 4, 8 and 11.

[9]   *The Guardian*, 28 January 1976.

[10]   D. Butler and D. Kavanagh, *The British General Election of February 1974*, Macmillan, London 1974, p. 202.

[11]   The following account of this inquiry is largely drawn from P. Seyd, 'Democracy within the Conservative Party?', *Government and Opposition*, vol. 10, Spring 1975, pp. 219–39.

[12]   Ibid., p. 220.

[13]   Butler and Pinto-Duschinsky, op. cit., p. 287.

[14]   See R. M. Punnett, *Front-Bench Opposition*, Heinemann, London 1973, pp. 265–6; and Rose, *Problem of Party Government*, pp. 391–402.

[15]   Butler and Pinto-Duschinsky, op. cit., p. 90.

[16]   R. Rose, 'Parties, factions and tendencies in Britain', *Political Studies*, vol. 12, no. 1, 1964, pp. 33–46.

[17]   Butler and Pinto-Duschinsky found that fifty-five parliamentary candidates in the 1970 election were members of the Monday Club; of these thirty were elected, ten for the first time (op. cit., p. 293).

[18]   P. Seyd, 'Factionalism within the Conservative Party: the Monday Club', *Government and Opposition*, vol. 7, no. 4, Autumn 1972, p. 487.

[19]   R. Rose, 'The Bow Group's role in British politics', *Western Political Quarterly*, 1961, vol. 14, no. 4, pp. 865–78.

[20]   Butler and Pinto-Duschinsky, op. cit., p. 293.

[21]   *The Economist*, 17 May 1975; *The Times*, 20 June 1975.

[22]   R. J. Jackson, *Rebels and Whips*, Macmillan, London 1968, ch. 7.

[23]   P. Norton, *Dissension in the House of Commons 1970–4*, Macmillan, London 1975, p. 610.

[24]   Ibid., p. 611.

[25]   H. Fraser, 'Tories need a new leader to heal the wounds and take the Party back to grass roots', *The Times*, 31 January 1975.

[26]   This was particularly the case in 1960 when seven out of the eight motions on foreign affairs specifically congratulated the actions of the Prime Minister.

[27]   A. Sampson, *Macmillan: A Study of Ambiguity*, Allen Lane, London 1967, p. 130.

[28]   See V. Bogdanor and R. Skidelsky (eds.), *The Age of Affluence, 1951–1964*, Macmillan, London 1970, pp. 219–20.

[29]   A. Gamble, *The Conservative Nation*, Routledge and Kegan Paul, London 1974, p. 166.

[30]   Ibid.

[31]   The Earl of Kilmuir, 'The path to the purge' (extracts from his memoirs *Political Adventure*), *The Sunday Times*, 5 April 1964.

[32] Ibid.

[33] See, for example, The National Union of Conservative and Unionist Associations' Handbook (henceforth referred to as Handbook), 1958 motion 303.

[34] See The National Union of Conservative and Unionist Associations, 80th Annual Conference, *Official Report*, 1961, p. 12. Cf. *Official Report*, 1957, p. 64. (In line with usual Conservative practice reprints of the Annual Conference Report will henceforth be referred to as *Verbatim Report*.)

[35] Gamble, op. cit., p. 188.

[36] See H. Macmillan, *Riding the Storm*, Macmillan, London 1971, ch. 14.

[37] See H. Macmillan, *At The End of The Day*, Macmillan, London 1973, ch. 1; and A. Roth, *Heath and the Heathmen*, Routledge and Kegan Paul, London 1972, p. 162.

[38] See J. Bruce-Gardyne, *Whatever Happened to the Quiet Revolution?* Knight, London 1974, pp. 56–7.

[39] See Bruce-Gardyne, op. cit., p. 47.

[40] See ch. 4 of this book. Also N. Harris, *Competition and the Corporate Society*, Methuen, London 1972, especially Part I and p. 243; R. E. Pahl and J. T. Winkler, 'The coming corporatism', *New Society*, 10 October 1974; M. Moran, *The Politics of Industrial Relations*, Macmillan (forthcoming); and M. Peston, 'Conservative economic policy and philosophy', *Political Quarterly*, vol. 44, 1973, pp. 411–24.

[41] Harris, op. cit., p. 229; P. Vander Elst, 'Radical Toryism – the libertarian alternative', *Political Quarterly*, vol. 46, 1975, pp. 65–72.

[42] See Harris, op. cit., p. 242–3.

[43] S. Brittan, *Steering the Economy*, Penguin, London 1971, p. 234.

[44] See J. Barnes, 'The record', in D. McKie and C. Cook (eds.), *The Decade of Disillusion*, Macmillan, London 1972, p. 12. It is important to note, however, that Barnes maintains that the new move towards planning was *not* inextricably bound up with entry to the EEC. Cf. J. Leruez, *Economic Planning and Politics in Britain*, Martin Robertson, London 1975, pp. 274–5.

[45] R. Rose, 'Tensions in Conservative philosophy', and R. Hornby, 'Conservative principles', in *Political Quarterly*, vol. 32, 1961, pp. 282 and 236 respectively.

[46] See Gamble, op. cit., pp. 64 and 135.

[47] See Bruce-Gardyne, op. cit., pp. 10–13; Lord Lambton, 'Why Mr. Heath should accept Sir Alec's terms for the election of a Tory leader', *The Times*, 20 January 1975; H. Fraser, 'Tories need a new leader'.

[48] P. Jay, 'In search of Conservative economic policy', *The Times*, 1 November 1968.

[49] Bruce-Gardyne, op. cit., pp. 60–2.

[50]   For the following pages on the Conservatives and the trade unions we are heavily indebted to Michael Moran for allowing us to consult the manuscript of his forthcoming book on *The Politics of Industrial Relations*. Chapters 1–6 were particularly helpful. References additional to the material found in Mr Moran's book have, of course, been separately noted.

[51]   Macmillan, *Riding the Storm*, op. cit., p. 715.

[52]   Fisher, op. cit., ch. 7.

[53]   Industrial Relations Bill, Consultative Document, Department of Employment and Productivity, HMSO, October 1970, p. 5.

[54]   It was to be an unfair industrial practice to strike, or threaten to strike to force an employer to discriminate in any way against a union or non-union member (ibid., p. 7).

[55]   A. V. Lowe in S. Young and A. V. Lowe, *Intervention in the Mixed Economy*, Croom Helm, London 1974, p. 123.

[56]   See Young and Lowe, op. cit., pp. 139–42.

[57]   See Young and Lowe, op. cit., pp. 127 ff. and 179.

[58]   See the report of her speech to her Finchley constituency officials in 'No Tory Left–Right split', *The Guardian*, 1 February 1975.

[59]   See J. Biffen, 'Tories, the State and the economy', *The Daily Telegraph*, 30 July 1975.

[60]   Speech by John Biffen at Eastbourne on 4 October 1975, reported in 'Heath's shadow over Blackpool', *The Daily Telegraph*, 6 October 1975.

[61]   See Nicholas Ridley, 'The struggle within the British mixed economy', *The Guardian*, 1 July 1976; and Timothy Raison, 'How Tories can show their nerve, *The Daily Telegraph*, 6 October 1975.

[62]   See 'Joseph wants new Bill of Rights', *The Observer*, 26 January 1975.

[63]   Sir Keith Joseph, 'Towards the good life', *The Guardian*, 27 January 1975.

[64]   See '278 Majority for 'back-up powers' after Tories abstain', *The Daily Telegraph*, 24 July 1975; and 'Tories clash on solving crisis, *The Observer*, 13 April 1975.

[65]   See his speech in *Hansard*, vol. 876, cols. 784–5.

[66]   National Union, Verbatim Report 1975, p. 90.

4 Grass roots Conservatism: motions to the Party Conference*

M. WILSON

Three important things happened to the Conservative Party in 1975. Firstly, Mrs Thatcher was elected the first woman to lead the Party. Secondly, this election heralded a success for the Party's right wing, a success which, according to one commentator, was 'for the first time this century within the Tory party, the result of an ideological battle inside the party.'[1] Thirdly, this success was widely attributed to the alleged sympathy for Mrs Thatcher, as an antidote to Heathism, on the part of the rank and file.[2]

The focus of this chapter will be the rank and file. More precisely it will be an examination of whether there is a link between rank and file attitudes, as manifested in motions to the Annual Party Conference, and the right wing ideology with which Mrs Thatcher is now identified. Inevitably this will also involve a consideration of whether the popular impression of a symbiosis between right wing militancy and Tory activists is correct, or whether, alternatively, the more restrained assessment of Rose is more accurate.[3]

Motions to the Annual Party Conference are, as Rose has said, a 'rich source of material for investigating the views of militants',[4] and yet, surprisingly, they have been largely disregarded by academics. As motions come directly from the constituencies they would appear to provide an extremely useful guide to rank and file opinion; they are arguably more representative than the conference debates, which in turn can be viewed as more representative than the motions chosen for debate.[5]

To begin we must briefly refer to the question of the Party's right wing ideology. There is, of course, much debate as to its exact nature but an interesting link that has recently been made is with the libertarian tradition inside the party.[6] Such a tradition, in the view of Greenleaf, consists of individuality, limited government, diffusion of power and a decentralisation of decision-making, and the rule of law.[7] Associated with this tradition is a

* The period covered is 1945–73. Because of the general election no conference was held in 1974.

64

firm belief in the workings of the free market economy. This does not, however, mean that the government should never interfere with the economy, for

> ... it may be that positive action is needed to remove obstacles or stop interference with the free flow of economic forces as when a system of controls is dismantled or a subsidy scheme abolished. Further it may be appropriate for government to adjust to this same end the framework of law within which industry and commerce operate, for instance, by the prevention of restrictive practices, the revision of trade union law, or the treatment of monopoly.[8]

However, the latter example of the libertarian tradition does not necessarily represent the full range of libertarian views on the workings of the market economy. Thus what Peston calls contemporary 'right-wing realism' within the Conservative Party is a 'laissez-faire philosophy' comprised of two parts. The first is 'the pure milk of economic liberalism based on perfect competition' and the second is 'the more adulterated variety which would give free rein to private business enterprise in whatever form, and however monopolisitc it appears.'[9] Nevertheless, as far as the rank and file are concerned, the evidence does suggest that it is the former and not the latter which is favoured. Thus in the question of the role of the State within the economy there is a close relationship between the views of Powell and those of the rank and file. Where Powell is not so representative of right wing libertarianism is in the area of the social services.[10]

Mrs Thatcher's relationship to the above views can be gleaned from her speeches and articles. An interesting example is the one she wrote for *The Daily Telegraph* in the 'My kind of Tory Party' series at the height of her election battle with Heath. Whilst this article is not, unsurprisingly, an exercise in clear theoretical thinking unmistakably dividing her from the centre–left advocates of Heathism, the emphasis certainly does distinguish her from other contributors to the series.[11] She commenced by admitting that the last Conservative government of 1970–74 'failed the people' – a failure for which she accepted her share of collective responsibility. Pledging herself 'to recognise the failures and to try to see that the mistakes are not repeated', she set out to identify positively herself with the constituency rank and file by decrying those politicians who saw themselves as 'professional efficiency experts' or 'amateur industrial consultants'. 'Politicians', she said, 'must work at every problem from the grassroots'. She clearly believed that her record as Secretary of State for Education and as leading Conservative spokeswoman against the Labour government's Capital Transfer Tax proposals was evidence that she was working in this manner. She maintained that such work was a freedom fight for *every* citizen against 'excessive State power' and for 'variety . . . individual choice . . . incentives . . . rewards . . . and a . . . wide distribution of individual *private* property.' That the latter had not been sufficiently recognised by certain Conservatives as 'one of the main bulwarks of individual freedom' was, she stated, one of the main reasons why the electorate had been unable to clearly differentiate Conservatives from the 'Socialists'. Her conclusions left the reader in no doubt that she was determined to remove this lack of clarity. Once more the various characteristics of 'freedom' were stated together with pleas for the 'maintenance of law and order' and the 'preservation of local rights in local communities.'[12] This was all heady material for the rank and file.

In this article there is, at the very least, an implied commitment to those bases of libertarianism which have already been outlined. The one major addition is that of law and order, which clearly involves the use of state power. Nevertheless, although this is strictly collectivism, i.e. it involves an expanding social and economic role for the State, it is extremely unlikely that a libertarian of the Right would object, since even the most ardent nineteenth century Liberal would have been willing to countenance the preservation of law and order as one of the few legitimate uses of state power.

Having now identified the Thatcherite version of right wing Conservatism we can proceed to the main business of the chapter: the extent to which the libertarian Right manifests itself in motions to conference. Debates at conference will only be referred to where they provide a useful expansion and commentary on the often tersely expressed principles of the various motions. The areas which will be analysed are those which have provided the major focus for British politics since 1945 – the management of the economy and the maintenance of the Welfare State – as well as those other domestic areas which have attracted distinctive rank and file contributions, e.g. immigration, and law and order. The concentration on domestic issues also stems from the fact that in analysing libertarianism and collectivism within the Party commentators have exclusively used such issues as their subject matter.[13]

However, it should perhaps be pointed out at this stage that although libertarianism will be shown to have been a major constituent of the rank and file's predominantly right wing attitudes, it cannot be denied that the rank and file has occasionally been willing to use the collectivist power of the State for what can only be termed right wing purposes. For example, there is the control of alleged political subversives within the educational system, the granting of state funds to aid private housing at the expense of council housing, and the restriction on immigration and state assistance for the repatriation of immigrants. Similarly, although the use of the collectivist power of the State provides the major opposition to the libertarian right – for example, in motions calling for extra state expenditure in regional policy, in the expansion of the road programme, and of educational and medical provision, and in the allocation of greater funds for local authorities with a high immigrant population – there are a number of motions (mostly in the social services area) which, though libertarian, could scarcely be included in the libertarian right classification. Examples of these are concerned with the abolition/diminution of the pensioners' earnings rule, the lowering of the tax threshold for the disadvantaged (e.g. widows) and the abolition of pre-scription charges for pensioners. These are referred to as libertarian (left).

Consequently, a five-fold classification of motions may be used:

(1) Libertarian (right);
(2) Collectivist (right);
(3) Collectivist (left);
(4) Libertarian (left); and
(5) Others.

The latter category contains three main types of motion; firstly, the utterly banal non-contentious motion containing no hint of what is required in the way of policy; secondly, ritualistic denunciations of the Labour Party's policies and actions, whether in opposition or government; and thirdly, those motions which, whilst supporting typical Tory aims, fail to suggest what line of action the State should take to achieve these aims.[14]

The above method of classifying Conservative motions and the fact that, as will be shown, there is a majority of libertarian (right) motions in many of the areas examined, does not immediately imply a conflict between the findings of this research and that of, say, Rose. Thus whilst there may be a frequent majority of libertarian motions, this does not mean that all libertarian (right) motions are necessarily militant in relation to the policy of the party leader-ship. Indeed, numerous libertarian (right) motions were regarded as desirable policy objectives by the party leadership: for example, the relationship between, on the one hand, those motions pushing for economic rents and a diminution of council house subsidies and, on the other hand, the Housing Finance Act of 1972.

As to methodology, it has to be appreciated that many of the motions for the major categories of management of the economy and the Welfare State are gleaned from a multiplicity of subject headings. This is especially the case in management of the economy where the subject headings of economic policy and taxation by no means cover all the relevant motions. Other subject areas cover trade unions, nationalisation and monopoly through to employment, cost of living and small businesses. Moreover, all subject headings are not mutually exclusive; for example, the taxation sections often contain motions which simply relate to health or medicine or education (usually in terms of a

67

call for tax relief) which have to be deducted from the sum of motions on taxation.

Management of the economy

The steep rise in the number of motions concerned with the management of the economy is an eloquent testimony to Critchley's 1973 statement that for the Conservatives 'contemporary politics is about economic management'.[15] Such reorientation coincided with the onset of Britain's present economic difficulties in the early 1960s, although the evidence also shows that there was an upsurge of rank and file interest in 1956 and 1957 (also years of economic difficulty).

These latter two years are of particular interest, not least because they contain some of the most forthright rank and file statements about what, since 1945, has been the dominant theme of the equally dominant libertarian (right) category of conference motions, that is, the reduction of taxation and/or its related theme of less government expenditure. Thus in 1956 motion 160 demanded:

> That the Government give urgent consideration to ways and means for lightening the burden of taxation on the middle-classes, having regard in particular to . . . concessions to individuals who do not avail themselves of 'welfare' facilities.[16]

Nevertheless, such motions did not mean that the rank and file did not seek to 'avail' themselves of certain other facilities offered by the government. An example of this is provided by the fact that in 1956 twelve motions saw the answer to the problem of inflation in the imposition of some form of prices and/or incomes policy. Such a policy was to find favour yet again with the rank and file in times of economic difficulty under a Conservative government.[17]

Furthermore, the rank and file has never been averse to asking the party leadership (whether in power or not) to commit themselves to policies which would clearly entail extra government expenditure, often of quite considerable amounts. Expansion of the road programme has always been a favourite, though recent developments in road traffic have meant, perhaps a little surprisingly, a recent turning towards public transport as the solution to the transportation problems of the middle-classes as well as of private industry.[18] In recent years regional aid – whether through direct subsidies to various depressed regions, or to industries contemplating setting up business in them – has attracted a considerable number of motions from rank and file representatives. Moreover, an occasional motion has, within itself, displayed the not inconsiderable art of pointing in both a libertarian (right) and collectivist (left) direction at the same time.[19]

Such a situation evoked a laconic comment from Richard Law (MP for Halifax and later Lord Coleraine) who was speaking to a 'resolution' (sic) submitted to the 1952 Conference which stated that 'public expenditure has increased, is increasing and ought to be diminished'. Whilst admitting that economy in public expenditure was 'the clue to everything', Law nevertheless went on to point out that the demands for public expenditure came not so much from the government as from the party rank and file. Thus he concluded:

> I would be prepared to bet that the Conference will pass this resolution unanimously and within the next forty-eight hours will pass some other resolution which recommends pouring another twenty or thirty millions of public money down the sink. If this Conference does not do that, it is a great advance, because it is the first Conference I have ever heard of that has not.[20]

This fact was not lost on the party leaders, who were quick to reiterate it at the height of the so-called revolt of 1956 and 1957. Such criticism could well have been levelled at the Party Conference at any time since that date and especially in 1973. That it has not been levelled in such a fashion clearly tells us something, if only implicitly, about the changed attitude of Party leaders to the rank and file.[21]

Thus on the predominant matters of taxation and public expenditure, together with the (numerically) more minor ritualistic denunciations of nationalisation, the Party rank and file consistently spoke with an unequivocal libertarian (right) voice to the Party leadership, despite the occasional protestations of the latter. Within these sections the most vehement expression of right wing libertarianism came in the support (for both social and economic reasons) of the notion of a property-owning democracy. The key elements in the pursuit of such an ideal were the expansion of home ownership; the spread of share ownership; an adherence to free market competition; a dislike of restrictive practices; and, above all, the furtherance of the interests of small business – that repository of all those virtues which the Conservative rank and file holds so dear.[22]

With the exception of the first of these, none of the aims *per se* was ever constantly voiced either in volume or in a libertarian (right) spirit. Perhaps one should not find this lack of decisiveness too surprising for, as Gamble has pointed out in connection with Heath's competition policy:

> The actual implementation of the competition policy could be expected

to favour their [i.e. the big public corporations', the banks' and the multinational companies'] interests more than it helped small business.[23]

Whilst it might be objected that the same could not be said of certain aspects of the competition policy (such as the abolition of monopolistic and other restrictive practices), this did not necessarily mean that the interests of small business would be furthered as a consequence. Thus it is not surprising to find, after repeated pleas to save the small businessman from the depredations of 'the larger companies and finance houses',[24] a plea

> That future Conservative policy with regard to countering monopoly, restrictive practices and resale price maintenance, must contain positive assurance to proprietors of small businesses and shops that they can expect a reasonable future in an expanding economy.[25]

It would appear that the rank and file felt that such 'a reasonable future' would be best achieved by relieving the small businessman of the worst excesses of various state-imposed burdens – noticeably taxation.[26] This is very much in line with what the Bolton Committee on Small Firms discovered to be the major element in the small businessman's attitude towards central government.[27] Thus unburdened, the small businessman, that 'backbone of the nation', would be free to fulfil his 'historical role' of providing the 'beneficial impetus to the national economy and the driving force behind the will to work.'[28]

Nevertheless, given that the small businessman was held to encapsulate all those virtues which Conservatives held dear, he could justifiably argue that the preservation and furtherance of his interests was as much a social as an economic necessity, an opinion very much shared by Mrs Thatcher. This view, which was put forth most eloquently in the late 1960s and early 1970s by leading Conservative writers,[29] was periodically referred to but nowhere more clearly than in motion 44, 1957, where the government was urged 'to make money more readily available' to present and prospective small business-men as 'the added responsibilities of ownership are powerful stabilising influences in our lives.' As this motion clearly demonstrated, such an attitude did not consider it inappropriate for a Conservative government to suspend the laws of free enterprise and competition if, in return, it was to receive such social benefits as outlined in the motion.

Moreover, it could be argued that these spokesmen of the 'unorganised middle-class' were more than willing to suspend their libertarian principles when the question arose of the State's relationship to that other category of large scale economic organisations by which they felt threatened, namely, the trade unions. Thus Seyd, in describing the Monday Club's post-1964 policies as representative of the liberal conservative tendency (which, he argues, began to assume prominence within the Conservative Party between 1966 and 1970), declared that:

> ... certain inconsistencies exist in the Monday Club's liberalism. Whilst demanding that individualism should be encouraged in economic and social policy it demands that the state's power should be increased in such fields as industrial relations or civil liberties. It is in favour of increasing the power of the policeman, the employer and the vice-chancellor and of diminishing the power of the demonstrator, the trade unionist and the student. Whilst expressing the class interest of its supporters with perfect clarity it fails to achieve the philosophical consistency of classical liberalism.[30]

Though generally acceptable, such a statement can be challenged when applied to the subject of trade unions. Thus it does not, for example, appreciate that for many Conservatives – certainly the rank and file – the trade unions, just like other great industrial organisations, were 'economic monopolies, whose power had to be curbed for the market in labour to function properly again.'[31] This was succinctly demonstrated in 1956 when the mover of motion 104 urged the Conservative government on towards 'the breaking down of all monopolies, whether by employer or employees.' Clearly, both large scale industrial companies and trade unions were regarded as equal subjects for any monopolistic or restrictive practices legislation. Any suggestion that the two were not being so regarded elicited cries of outrage as demonstrated in the same year by motion 180:

> ... this Conference, whilst welcoming the initiation of measures against restrictive practices by industrial undertakings, deplores the continued conciliation and appeasement of trade unions, as constituting a sectional approach to a national problem, and calls upon the Government to promulgate legislation to curb . . . irresponsible restrictive practices . . . which threaten the country's economic survival.

This attitude, though somewhat conditioned by the special circumstances of 1956, was characteristic of the rank and file's attitude towards the trade unions for most of the post-1945 years. That is not to deny that many of the debates of the 1950s concerning industrial relations and related matters revolved round calls for greater voluntary harmony in industry, a better 'human' approach to industrial relations, and government encouragement of schemes such as profit sharing, wider share ownership, and disclosure of company information to workers, etc. However, not only is it questionable whether all of the participants regarded such discussion as being of central importance,

71

but also whether such debates were altogether representative of the underlying rank and file opinion. In this connection it is revealing to note that in
1957 a 'practising trade unionist', speaking to a motion which urged 'Her
Majesty's Government to get to grips with the problems which arise between
management and labour in industry in the spirit of the 'Industrial Charter'
and with the realisation that the country expects a sense of united purpose
from all those engaged in industry', declared himself to be '. . . very disturbed
by the violent phraseology of some of the Motions on Industrial Relations . . .
You cannot seek a solution to the sore problems of industrial relations by
repressive legislation as many of the motions suggest.'[32]

Certainly, the libertarian (right) predisposition towards direct government
action (including legislation) against the various trade union 'malpractices'
was always a stronger feature of rank and file opinion than of Party leadership
opinion. Although the most consistent examples of the rank and file attitude
were mainly confined to issues such as the closed shop, the pre-strike ballot,
the political levy and the fight against union victimisation, there were motions
as early as 1948 and 1949 which called for direct government action (in the
latter year, abolitionist legislation) against unofficial strikes. Such calls
became increasingly vehement from the late 1950s onwards as unofficial strike
action became a more significant part of an increasing labour problem.

In conclusion, it can be seen that there has been a strong disposition towards
the libertarian (right) in conference motions concerning the management of
the economy. Nevertheless, this has been most marked in the area relating to
taxation and government expenditure and the trade unions, both of which
have covered a large proportion of all management of the economy motions.
However, such motions have not necessarily implied a minimisation of state
interference – certainly not in the case of trade unions. Such willingness to use
the power of the State has also been present, though for differing motives, in
numerous motions calling for state expenditure as a positive aid to various
industrial and regional interests.

The Welfare State

Social security

Social security has been a matter of great concern to rank and file Conservatives involving as it does the public expenditure of a significant proportion
of national income.[33] Nevertheless, one must be careful to separate the
issue of pensions from the main body of rank and file opinion on social
security spending. In the case of the former, the rank and file has consistently
shown itself willing to increase the amount of state benefits accruing to a

rapidly growing proportion of the populace. Important factors in explaining this position are, firstly, the periodically high proportion of collectivist (left) motions on pensions concerned with Armed Forces pensions; secondly, the fact that many references to the problems of pensioners are associated with the problems of elderly middle-class people living on fixed incomes in a time of inflation; and thirdly, the desire not to make pensions a subject of acute political controversy.

In addition to actually providing more state benefits, a significant section of rank and file opinion has constantly sought to improve pensioners' income by releasing them from state restrictions on their earning power. The classic example of this is provided by the large number of libertarian (left) motions calling for the easing or abolition of the earnings rule. Moreover, in the prosperous mid-1950s the motions relating to this rule were usually linked with a call for a flexible attitude towards the retirement age principle in an era of labour shortage. However, as prosperity receded and Britain's economic difficulties increased, the calls for a flexible retirement age principle disappeared and in 1972 there were even motions calling for the government to introduce legislation requiring a lowering of the retirement age as a contribution to the eradication of unemployment. It is interesting to note, however, that this reversal in attitude was not accompanied by a decline in the number of motions calling for an easing/abolition of the earnings rule.

The small minority of pensions motions relating to the libertarian (right) category mainly contented themselves (as did many of the motions on other aspects of social security) with calling for the encouragement of private schemes, accompanied occasionally by calls for the introduction of greater selectivity and the chance to opt out of the National Insurance pension scheme.

In the remaining area of social security (which in both motions and debates was frequently intertwined with a discussion on the state of the social services generally) there is a marked rise in rank and file interest, which was dominated by a libertarian (right) orientation. It is true that there had always been a fairly regular (though small) supply to conference of those motions which were concerned mainly with either the independence/character/morale sapping nature of social security or with the abuse of social security by feckless individuals. Particularly good examples of such attitudes are to be found in motion 153 of 1948 and motion 336 of 1969, the latter of which stated

> That this Conference, knowing full well that the Welfare State has reached the stage where it is damaging the moral fibre and financial stability of the nation, urges the Conservative Party to reappraise the whole position and substitute a system designed to encourage individual responsibility. . . .

Concern with abuse of the social security system has also been a constant theme of conference motions. As early as 1949 the mover of motion 83, which 'pledged' the Conference 'to humanise the social services wherever possible by creating local responsibility', and which was 'certain that economies can be affected by cutting down administrative costs', concluded that the major way to achieve the latter was to put an end to abuse. Regularly expressed concern at such 'abuse' eventually led to an assertion in 1960 that 'the time has arrived when a Select Committee or some such organisation should be set up to review and report on the obvious abuses which are occurring in the admini- stration of National Assistance.'[34]

Nevertheless, these references were as nothing compared to the massive upsurge in the numbers of libertarian (right) motions from 1965 onwards. Harris has talked of a shift in the emphasis of Conservative policy during this period as the government disentangled itself from public welfare in favour of private schemes,[35] and Gamble has described the important role of the rank and file in changing the Party's policy towards the social services during the years of opposition. Such a policy, he says, came to regard 'welfare provision' as

> the new field where property-owning democrats were expected to exercise their independence through . . . the crusade for selectivity rather than universal welfare benefits that had taken root in the party during the 1950's.[36]

Such a statement, whilst perhaps not conveying the sense of the growing number and ferocity of motions illustrating the rank and file's abhorrence of the abuse of social security and the character-sapping nature of such a system, certainly illustrates more vividly than does Harris the highly charged feeling of the rank and file regarding the social services from the mid-1960s onwards.

The centrality of this feeling to the enunciation of a distinctive Conservative philosophy was clearly revealed in 1970 by the mover of a unanimously approved motion calling for the British system of social security to encourage effort rather than idleness and the stamping out of abuses whilst still protecting the genuinely needy:

> Nowhere is there greater opportunity to make fundamental changes . . . by tearing down the shackles of socialism, and, in particular, the idea that the state is the all-embracing provider . . . than in the welfare state.[37]

Such thoroughgoing selectivists were often incensed by what they regarded as the woolly thinking of some would-be selectivists. Thus in 1965 Mrs Peggy

Fenner (Newcastle-under-Lyme) – whilst supporting a motion which aimed at reaffirming 'the basic Conservative principle of caring for those least able to care for themselves' and which sought to stress 'the need to strengthen the structure of social service to make better provision in cases of special and individual hardship' – was nevertheless moved to point out that the motion made a

> major omission . . . in that it makes no reference at all to the need to reject what is referred to variously in many other motions on the subject as flat rate social security benefits, blanket payments and indiscriminate aid for all, with no reference to the need to be more selective with social benefits . . . discriminating selective action needs to be taken in our social services not only . . . because it is the proper function of the welfare services . . . to give the greatest care and benefit to those in greatest need . . . but because the blanket welfare of the Welfare State will sap our British national character and further permit totalitarian principles to brainwash our society.[38]

Closely associated with the drive towards selectivism was the rank and file's desire to do something about what they believed was widespread abuse of the social security system. Concentration on such 'abuse' developed during the late 1960s and early 1970s. Particular hostility was reserved for the 'exploitation' of the system by strikers. The almost obsessional peak of this hostility came in the year of labour upheaval, 1972, and in the subsequent year. In 1972, of the ninety-four motions on social security (other than pensions), forty-eight were explicitly concerned with the abuse of the social security system and steps likely to reduce such abuse. Of these, thirty-nine were directed at strikers and/or their unions by aiming to deny the payment of any social security benefits to the families of strikers; by seeking to recover the payment of such benefits from the unions concerned in the strike; or by making social security payment to strikers on a loan basis only. In 1973 the figures were 112 : 50 : 41 respectively. It is significant that in both 1972 and 1973 the Tory Minister for Health and Social Security, Sir Keith Joseph – that scourge of the scroungers[39] – was extremely noncommittal, to say the least, on this topic. Thus in 1973, speaking in the debate on social services and health, Sir Keith declared:

> Robin Page wants us to turn benefits to strikers' families into loans. The motions on the order paper range from that proposal to a complete withdrawal of any benefits to strikers' families. I have asked the Conference once before, last year, to recognise – and I do ask you again – that this is a very much more complicated problem than it looks . . . This

Conference would be the first to howl if we really did have pictures on television of children going hungry for lack of benefit. . . .[40]

Consequently, the inclusion in the February 1974 election manifesto of a plan concerning the cessation of state benefits to strikers' families is all the more interesting.

In conclusion it can be said that not only have the views of the party activists – on social security specifically and the philosophy of the social services generally – been, almost without exception, predominantly of the libertarian (Right) persuasion, but that it is in these areas that some of the most distinctive expressions of rank and file libertarianism (Right) are to be found.

Health

Concern with the health service has commanded only low priority with the rank and file. Moreover, most of the non-libertarian, non-collectivist motions which are annually a large proportion of all health motions are either extremely vague or non-contentious, as manifested in motion 464, 1971.

Amongst the libertarian (right) motions are hardy perennials calling for the encouragement of private health insurance schemes specifically through the provision of tax relief for such schemes and the availability of National Health Service priced medicines for private patients. Most of such motions either ignore or are indifferent to the National Health Service itself but in the 1970s there has been some attempt in such motions to present the encouragement of private schemes as an aid to the National Health Service. Thus motion 502 in 1972 advocated the provision of National Health Service priced medicines for private patients 'so affording some relief to the over-burdened National Health Service by encouraging more private patients', and motion 508 in 1973 declared that ' . . . this Conference, mindful of the soaring demand and increasing cost of providing a National Health Service, would encourage private provision by making health insurance premiums tax deductable'.

Clearly the mover of the latter motion either ignored or was ignorant of Lord Balneil's speech in the 1969 social security and health debate in which he said that:

Tax relief for health insurance . . . is a proper objective for the Conservative Party, but it is subordinate to our wider aim of an overall reduction in direct personal taxation, which is the immediate objective of the Conservative Party. . . .[41]

Such a reply was, nevertheless, more moderate towards the rank and file's wishes than either of the responses of the relevant Conservative ministers (in

1960 Enoch Powell and in 1973 Sir Keith Jospeh) to similar requests. In the first case a request for the provision of NHS medicines for private patients was simply ignored by Powell.[42] In the second case Sir Keith Joseph was faced with, amongst others, a rousingly radical demand by Peter Morgan of Luton to

> give private enterprise a bit of a chance in the field of Health . . . We ought – it is in the spirit of Conservatism to have this – to have a choice when it comes to the National Health Service or a private scheme. This proposal is in the spirit of a free market; it is in the spirit of Conservatism; and it is in the spirit of Capitalism, the badge of which we are so proud to wear.

Sir Keith's reply was straightforward:

> I do not think we should follow Peter Morgan's advice. Private health insurance does not cover old age; it does not cover for mental illness or for mental handicap. Only 5 per cent of the cost of the National Health Service is borne on the stamp, so I hope you will not think his advice is right.[43]

Nevertheless, despite the nature of the rank and file language contained in the motions and speeches here referred to, the evidence does show clearly that the National Health Service has not attracted an extreme right wing ideological commitment from the rank and file, although there is a balance in favour of the right wing orientation. More interestingly, all the motions associated with the latter orientation can be comfortably categorised as libertarian, though there is not the same correlation between collectivism and a 'leftist' orientation. The libertarian (left) motions mainly relate to exemption of various groups from certain charges. The most numerous examples of such motions are those requesting the exemption of various groups (such as women over sixty, pensioners generally, and sufferers from pulmonary tuberculosis) from prescription charges.

Housing

In contrast to other devices which aim at achieving a property-owning democracy (such as co-partnership, wider share ownership, profit sharing), the encouragement of home ownership has played a significant part in rank and file thinking since the war. Indeed, in 1958 the mover of an almost unanimously approved motion reaffirming 'the faith' of conference in 'the wider private ownership of house property' believed it to be central not only to Conservative thought but also to 'our civilisation'. This was so because such ownership provided for the 'healthy growth' of the family which was 'our only sure bulwark against barbarism of mind and character' as exemplified by 'the power of alternative types of social grouping, based on the exclusive self-interest of members . . . akin to the social organisation of jungle beasts, and liable when given power to behave as savagely.'[44] Unfortunately, as in this particular passage, a significant number of motions have contented themselves simply with praising the concept of a property-owning democracy and the importance of encouraging and assisting home ownership, without defining the role of the State in this.

Nevertheless, there have been large numbers of motions which do contain sufficient substance to be classified, amongst which the libertarian (right) has been consistently dominant. That it has been so, even in periods when the Conservatives were in power, is to a large part explained by the presence of two major themes in rank and file motions in the 1950s. Firstly, the campaign against the Rent Restriction Acts which culminated in the 1957 Rent Act, and, secondly, the succeeding campaign against the abolition of Schedule A tax, which continued until the tax was abolished in 1963.[45] The motions on rent restrictions formed a significant part of all motions on housing prior to 1957. Thus in 1952 the proportion was 40 per cent; in 1953, 36 per cent; in 1955, 13 per cent; in 1956, 67 per cent. 1954 was the year of the Housing Repairs and Rent Act which evoked only one approving motion from the rank and file. 1953 and 1955 were interesting years in that there was a significant number of related motions on the question of rent restriction. As manifestations of faith in the free market, motions on rent restriction provided an important back-cloth to the passage of the 1957 Rent Act.[46] Nevertheless, the campaign against Schedule A tax was the larger and the more consistently pursued. For example, in 1957 motions on the tax represented 25 per cent of all housing motions; in 1958, 47 per cent; in 1960, 82 per cent; and in 1961, 79 per cent. In 1962 there were two motions which, though welcoming the Conservative leadership's commitment to abolition, also urged quick implementation of this commitment. The campaign against Schedule A tax has indeed been quoted as one of the classic instances within the Conservative Party of rank and file pressure forcing the leadership's hand.[47]

However, the successful culmination of these two campaigns has not meant the cessation of motions calling for further cuts in rent restrictions and taxation relief for either present or prospective house owners. On the contrary, this has been particularly the case during the 1960s and 1970s in those motions calling for the provision of economic rents. Most of these motions, however, have referred to the charging of economic rents on council housing and the directly associated question of the council house subsidy. Such concerns have a long tradition in post-war rank and file attitudes towards housing (the sale of council houses is another), as is shown, for example, in 1953 by motion 95. Moreover, it is interesting to note that collectivist (right) motions have throughout this period used the council housing subsidy as a lever to gain more state money for the private sector. Thus in 1947 motion 77 requested:

> That when the Conservative Party is returned to power . . . it shall be part of their policy that houses built for owner-occupation by private enterprise shall receive a subsidy comparable in its effects to the subsidy granted to local authorities . . .

By the 1960s however, not only had the rank and file's attitude towards the subsidy become more radical but its erosion was also linked with the provision of more funds for the private sector. Thus in 1965 motion 63 requested

> the next Conservative Government . . . to consider the introduction of legislation, subject to necessary safeguards, on the following lines:- the payment of a grant to assist towards the deposit for house purchase . . . the limitation of Exchequer housing subsidies to those local authorities who operate an approved differential rent scheme.

Whilst the Conservative government of 1970-74 did not satisfy all such requirements, the big step it took towards satisfying rank and file views on economic rents was revealed by the widespread approval shown in housing motions that year towards that government's Housing Finance Act of 1972.

Education

The Conservatives have always regarded education as an area in which public expenditure should be expanded. This was very noticeable in the years of Crowther and Robbins in the early 1960s. The vast majority of the motions calling for additional public expenditure are concerned with the public sector of education and are thus of a collectivist (left) nature. Nevertheless, this has not prevented certain rank and file representatives from calling for the use of state funds to bolster private education, nor has it prevented them from occasionally wishing to use the power of the State to root subversive political influences from key positions in the state education sector.[48]

Libertarian (right) views have tended to be constantly grouped around two major themes; firstly, the call for income tax relief for those parents wishing to educate their children privately; and secondly, the pledges to fight comprehensivisation as, in particular, a restriction on the freedom of choice. The first of these themes has been the most consistently expressed whilst the second, with certain notable exceptions (particularly in 1958), has been mainly concentrated in the post-Circular 10/65 era and has provided the main focus of rank and file attitudes on education in this period.

In the 1950s and early 1960s an interesting association with the first of the above themes is to be found in the call for the abolition of the means testing of middle-class families whose children wanted and were able to pursue higher education. Thus in 1958 motion 188 asked 'That this Conference urges Her Majesty's Government to abolish the means test imposed on parents who are given a grant for the education of their children.' Two years later Dudley Smith MP (Brentford and Chiswick), moving that the means testing of student grants should be ended in line with the majority report of the Anderson Committee, declared that:

> . . . these means tests are pressing very severely on some parents of the middle income group . . . I [have] received a number of interesting letters, one of which came from a man in Bristol, who is privately educating four children. I should like to quote a brief extract from it: 'It seems to be assumed that, because, on paper, the gross income of a middle class family appears larger than that of a working class family, the grant can be cut to next to nothing and the value of the Exhibition is completely cancelled out, being regarded as relief to the State and not the parent or the boy. No regard seems to be given to the fact that professional men have to spend more to maintain the living standards required by their job.'[49]

This essentially libertarian (right) appeal for greater relief to match greater financial responsibilities was, however, seen by one of the members of the rank and file as a dangerous erosion of pure libertarianism:

> I consider the proposal to abolish the parents' income test in relation to student grants wrong on three grounds – in principle, morally and financially. On principle it is against the Conservative ideas of self-reliance and independence. Morally, we would be hypocritical as a party to demand that council house tenants should not receive a rate subsidy on their rents because of the size of income going into the council houses, if at the same Conference we were to demand that well-to-do parents should receive a subsidy towards the education of their children . . . Financially, it is wrong because it increases the financial burden on the taxpayer and ratepayer . . . You cannot have a reduction in taxation and at the same time demand additional help from the Government for sections of the population.[50]

The speaker's appeal for consistency was ignored, however, and the motion carried by an overwhelming majority.

Nevertheless, the Conservative rank and file did have a clear signpost in the fight against comprehensivisation and for the freedom of choice. Thus in 1972 the mover of motion 255, whilst declaring his belief in 'equality of opportunity of education', nevertheless expressed the belief 'that the wishes of parents and the potentialities of a child must be taken into account when the move from primary to secondary education takes place.' Any attempt 'to use a child's ability to further social engineering is heading straight for the totalitarian collectivism that rules behind the Iron Curtain.'

It is interesting to note, however, that a number of speakers in debating the issue implicitly highlighted the question mark that has often been held against the views of the Right in general: is it a philosophy *per se* or largely a set of reactions to the Left? Thus, in 1972, the opening speaker on the education debate bemoaned the fact that

> Too often the Socialists are making the running on policy in education. We in education committees are continuously faced with left wing demands for comprehensive this and comprehensive that, and for their own policies to be brought in. Too often we as a party . . . do not have enough positive alternatives to put in the field of education.[51]

A year later another opening speaker in the education debate was also expressing similar fears but was much more confident about the Conservative response, namely a more vigorous implementation of 'one of the cornerstones of modern Conservatism . . . the provision of choice for all [in education].'[52] Happily for this speaker Mrs Thatcher, the then Minister for Education and Science, was able to confirm that he was right, though, like innumerable Conservative ministers before her, she was much more cautious about the means of implementing the theory.

Immigration

Immigration, although it has strong links with foreign policy and British imperial traditions, nevertheless has strong domestic implications for the rank and file, associated as it is, in their minds, with many of the social and economic problems of British urban life. Thus in a short but significant immigration debate in 1958 one of the leading Conservative advocates of immigration restriction, Norman Pannel MP (Liverpool Kirkdale), quickly articulated many of the rank and file fears about the 'coloured Colonial Immigrants'. Firstly, the immigrants were spongers – 'of the 200,000 now here, some 10 per cent roughly are unemployed and many thousands of them are on National Assistance, never having been able to work in this country.' They exacerbated the housing problem and caused health problems – 'the majority of them . . . come here with no means or provision for housing and live in squalid, crowded conditions in the slums of our cities, all of which gives rise to grave social problems.' Finally, there was the moral threat – 'In the Metropolitan Police District of London there were 130 convictions for living on immoral earnings in 1957. Of these, 66, or no less than 50 per cent, concerned immigrants from the Commonwealth.'[53] Such fears were elaborated and supplemented in further debates on immigration and also in debates which dealt with related areas of interest, for example, social security and health. This is illustrated by the opening speech in the 1958 debate on social and health services in which Mrs J. Adams from Solihull bemoaned the fact that what had become virtually extinct diseases in Britain now stood a chance of reappearing because of the 'unlimited number of immigrants landing here without a medical examination . . . [going] to live in very, very crowded conditions . . . breeding grounds for disease.' She concluded, with some disgust, that she was 'a bit fed up with all this Mother Country Stuff, because after all, common sense must never be over-ruled by sentiment.'[54] The response of the rank and file was forthrightly collectivist (Right). The State was to be used to restrict immigration, ranging from medical and literacy tests, proof of employment, restriction of work permits, quota schemes, through to calls for outright restriction (which were not quelled by the passage of the 1962 Commonwealth Immigration Act).

It is true that there were also a number of motions seeking seemingly to help the immigrant within Britain.[55] Nevertheless, many 'friendly' motions had an unpleasant sting in their tail. Motion 511 of 1968, 'whilst regretting the increasing signs of racial prejudice and intolerance', believed that these stemmed in large part 'from the inadequacy of housing, education and medical facilities available in areas with a high concentration of immigrants.' Thus it called upon the Conservative Party

> to issue a detailed statement of policy which will include the following points:
> (a) The provision of special financial assistance to those areas with a large immigrant population so that they may provide housing, educational and medical facilities adequate to their needs.
> (b) The effective curtailment of further immigration for at least five years.
> (c) The provision of financial assistance to those immigrants who wish to return to their country of origin.

The latter type of 'assistance' was more typical of the kind of 'help' that the rank and file were prepared to extend to the immigrant population after 1968.

Libertarianism reared its head in two major forms. The libertarianism of a leftward persuasion is mainly to be found in that periodically small number of motions calling for the protection of the rights of those immigrants who were qualified to remain in Britain.[56] In contrast, the more numerous libertarian (Right) motions were almost exclusively those concerned with denouncing the 1968 Race Relations Act as an infringement of personal liberty.[57]

Law and order

Reference has been made earlier to the fact that the use of law to maintain social order is one example of the use of the collectivist power of the State to which a libertarian of the Right would not object. It is interesting to note the extent to which, especially from the mid-1950s onwards, conference motions wished to use the power of the State to detect, deter, or punish the manifestations of crime by increasing support for the police or by imposing severer penalties: collectivist (right); or alternatively, by seeking out and eradicating the causes of crime: collectivist (left). The overwhelming majority of motions were of the former variety. A typical example is motion 22 of 1971 which stated 'That this Conference is concerned at the present level of violent crimes in this country and urges Her Majesty's Government to strengthen our police forces and to introduce far sterner penalties to dissuade possible future offenders.'

Of greater interest in analysing the debate between libertarianism and collectivism are those motions which deal with the question of the relation of the State to moral order. Although the rank and file was probably not acquainted with the intricacies of the Hart vs Devlin debate, there was little doubt where it stood on the question of the enforcement of morals. The State should act firmly and positively to resist the erosion of the traditional moral order by the insidious incursion of the permissive society with its tolerance of pornography, drugs, homosexuality and abortion. An illustration of this viewpoint is provided by motion 1242 of 1969 which demanded:

> That this Conference takes note of the public anxiety over increased crime, drug-taking, obscenity and other excessive permissiveness and calls upon the Conservative Party when in power to uphold civilised values both in legislation and in standards of public leadership.

The rank and file was never predisposed to appreciate the illogicality of demanding such action whilst at the same time liberally sprinkling references to individual freedom throughout so many other motions and debates.[58]

What can be concluded from the above picture? Firstly, it would be a mistake to regard the Party Conference as being solidly behind libertarianism of the Right throughout the period. This can be demonstrated by examining that category of motions which Rose has called 'consumerism' – the desire for more from the government coffers – side by side with 'principled' calls for retrenchment in government expenditure. Nowhere is this more apparent than in those motions relating to management of the economy, particularly in the years of post-1960 Conservative governments. One is on safer ground, however, in regarding the social security system as a much more solid redoubt of right wing libertarianism. Here at least Mrs Thatcher would appear to have found an unequivocal echo of her views on 'shirkers'.

However, such would not be her experience if she tried to discover widespread libertarian (right) support for another of her major policy positions – sympathetic government action towards small businessmen, those stalwarts of the Tory rank and file. In only one year – 1969 – has the number of motions on small businesses *per se* gone into double figures. This might well be indicative of the fact that a section of the community which is usually identified solidly with one political party suffers the worst of all worlds – complete disregard on the part of the opposing party and complacent lethargy on the part of the friendly party. Add to this the historical difficulty of organising the notoriously individualistic small business community and one perhaps does not find it so unexpected that its political and electoral significance for the Conservative Party is not reflected in the motions. Nevertheless, at the other end of the industrial spectrum the preponderance of libertarian (right) motions on the question of trade union affairs would seem to support Thatcherite individualism, though, as we have seen, the policy of her Shadow Cabinet on this question has been rather confused.

Further confusion is added by the prevalence of collectivism – both of the left and right wing varieties – amongst conference motions. In the former case pensions, especially, have proved to be an area where the rank and file was prepared to use state resources on an expanding scale, though the social class of the recipients of such largesse was often confined to the ranks of the middle-classes. Left wing collectivism also formed a considerable proportion of all the motions on health and education, though in the periods of opposition the latter tended to attract a majority of libertarian (right) motions. Moreover, the increasing contentiousness of educational issues in the political arena at the end of the period was reflected in the increasing right wing libertarianism of both motions and debates.

Right wing collectivism is most noticeable in the areas of law and order and immigration. The first is unexceptionable and can easily be squared with the conscience of even the most ardent Conservative liberal. Such is not necessarily the case when one comes to the area of immigration, necessitating as it does positive state discrimination against certain sections of the community. Perhaps it would help in this, as in the other areas referred to, if one were to drop the search for intellectual consistency amongst the rank and file and regard it as merely expressing what – with reference to the Monday Club – Seyd has seen as a perfectly consistent class interest. Yet even here one must be careful. The Monday Club – not without considerable sympathetic support amongst the Conservative rank and file – has been seen to be antagonistic towards the extension of state power even in the area of immigration control, as was shown by its opposition to the State's assumption of retrospective powers in the 1971 Immigration Act.[59].

The scene is further confused when one sees that throughout the period – no matter how numerous and how voluble the rank and file's opinions on important domestic issues – whenever the leadership felt itself embarrassed by an extremist rank and file position, it had little difficulty in rendering it ineffective. Moreover, it had little difficulty, whether in opposition or government, in persuading the rank and file to vote for motions which, if not directly in contrast to the feelings of the rank and file, were often largely irrelevant to what it appeared to consider the real issues. This suggests the operation of a number of factors within the Conservative Party, either singly or in combination. Firstly, the influence of the leadership was and is still strong. Secondly, the rank and file's principles are not as strongly held as rhetoric would have the reader believe. Thirdly, the 'politicised' sections of the rank and file are in a minority vis-à-vis the 'non-politicised' sections. The latter is a point worth particular consideration in view of the numbers of constituency parties which do not submit motions and also the proportionately large numbers, in nearly all sections, of banal and non-contentious motions.

Nevertheless, from a numerical point of view it is clear that the motions of a right wing libertarian line have played a major role in virtually every Conservative Party Conference since the war, particularly in the years of opposition. However, at the same time, one is faced with the considerable numbers of banal and non-contentious motions; with those from a collectivist viewpoint – whether of right or left; and with the ideologically confused motions – particularly in the sphere of management of the economy. The presence, in large numbers, of such motions throughout the period inhibits any description of Conservative Party Conferences as essentially gatherings of right wing libertarians. It would appear, despite certain reservations, that the Conservative Party Conference has been and is surer of its class interest than its ideological consistency.

Notes

[1]   See '... and for her own party,' *The Economist*, 15 February 1975. Where the term ideology is used in this chapter it will not be in a sophisticated way but simply to refer to the ideas deployed by various Conservatives: in this connection see W. H. Greenleaf, 'The Character of Modern British Conservatism', in R. Benewick, R. N. Berki and B. Parekh (eds), *Knowledge and Belief in Politics*, Allen and Unwin, London 1973, p. 178.

[2]   The facilities for the consultation of constituency opinion under the new arrangements for the election of the party leader did not, unfortunately, lead to an unambiguous assertion of rank and file opinion in the leadership election – see P. Seyd, 'Case study – democracy within the Conservative Party', *Government and Opposition*, vol. 10, 1975, pp. 219–37. Butt, however, seemed more certain about rank and file sympathy for Mrs Thatcher – see his article on 'The good that can come from the Tories' cash shortage', *The Times*, 13 March 1975.

[3]   R. Rose, 'Who are the Tory Militants?', *Crossbow*, vol. 5, no. 17, 1961, pp. 35–9. He describes the motions as 'resolutions'. This is, in one sense true in that they are resolutions which constituency parties submit to Party conferences. However, the term 'motion' is the one used in respective Conservative Handbooks and thus in this chapter the word 'resolution' will only be used to describe those motions chosen for debate at conference and subsequently passed by it.

[4]   Ibid. Basing his assessment on an analysis of motions submitted to party conferences from 1955 to 1960, Rose came to the conclusion that the views of the party activists were not as militant in reality as they were in 'the fertile brain of journalists.'

[5]   On the relationship between debates and motions chosen for debate see A. Gamble, *The Conservative Nation*, Routledge and Kegan Paul, London 1974, p. 81.

[6]   See P. Vander Elst, 'Radical Toryism – the libertarian alternative', *Political Quarterly*, vol. 46, 1975, pp. 65–72; M. Peston, 'Conservative economic policy and philosophy', *Political Quarterly*, vol. 44, 1973, pp. 411–24; and P. Seyd, 'Factionalism within the Conservative Party: The Monday Club', *Government and Opposition*, vol. 7, 1972, pp. 464–87.

[7]   Greenleaf, op. cit., pp. 181–2.

[8]   Ibid., p. 204.

[9]   Peston, op. cit., p. 411.

[10]   See pp. 72–6 and also pp. 105–6 of this book.

[11]   See, in particular, the contributions of Carr, Prior, Whitelaw, and Heath, *The Daily Telegraph*, 29 January, 31 January, 1 February and 3

February 1975 respectively. Mrs Thatcher's article was published on 30 January.

[12] I would like to thank *The Daily Telegraph* for giving me permission to reproduce quotations from the article. All emphasis is as in the original.

[13] It is not the aim of this chapter to discuss the nature of collectivism. For a discussion on its nature within the Party see Greenleaf, op. cit., pp. 182 ff and the debate on the Industrial Charter, Verbatim Report, pp. 46–54.

[14] As an illustration of the first type of these motions see motion 195, Handbook 1958; for the second type, see motion 494, Handbook 1970; for the third type, see motions 3 and 12, Handbook 1958.

[15] J. Critchley, 'Stresses and strains in the Conservative Party', *Political Quarterly*, vol. 44, 1973, pp. 401–10. The explanations of the relatively significant dips in 1965, 1970 and 1971 may reflect electoral considerations in the first two cases (a reluctance not to embarrass in 1965 and complacency in 1970). 1971 may reflect a feeling of satisfaction that the Selsdon Man experiment was still healthy.

[16] Handbook 1956. Where the number and year of the motion is cited no reference will be made to the Handbook in the chapter endnotes.

[17] In 1973 the balance was 44 to 10 in favour of the controls over incomes which the government had introduced in that year.

[18] There was a majority of motions against Beeching in 1963 but 1973 represented the height of support for the public transportation system. It is interesting to compare motion 125 of 1963 with motion 910 of 1973 – both seemed to appreciate that the costing of transportation was not simply a matter of commercial profit and loss.

[19] A particularly good example is motion 741 of 1968.

[20] Debate on the economic situation, Verbatim Report 1952, pp. 42–52.

[21] See Seyd, 'Factionalism within the Conservative Party.' Critchley, op. cit., has dryly observed that it is 'difficult to defer to our leaders when we now elect them. The embourgeoisement of the Conservative Party in the House of Commons, and beyond it, has made the task of the party management more difficult.'

[22] See Gamble, op. cit., p. 59. The last three factors were quite frequently linked together in the mind of the rank and file – see motion 108, Handbook 1949.

[23] Gamble, op. cit., p. 133.

[24] Motion 369, Handbook 1957. On liberal Conservative attitudes towards monopoly see N. Harris, *Competition and the Corporate Society*, Methuen, London 1972, p. 128.

[25] Motion 251, Handbook 1965. It is interesting to note that apart from three motions in 1951 denouncing Labour plans for abolishing many aspects

of RPM, there were very few motions pertaining to it *per se* and those that were submitted were in favour of its abolition.

[26] Apart from 'disguised' small business motions in the taxation schemes, those motions dealing exclusively with the question of small businessmen show a comfortable majority of libertarian (Right) motions over all others. This is mainly due to the acceleration, from the late 1960s onwards, of the number of motions calling for a diminution of the tax burden on small businesses.

[27] 'Small firms', Report of the Committee of Inquiry on Small Firms, Cmnd. 4811, HMSO London 1971, p. 193.

[28] See motion 210, Handbook 1961 and motion 1065, Handbook 1969.

[29] For the views of Angus Maude see Gamble, op. cit., p. 105. Peregrine Worsthorne's pertinent views on the 'social virtue of capitalism' are contained in his essay 'Priorities for capitalism' which is part of the four-part CPC pamphlet (no. 350) 'Conservativism today', 1966, pp. 17–30. See also B. Patterson, 'The character of conservativism', CPC no. 532, London 1973, pp. 18–21.

[30] Seyd, 'Factionalism within the Conservative Party', p. 480.

[31] Gamble, op. cit., pp. 156–7.

[32] See Mr Beaman's speech in the industrial relations debate, Verbatim Report 1957, pp. 87–93.

[33] See, for example, the debate on pensions and allowances, Verbatim Report 1963, pp. 33–9. Believing themselves largely independent of the Welfare State, the rank and file occasionally expressed the belief that, in return, they should receive financial concessions from the State (see e.g. motion 160, Handbook 1956). Furthermore, they have always regarded the level of provision of the Welfare State as being contingent on national prosperity and not as a factor in creating it (see, for example, motion 3, Handbook 1949 and motion 429, Handbook 1966 – 'That this Conference believes that a country which has failed to achieve economic efficiency cannot afford social extravagance').

[34] Motion 150, Handbook 1960.

[35] Harris, op. cit., p. 270.

[36] Gamble, op. cit., pp. 59–60.

[37] David Lewis in the debate on social security and health, Verbatim Report 1970, pp. 48–54.

[38] See the debate on social policy and the cost of living, Verbatim Report 1965, pp. 89–96.

[39] Following the Report of the Committee on the Abuse of Social Security Benefits, Cmnd. 5228, HMSO 1973, the DHSS decided to appoint

sixty new special investigators. See Ruth Lister's article on this committee in *Poverty*, no. 26, Summer 1973, pp. 9–11.

[40] See the debate on social services and Health, Verbatim Report 1973, pp. 89–99.

[41] Verbatim Report 1969, pp. 52–9.

[42] See the debate on the health Service, Verbatim Report 1960, pp. 125–30.

[43] See the debate on social services and health, Verbatim Report 1973, pp. 89–99.

[44] See the debate on home ownership, Verbatim Report 1958, pp. 32–8.

[45] For the background to the Rent Restrictions Acts and their relationship to the 1957 Rent Act, see J. Barnett, *The Politics of Legislation – The Rent Act 1957*, Weidenfeld and Nicolson, London 1969, pp. 19–29. As for the campaign against Schedule A tax, this only really started in earnest in 1957. Nevertheless, there had been references to its abolition/diminution as early as 1948 (motion 77, Handbook 1948).

[46] See Barnett, op. cit., pp. 71–3.

[47] See J. O'Sullivan, 'Shuffling to the Right', *The Spectator*, 22 March 1975, pp. 338–9.

[48] For an example of the former see motion 178, Handbook 1955. On the latter see motion 113, Handbook 1954 and motions 318–22, Handbook 1972.

[49] See the debate on education, Verbatim Report 1960, pp. 28–36.

[50] Ibid.

[51] Verbatim Report 1972, pp. 59–65.

[52] Verbatim Report 1973, pp. 108–15.

[53] Verbatim Report 1958, pp. 149–51.

[54] Verbatim Report 1958, pp. 145–9.

[55] See for example motion 526, Handbook 1968.

[56] For example, motion 654, Handbook 1969.

[57] For example, motion 493, Handbook 1968.

[58] See Gamble, op. cit., p. 112; also motion 652, Handbook 1969 and motion 493, Handbook 1968.

[59] See Derek Humphry, 'Did M.P.s blunder into double-cross of immigrants?', *The Sunday Times*, 17 June 1973.

Appendix 4.1*
Management of the economy

Year	Total of motions submitted	Total of motions on management of economy	Libertarian (right)	Collectivist (right)	Libertarian (left)	Collectivist (left)	Others
1945	52	7	3	–	–	3	1
1946	67	8	4	1	–	2	2
1947	125	34	11	–	–	20	3
1948	178	35	25	1	–	8	2
1949	143	42	27	3	–	2	10
1950	149	30	21	1	–	4	4
1951	187	37	17	3	–	1	16
1952	186	33	13	2	–	6	12
1953	212	37	21	–	–	–	16
1954	252	36	21	–	·–	6	9
1955	292	54	29	–	–	12	13
1956	394	107	56	–	–	7	44
1957	412	122	61	1	–	22	38
1958	447	53	31	2	–	10	10
1960	415	91	53	–	–	18	20
1961	536	66	31	–	–	7	28
1962	532	103	41	–	–	32	30
1963	535	100	45	–	–	32	23
1965	616	80	70	–	–	4	12
1966	534	140	107	–	–	17	16
1967	712	204	165	1	–	16	22
1968	1,031	240	195	–	–	21	24
1969	1,250	200	146	3	–	18	33
1970	900	121	67	–	–	23	31
1971	766	117	73	–	–	16	28
1972	1,062	182	69	–	–	46	67
1973	1,304	231	88	1	–	97	45

* Figures for 1959 and 1964 are omitted in all the appendices. No conference was held in either of these years due to the timing of the general election. For the same reason there was no conference in 1951. However, this did not prevent the submission of motions and the publication of a handbook – hence the inclusion of this year in the appendices.

Appendix 4.2

Trade Unions

Year	Total of motions submitted	Total of motions relating to TUs	Libertarian (right)	Collectivist (right)	Libertarian (left)	Collectivist (left)	Others
1945	52	1	–	–	–	–	1
1946	67	3	–	–	–	2	1
1947	125	6	2	–	–	–	4
1948	178	14	7	1	–	–	6
1949	143	14	3	2	–	3	6
1950	149	8	1	–	–	–	7
1951	187	15	3	–	1	2	9
1952	186	6	1	–	–	1	4
1953	212	10	4	–	–	3	3
1954	252	14	2	–	–	6	6
1955	292	34	6	1	1	8	18
1956	393	29	10	4	1	1	13
1957	412	28	6	8	–	4	10
1958	447	35	21	–	–	1	13
1960	415	16	10	–	–	2	4
1961	536	41	29	–	–	2	10
1962	532	43	25	–	–	13	5
1963	535	31	18	–	–	6	7
1965	616	48	37	–	–	1	10
1966	534	37	34	–	–	1	3
1967	712	21	10	5	–	4	2
1968	1,031	37	23	6	–	4	3
1969	1,250	81	57	12	–	3	9
1970	900	46	26	4	–	4	12
1971	766	28	12	6	–	6	4
1972	1,062	57	34	10	–	3	10
1973	1,304	24	12	5	–	1	6

Appendix 4.3

Social Security

Year	Total of motions submitted	Total of motions on social security	Libertarian (right)	Collectivist (right)	Libertarian (left)	Collectivist (left)	Others
1945	52	2	1	–	–	1	–
1946	67	–	–	–	–	–	–
1947	125	1	–	–	–	–	1
1948	178	4	2	–	–	2	–
1949	143	1	1	–	–	–	–
1950	149	–	–	–	–	–	–
1951	187	–	–	–	–	–	–
1952	186	2	1	–	–	–	1
1953	212	1	1	–	–	–	–
1954	252	1	1	–	–	–	–
1955	292	1	1	–	–	–	–
1956	393	4	3	–	–	1	–
1957	412	–	–	–	–	–	–
1958	447	1	1	–	–	–	–
1960	415	1	1	–	–	–	–
1961	536	3	1	–	–	–	2
1962	532	5	5	–	–	–	–
1963	535	2	2	–	–	–	–
1965	616	41	32	–	–	6	6
1966	534	13	11	–	–	2	–
1967	712	28	26	–	–	–	2
1968	1,031	26	20	–	–	–	6
1969	1,250	82	71	–	5	6	–
1970	900	29	23	–	–	6	–
1971	766	52	30	–	8	7	7
1972	1,062	94	60	–	4	14	16
1973	1,304	112	62	–	2	34	14

Appendix 4.4

Pensions

Year	Total of motions submitted	Total of motions on pensions	Libertarian (right)	Collectivist (right)	Libertarian (left)	Collectivist (left)	Others
1945	52	–	–	–	–	–	–
1946	67	–	–	–	–	–	–
1947	125	1	–	–	–	–	1
1948	178	–	–	–	–	–	–
1949	143	1	–	–	–	1	–
1950	149	4	1	–	1	2	–
1951	187	5	–	–	–	2	3
1952	186	3	–	–	–	3	–
1943	212	11	–	–	3	4	4
1954	252	32	3	–	12	13	4
1955	292	25	–	–	6	16	3
1956	394	21	2	–	8	9	2
1957	412	23	2	–	5	15	1
1958	447	21	3	–	11	4	2
1960	415	26	–	–	10	13	3
1961	536	36	1	–	5	28	2
1962	532	59	–	–	15	40	4
1963	535	55	1	–	6	44	4
1965	616	55	3	–	3	48	1
1966	534	11	–	–	1	9	1
1967	712	16	–	–	5	11	–
1968	1,031	14	3	–	5	6	–
1969	1,250	15	7	–	1	7	–
1970	900	16	6	–	1	9	–
1971	766	26	2	–	5	10	–
1972	1,062	16	1	–	5	10	–
1973	1,304	46	2	–	22	21	1

Appendix 4.5

Health

Year	Total of motions submitted	Total of motions on health	Libertarian (right)	Collectivist (right)	Libertarian (left)	Collectivist (left)	Others
1945	52	2	1	–	–	1	–
1946	67	–	–	–	–	–	–
1947	125	1	–	–	–	–	1
1948	178	1	–	–	–	–	1
1949	143	3	2	–	–	1	–
1950	149	4	–	–	–	–	4
1951	187	7	2	–	–	3	2
1952	186	1	1	–	–	–	–
1953	212	5	2	–	1	–	2
1954	252	–	–	–	–	–	–
1955	292	4	1	–	–	–	3
1956	394	4	2	–	–	1	1
1957	412	15	3	–	–	6	6
1958	447	6	2	–	–	1	3
1960	415	16	7	–	–	1	8
1961	536	17	3	2	–	–	12
1962	532	16	–	6	–	–	10
1963	535	11	2	–	–	–	9
1965	616	11	5	–	–	–	6
1966	534	7	–	–	–	2	5
1967	612	17	9	–	–	4	4
1968	1,031	21	7	–	1	3	10
1969	1,250	32	9	–	–	11	12
1970	900	26	12	–	–	6	8
1971	766	17	5	–	–	3	9
1972	1,062	11	4	–	1	–	6
1973	1,304	35	3	–	–	8	24

Appendix 4.6

Housing

Year	Total of motions submitted	Total of motions on housing	Libertarian (right)	Collectivist (right)	Libertarian (left)	Collectivist (left)	Others
1945	52	3	–	–	–	1	2
1946	67	1	1	–	–	–	–
1947	125	4	1	1	–	–	2
1948	178	6	5	–	–	–	1
1949	143	3	1	–	–	–	2
1950	149	19	3	–	–	–	16
1951	187	12	4	–	–	–	8
1952	186	15	10	3	–	–	2
1953	212	33	24	4	–	–	5
1954	252	12	7	2	–	–	3
1955	292	16	13	–	–	–	3
1956	394	15	11	3	–	–	1
1957	412	24	19	4	–	–	1
1958	447	45	29	7	–	–	9
1960	415	65	57	–	–	4	4
1961	536	48	40	1	–	5	2
1962	532	50	18	8	–	8	16
1963	535	44	20	–	–	14	10
1965	616	62	23	3	–	13	23
1966	534	39	8	–	–	1	30
1967	712	60	36	–	–	7	17
1968	1,031	34	25	–	–	3	6
1969	1,250	87	48	8	–	10	21
1970	900	54	29	3	–	9	13
1971	766	45	25	2	–	8	10
1972	1,062	100	54	6	–	15	25
1973	1,304	119	62	11	–	20	26

Appendix 4.7

Education

Year	Total of motions submitted	Total of motions on education	Libertarian (right)	Collectivist (right)	Libertarian (left)	Collectivist (left)	Others
1945	52	–	–	–	–	–	–
1946	67	–	–	–	–	–	–
1947	149	1	–	–	–	–	1
1948	178	1	–	–	–	1	–
1949	143	3	2	–	–	1	–
1950	149	6	2	–	–	2	2
1951	187	5	4	–	–	1	–
1952	186	9	6	–	–	–	3
1953	212	13	5	2	–	3	3
1954	252	16	5	2	–	4	5
1955	292	17	7	3	–	3	4
1956	394	21	14	1	–	1	5
1957	412	19	9	–	–	2	8
1958	447	34	25	–	–	2	7
1960	415	23	9	–	–	8	6
1961	536	20	4	2	–	8	6
1962	532	24	2	–	–	11	11
1963	535	28	–	–	–	18	10
1965	616	49	44	1	–	3	1
1966	534	51	38	1	–	7	5
1967	712	55	39	–	–	9	7
1968	1,031	80	28	–	–	30	22
1969	1,250	102	46	3	–	23	30
1970	900	57	27	–	–	15	15
1971	766	72	32	5	–	9	26
1972	1,062	97	41	13	–	16	27
1973	1,304	117	72	–	–	13	32

Immigration

Year	Total of motions submitted	Total of motions on immigration	Libertarian (right)	Collectivist (right)	Libertarian (left)	Collectivist (left)	Others
1945	52	–	–	–	–	–	–
1946	67	–	–	–	–	–	–
1947	125	–	–	–	–	–	–
1948	178	–	–	–	–	–	–
1949	143	–	–	–	–	–	–
1950	149	–	–	–	–	–	–
1951	187	–	–	–	–	–	–
1952	186	–	–	–	–	–	–
1953	212	–	–	–	–	–	–
1954	252	1	–	1	–	–	–
1955	292	6	–	6	–	–	–
1956	394						
1957	412	3	–	3	–	–	–
1958	447	6	–	6	–	–	–
1960	415	7	–	7	–	–	–
1961	536	38	–	37	1	–	–
1962	532	2	–	2	–	–	–
1963	535	3	–	3	–	–	–
1965	616	32	2	27	–	3	–
1966	534	5	–	5	–	–	–
1967	712	9	–	9	–	–	–
1968	1,031	80	8	60	2	7	3
1969	1,250	31	5	17	2	2	5
1970	900	18	6	7	2	3	–
1971	766	17	–	13	–	1	3
1972	1,062	29	6	19	–	1	3
1973	1,304	53	6	43	2	2	–

Appendix 4.9

Law and Order

Year	Total of motions submitted	Total of motions on law and order	Libertarian (right)	Collectivist (right)	Libertarian (left)	Collectivist (left)	Others
1945	52	–	–	–	–	–	–
1946	67	–	–	–	–	–	–
1947	125	–	–	–	–	–	–
1948	178	–	–	–	–	–	–
1949	143	–	–	–	–	–	–
1950	149	2	–	–	–	1	1
1951	187	1	–	–	–	–	1
1952	186	5	–	–	–	5	–
1953	212	3	–	1	–	1	1
1954	252	–	–	–	–	–	–
1955	292	–	–	–	–	–	–
1956	394	35	35	35	–	–	–
1957	412	4	–	2	–	1	1
1958	447	32	–	26	–	2	4
1960	415	24	–	17	–	2	5
1961	536	66	–	57	–	8	1
1962	532	25	–	18	–	5	2
1963	535	18	–	7	–	11	–
1965	616	15	–	15	–	–	–
1966	534	24	–	24	–	1	2
1967	712	26	–	19	–	5	2
1968	1,031	28	–	20	–	2	6
1969	1,250	54	–	41	–	2	11
1970	900	55	–	42	–	6	7
1971	766	78	–	59	–	14	15
1972	1,062	80	–	61	–	4	15
1973	1,304	123	–	101	–	3	19

5 The nature of Powellism

K. PHILLIPS

One of the most interesting and most publicised developments in British politics since the mid-1960s has been the emergence, to considerable prominence, of Enoch Powell. Several collections of his speeches and writings have been published, his biography has been written, and many critical reviews of his political ideas have appeared. It is not intended here to duplicate any of these, although use will certainly be made of Powell's own words, aspects of his political career will be examined, and, it is hoped, a basis for rational and informed criticism of his thought will be provided. However, the central focus here is rather the new term that has gained wide currency in British political volcabulary as a result of Powell's emergence – 'Powellism'.

From the various ways in which the term has been used, it is possible to suggest at least three different meanings of Powellism according to the contrasting perspectives of those using the term. From an ideological viewpoint, the term is sometimes conferred upon Powell's political ideas because they are seen as achieving sufficient depth and internal consistency to provide a more or less universal guide to political conduct. From a political perspective, the term has been used more simply to suggest that Powell's ideas can be distinguished from other sets of ideas associated with an existing political party or faction and therefore in need of a separate title of their own. Finally, the term has commonly been used to describe the impact of Powell and his ideas on the electorate. These three alternative usages of the term Powellism provide a useful basis for an analysis of Powell's political ideas which, it is suggested here, are essentially contained in three major themes.

The first of these themes is embodied in his approach to a key policy issue of the post-war period, an issue with which he was closely involved as Minister of Health between 1960 and 1963, that of the role of the State in social welfare. Behind the numerous statements he has made over the years concerning this area there has been a central concern with the fundamental question of the principles that should govern the role of the State.

His position on the question can be analysed on two levels. On the general level lies his prescription that the role of the State in the field of social welfare should be limited. On the more theoretical level lies his definition of the principles which should determine the parameters of limited social provision

99

by the State. The first of these two levels of analysis involves an examination of his justification of non-state provision and also of his attack on political notions which serve to justify a wider role for the State than that which he proposes.

Powell has expressed the justification of non-state provision of social welfare in terms of a 'defence of institutions which are local and autonomous.'[1] The great value, to Powell, of local and autonomous provision of social welfare is that it ensures a corresponding diminution of bureaucracy and centralisation which in turn is a safeguard against rigidity.

The need to avoid rigidity and to encourage, on the other hand, spontaneous development and change is a central tenet in his approach to the social services. His Conservative Political Centre pamphlet on the Welfare State is, in the main, a direct attack on the inertia and institutionalisation which he believes characterises the provision of social services by the State.[2] Such inertia and institutionalisation are seen as having their roots in vested political interest where pressure is strongest to retain unchanged that which already exists.

This politics of inertia, Powell argues, has resulted in excessive social services in some areas and inadequate provision in others. By way of example of excess provision, Powell frequently points to housing and is fond of relating the 'natural history of the upas tree of housing as a social service.'[3] To Powell, the 'twin evils' of rent control and housing subsidy are anathema, and the 'sum total of misery and squalor' caused by them 'baffles calculation.'[4] In his view, the only success which governments have had through their housing policies has been 'in organising a never-ending, self-perpetuating shortage of housing.'[5] In part, Powell explains the continued existence of rent control and housing subsidy as a result of institutionalisation. They were introduced at the end of the First World War and re-introduced following the Second World War, in both cases to temporarily bridge the gap between pre-war and supposedly inflated post-war rents. But once institutionalised, the politics of inertia resulted in their retention.

Although Powell posits housing as 'the extreme instance of irrationality among all the social services,'[6] he finds examples of inertia and institutionalisation in many others. They are particularly manifest, he suggests, in the National Health Service. Indeed, as Minister of Health, he put forward the view that there is a basic and unresolvable conflict between the characteristics of a comprehensive state service and the possibilities of social change and medical progress: 'In this changing world poor Leviathan is left lumbering behind.'[7]

The need to encourage flexibility and spontaneity in the social services by the harnessing and development of private provision alongside public provision is only part of Powell's justification of a limited role for the State. Of equal importance is his rejection of two political notions which he sees as implying a threat to his general prescription: the political notions of rights and equality.

With an intensity similar to that of Bentham, Powell lambasts those who claim that the individual has a right to social services in order to attain and protect an adequate standard of living: 'This translation of a want or need into a right is one of the most widespread and dangerous of modern heresies'.[8]

The great heresy to Powell of resorting to the claiming of a right to certain social services is that it results in the total distortion of market mechanisms in their provision. Such a distortion occurs because demand is no longer relative to price but is universal, and because supply of the service is no longer free but subject to compulsion. Such compulsion follows because the corollary of a right is that of a duty, and the imposition of a duty requires the extension of state powers to ensure its fulfilment. For Powell, the necessary connection between the acceptance of the notion of a right applied to social provision and the limitless opportunity for the extension of state control has a further corollary, that of civil violence:

> The state which undertakes, and is accepted as undertaking the obligation to meet the general needs of the citizens is particularly vulnerable to violent agitation, for one simple reason – the obligation it has accepted is by its nature unlimited. It follows that the material for dissatisfaction is likewise unlimited.[9]

The unlimited role of the State is also seen as fostering animosities between one section of potential recipients and another.

Powell has equally vehemently attacked the notion of equality as a basis for state provision of the social services. He understands the notion of equality to mean the attempt to promote uniformity: the 'aim at averaging everything and everybody'.[10] Such a justification for state provision carries with it the two connected evils of, on the one hand, state compulsion and the elimination of all scope for choice and intiative, and, on the other hand, the failure to meet the requirements of those in greatest need.

The first of these evils is seen as a logical result of egalitarianism, since private provision implies choice and choice itself implies variation. The second follows because Powell sees egalitarianism as the bedfellow of universal, as opposed to selective, social benefits. He has stridently attacked the universal provision of benefits, his argument being as follows:

> The most obvious effect is that the community cannot afford as high a standard for the minority of its citizens who are actually dependent on it

101

for their individual needs as it could do if it was not to cater for everybody's needs. Benefits for all are the enemy of care for the few.[11]

It is this attack on universal benefits that has perhaps been most misunderstood popularly, the misunderstanding being to assume that Powell wishes to see the Welfare State, as it exists at present, demolished and all social welfare provided solely on the basis of needs as measured by some form of testing.

This is not in fact his position. Indeed he categorically rejects it as far as education is concerned, partly because it is easier to secure compulsory attendance where fees are not charged, and partly because education provision is less open to abuse. More importantly, he has suggested that education satisfies the following principle which should govern the question of means testing: 'The more easily a service approaches to a public and general benefit and recedes from a personal one, the more natural is its provision without charge or test of means'.[12]

Of the other social services, those in the health field are seen as the other major area where the above principle is satisfied.

It is with regard to social benefits which are more clearly personal and where there is dispensing of monetary payments as opposed to payments in kind that Powell is most in favour of an enquiry into means. Indicative of his attitude to such benefits is his position with regard to retirement pensions. With Iain Macleod, he traced the development of pension provision in an early CPC publication, and emphasised in particular how the Beveridge principle (that pensions should be insurance-based and fixed on an assessment of a subsistence minimum) had been eroded by inflation. The result, as the authors point out, was a greater reliance by those pensioners living below subsistence incomes on national assistance for which they were subject to a means test. Such a development was viewed as a 'most unwelcome fact.'[13] Two clear alternatives to this position were posited. Firstly, the abolition of the insurance principle in favour of the exclusive use of national assistance to bring the income of the retired up to subsistence level where necessary. Secondly, restoring the insurance benefit on an actuarial basis to subsistence level or slightly above. While the authors favoured the latter course of action with regard to the eventualities of sickness, unemployment and death, they were sceptical of its possibilities with regard to pensions because of the expense to the public purse over a considerable length of time of covering 'late entrants' to a totally actuarially-based pension scheme. They also saw it as increasingly unnecessary, given the growth of private insurance schemes and of personal savings. The solution they suggested was not to return to the Beveridge subsistence principle, but rather to the principle embodied in the 1908 Act:

We . . . appear to be led to ask whether the insurance pension should not again be regarded in the light in which it was originally presented – not as a self-sufficient basis for retirement, but as 'a basis so substantial that it will encourage people to try and add to it and thus achieve independence'.[14]

Since the publication of these views, Powell has appeared to move towards supporting the first of the alternatives mentioned above, and he has done so by increasingly emphasising the deleterious effect state provision of pensions has had on the development of private pension schemes, which he believes have become increasingly viable with increasing affluence.

The role of the State in this field should be to provide a generous guaranteed minimum pension only to those in need of it; this needs to be ascertained by investigation, and the pension to be paid as a supplement to existing income in order to bring the individual up to subsistence level. Such a view runs totally counter to recent Conservative and Labour Party proposals with their aim of providing a comprehensive system of pensions based on graduated contributions and assessed on level of earnings. Powell's attitude to this alternative has been clearly stated by Utley: 'To Powell, these tendencies are abhorrent. The function of State policy towards the aged is to achieve reasonable redistribution, not to impose the duty of providence'.[15]

This example provides insight into two other important aspects of Powell's view of the social services. The first is the point made by Utley with regard to redistribution. Powell is aware that an element of redistribution is essential to social services but rejects the view that the major objective should be to reduce inequalities of gross incomes.[16] It is more important to give a higher standard of assistance to a minority who are dependent on the community, and to give the general citizen greater rather than less control over the disposal of his income.

The second point of wider relevance is his notion of the 'minimum': that the role of the State should be to secure a minimum standard of life below which no one should fall. This is his principal response to the egalitarian argument: 'The emphasis is upon minimum – not in the sense of least possible, but as the opposite to average or uniform: the social services are not to be a levelling instrument'.[17]

Given Powell's notion of the minimum, it only remains to determine the factors which should decide the level of that minimum and the range of needs that it should cover. We thus come to the theoretical question raised by Powell's advocacy of the limited and selective Welfare State: the criteria by which the limits are to be set, both in quantitative and qualitative terms.

Powell establishes the parameters of the State's role in social welfare in terms of both economic and social criteria. The economic criteria are two-fold: those of market forces and national wealth.

His application of the former to the social services has been clearly stated:

> In this sphere . . . the Conservative urge towards 'less government' . . . does not mean dismantling the national health service or the state education system or withdrawing the state's ultimate guarantee of security against want. What it does mean is that where economic forces will provide services within this area, we shall see that they are not choked or driven out by the ever growing appetite of the state, but rather that the state withdraws as the action of individuals, expressing itself through market forces, advances.[18]

Earlier in the same speech Powell made it clear that by such 'economic forces' he meant 'commercial principles' operating in a free market. He has applied this principle of market forces as the determinant of the areas of social welfare in which the State ought *not* to intervene to a considerable number of social services at present encompassed within the Welfare State. We have already seen its application to social security in Powell's advocacy of a greater reliance on private provision based on commercial principles of insurance. He has also indicated that the principle has some application to the area of education. The possibility of its application to this area is based on a prior distinction he makes between two kinds of education: that where knowledge is imparted as a clear means to an end; and that where knowledge is imparted for its own sake. It is the first kind of education, which he sees as encompassing an increasing proportion of further and higher education, that could be 'self-financed and self-determined', especially where the ends are themselves the reflection of economic demands: 'Like other investment undertaken on the prospect of direct economic return, these could, and increasingly should, be financed without call on public funds'.[19]

But of all the social services, housing is the one where Powell has most consistently advocated the application of market principles, for it would end the housing shortage, make for a better use of resources, and ensure a satisfactory level of rents.

The other economic criterion that Powell has applied to the question of the limits on state involvement in social welfare is, stated simply, that the level of provision should be determined by what the nation can afford in terms of its wealth and the taxable capacity of its members.

Powell's emphasis here is entirely consistent with his theory of inflation, but it is also significant because it embodies the rejection of a frequently stated belief that increased expenditure on social services is justified because it promotes economic growth. 'Growth theory', as he has called it, has been described by Powell as 'bunkum'[20] and a 'widespread heresy of our times'.[21] Powell has been particularly vociferous in denying its application to expenditure on health and education. With regard to health it is his view that growth theory is 'in nearly all circumstances in error'[22] because there is an obvious and logical limit beyond which gross domestic product per head will not be increased by further outlays on health. It is also misguided because the achievement of such a limit would mean an emphasis on those health services which have a direct economic benefit, such as immunisation, at the expense of those which do not, such as geriatrics. He has described this development as implying a change from a health service to a veterinary service. He also regards it as an impossibility given the close connection between all aspects of the health services.

The true relationship between the health services and economic growth is, for Powell, the exact opposite to that of the growth theorists: 'It is not the health services which produce wealth, but wealth which makes possible expenditure upon the health services'.[23]

He reaches the same conclusion with regard to education[24] but goes further by claiming that growth theory in education is a major cause of student unrest and of the withering away of academic freedom.[25]

But he does not determine the limits to state action in social welfare solely in economic terms. 'Market forces' are a negative determinant in suggesting what the State ought not to be involved in; national wealth is a positive determinant but only in suggesting the correct level of expenditure by the State, not in determining the *range* of social services to be provided. In seeking an answer to this question, he resorts to his view of the nation as a community which has inherited a certain number of responsibilities for its members based upon a regard for fellow wellbeing:

> A great part of the efforts of a civilised community are devoted to purposes which are not economic at all but humane and human, altruistic if you please. Look at our vast expenditure . . . upon the National Health Service . . . It is completely, triumphantly, justified on the simple ground that a civilised, compassionate nation can do no other. It, and all the other social services, is the corporate recognition by the community of its common obligation to its individual members.[26]

In this way Powell translates nineteenth century paternalism into democratic terms. The State exists to provide those services which are deemed necessary by its members upon the basis of philanthropic consideration to ensure a tolerable living standard for all and which would not otherwise be provided.[27]

Powell's views on the social services are therefore complex, but taken together they can be seen as forming a coherent body of thought. Central to his view is the notion of the limited and selective Welfare State. For Powell no great advantage automatically accrues from state provision of social welfare. In all cases where private and independent agencies can carry out the provision of social welfare services operating under market conditions then the State ought not to intervene, and in those cases where provision can be made by independent agencies acting under charitable or similar motives the State ought to encourage them. This is advocated with regard to the first situation because it is more efficient, and for both situations because it allows greater flexibility and a wider area of choice for the individual. Where neither of these situations exist, then there is a place for state action but only on the grounds of corporate philanthropy – the community's view, as expressed by governments, of what is necessary to ensure the wellbeing of its members – and not on the grounds of either political theories of rights or equality, or economic theories of growth. Such theories are either misguided or lead to an ever-expanding role for the State which in turn on the one hand, destroys, choice, flexibility and efficiency, and, on the other hand, breeds dissatisfaction and in certain cases civil violence. Corporate philanthropy, as well as being limited to situations in which market forces and independent charity are not applicable, should also be limited to a regard for what the nation can afford. Such philanthropy should also be selective where services are essentially a benefit to the individual personally rather than to society generally, in the sense of being applied only to those in need. In these cases it should also be based on the concept of minimum standards to secure the satisfaction of defined needs. These limitations require that the range and level of social provision need to be constantly adjusted to meet the changing circumstances within society and the economy. For Powell there are no universal or fixed parameters to the Welfare State.

While Powell's position on social welfare is difficult to classify in terms of common political labels, his economic ideas are readily identifiable as an almost classical exposition of economic liberalism. Historically, the basis of this doctrine has been rooted in the interconnection between two sets of political and economic theories: certain views on the role of the State in economic affairs and others on the workings of the economy. In order to make Powell's particular exposition of the doctrine clear, these two strands will be examined separately.

A central theme in his speeches and writings on economic policy concerns the question of the role of the State in the economic affairs of a nation. Of his innumerable statements on this question there are two which set forth his position most explicitly: one is an article for the Bow Group journal, *Cross-*

bow, published in 1960;[28] the other is the text of a speech given to the Cambridge Union in 1968.[29]

In the *Crossbow* article, he lays down the view that for the Conservative, the role of the State in the economic field should be minimal: 'The Conservative, in principle denies, in practice minimises, Government intervention in the economic field'.[30] In his speech, the inclusion of the term 'intervention' in the above quotation takes on an added meaning for it is contrasted with the term 'regulation'. With the latter, it is argued, the State has a rightful role to play in the economic field. The distinction lies in the breadth of the effect: regulations are general and limited in nature; intervention is particular and universal and vests the State with the power and responsibility to direct the economic activities of its members.

Powell's main thesis then is that the role of the State in the economic field should be limited to regulation alone. But what is meant by the 'economic field'? Powell is too good a logician to leave such terms undefined. In the *Crossbow* article he offers the following definition: 'By the economic field, I mean all matters in which the difference between success and failure, right judgement and wrong depend on economic criteria'.[31] In his Cambridge Union speech, he is even more explicit and clarifies what is meant by economic criteria in this context: 'I mean a choice between alternatives which can be compared on a common and normally on a monetary scale.'[32] Excluded from his regulatory principles then are a wide number of decisions which, although they may affect the economic field, are, given his tight definition of this term, non-economic and thus open to a degree of intervention by the State. However, the extent of this intervention must, as we have seen from the example of social welfare, be determined by other principles.

The economic theory that forms the other strand of Powell's economic liberalism is his belief in the classical theory of free enterprise and the free market, or, as he is not afraid to call it, capitalism: 'Often when I am kneeling down in church, I think to myself how much we should thank God, the Holy Ghost, for the gift of capitalism'.[33] This is not the place to examine in any detail the classical economic theory to which Powell subscribes, although we shall have occasion to examine Powell's application of it to the question of inflation. Of greater interest is the justification he offers to support his belief in economic liberalism. This is likewise couched in both political and economic terms.

From a political standpoint, economic liberalism is seen by Powell as bringing with it the virtues of freedom, humanity, justice and democracy. With regard to freedom, Powell has written:

I happen to believe that when a society's economic life ceases to be

107

shaped by the interaction of the free decisions of individuals, freedom is in a fair way to disappear from other sides of its existence as well. The terms 'free democracy' and 'free society' are to me interchangeable.[34]

Economic liberalism is also seen as providing the key to a more humane political system because, being most productive, it can afford a greater expenditure on social welfare, It is also more just since 'The market is the fairest standard, impartial and impersonal, treating like things alike, which is the essence of justice'.[35]

It is also the lynchpin of democracy:

The free enterprise economy is the true counterpart of democracy: it is the only system which gives everyone a say . . . In this great and continuous general election of the free economy, nobody, not even the poorest, is disenfranchised: we are all voting all the time.[36]

Additionally, economic liberalism is seen as being congruent with 'the grain of human nature and of circumstances'.[37]

From an economic standpoint, economic liberalism is justified because it is the most efficient method of employing, and co-ordinating the use of, a nation's resources, both human and physical.

Powell contrasts his adherence to economic liberalism with, on the one hand, state socialism, and, on the other, the mixed economy. To the former he is totally opposed, but towards the latter he is somewhat ambivalent. On certain occasions, he has suggested that economic liberalism can co-exist with a mixed economy,[38] on other occasions that the two are mutually exclusive.[39] If anything he has moved increasingly to the latter position.

While there is a degree of ambivalence in Powell's position on the relationship between a totally free economy and a mixed economy, there is no such ambivalence in his attitude to another form of 'halfway house': 'collaboration'. He has been a consistent critic of attempts by governments to bring organised business and labour groups into economic decision-making. He denounces such attempts, which are often based on an appeal to the national interest, as both a negation of the rule of law and of the true function of business and labour organisations, which is to safeguard the interests of their members not those of the nation. In more strident terms he argues that because of such collaboration:

We are today in imminent danger of slipping unawares into that form of state socialism which is known as fascism, whereby the control of the state over individuals as exercised largely through corporations which purport to represent the various elements of society, and particularly the employers and employees.[54]

108

Having described Powell's formulation and justification of economic liberalism, it is necessary to examine its application. For this purpose his attitude to inflation is taken because its causes and effects have been a preoccupation of his political career both in and out of office. Powell has consistently held the view that one of the prime regulatory functions of the State is responsibility for the money system in the sense that it is the State's 'duty to secure and preserve the integrity and stability of the medium of exchange on which depends all the economic dealings of man with man'.[41] His understanding of this duty has, however, from 1957 developed into a firm advocacy of, on the one hand, the monetarist theory of the causes of inflation, and, on the other hand, the value of a floating exchange rate.

Powell has commented most succinctly on the monetarist theory of inflation as follows:

> The truth is that the rise in the cost of living is due neither to British trade unions, nor to British industry, nor to the British economy: it is due wholly and solely to the British Government . . . When the expenditure of the Government is rising faster than the national income, it is odds-on that what it spends will exceed what taxation brings in and that the public will not be willing to lend it sufficient extra money to meet its expenditure . . . As a result vast quantities of additional money [are] pumped into the economy. If trade unions had never been invented and if the population had consisted of Benedictine monks, the consequence would still have been, inevitably and automatically, the rise in prices (including wages) which we have experienced.[42]

Such a view of the cause of inflation leads Powell, as the quotation suggests, to reject the view that trade unions are responsible for inflation and also to attack attempts to curb free collective bargaining through prices and incomes policy. He has described such policies as 'A nonsense, a silly nonsense, a transparent nonsense. What is more and worse, it is a dangerous nonsense'.[43] Prices and incomes policies are a 'silly nonsense' because they leave untouched the true causes of inflation – government expenditure, and the supply of money over which the government already possesses total control. They are a 'dangerous nonsense' because they fly in the face of the proper functioning of the economy. Taking wages as an example, Powell points out that these need to vary according to different employments, and within different employments, at different rates, and according to time and place in order to satisfy the changing supply and demand for labour. Such wages can only be determined empirically and any attempt to control them by other than free market forces will totally upset the workings of a free economy and endanger the benefits which, as we have seen, Powell associates with it. In a similar vein to his attack on national planning, he also points out that prices and incomes policies with their attempt to relate incomes to production imply the ridiculous claim that the rate of production can be foreseen. To Powell, the only mechanism capable of doing this is the free market: 'The largest and most wonderful computer the world has ever known'.[44] He has also pointed to the problems involved in such policies when enforcement becomes necessary, and the unjustifiability of freezing an existing pattern of incomes which has no validity in its own right beyond being a reflection of the forces of supply and demand at one point in time.

As for that other 'nonsense', the search for surplus in the nation's balance of payments, there are three dangers: an unnecessarily high rate of interest, the holding of money rather than the creation of additional resources, and the financing of further inflation. The solution for Powell is a floating exchange rate in order that the level of the nation's currency should be governed by the same economic forces governing the price of other commodities: supply and demand.

Powell's belief in economic liberalism can thus be seen as containing both an appeal to a normative order based on individual freedom, humanity and justice, and an empirical key to the economic problems facing the contemporary nation. For Powell, economic liberalism is both a guide to thought and action.

From an analysis of Powell's position on social welfare and economic policy two underlying dimensions of his political thought have been distinguished: those of social philanthropy and economic liberalism. But his political thought contains a third and equally vital dimension – that of nationalism. It forms the basis of his response to such diverse policy issues as defence, the Common Market, Ulster and immigration. That Powell has given prominent consideration to the need for a nationalistic approach to British politics is shown by his various statements to this effect in writings and speeches, of which the following are examples:

> I believe that, in order to live a full and satisfying life, a man needs to have a picture not only of the community to which he belongs and of his place in it, but also of the place and destiny of that community in the outside world. This is, as it were, the frame of reference within which his life is lived, which gives it – humanly speaking – a meaning and a purpose beyond the narrow confines of place and date. If you care to call this patriotism, so much the better. I would like to see the word in use again, we surely need the thing.[45]

> Every nation, to live healthily and to live happily, needs patriotism.[46]

I suppose there can be no issue more basic than the existence and the identity of the nation itself . . . nationhood, with all that word implies, is what the Tory Party is ultimately about.[47]

. . . the Tory Party . . . [is] the nationalist party '*par excellence*'.[48]

'Patriotism', 'nationhood', 'nationalism' (Powell uses the words interchangeably) are for him of fundamental importance both to the integrity of the individual and to the success of a nation. What he means by the terms is perhaps best stated in the introduction to a book he wrote with Angus Maude in which he attempts to bring out the salient features of the British nation. In this instance, he refers to national consciousness:

Self-consciousness . . . is the essence of nationhood . . . To this collective self-consciousness there are two aspects, one looking inwards, the other outwards; one the sense of unity, the other a sense of difference. The sense of unity implies the relationship of parts to a whole . . . National consciousness is also a sense of difference from the rest of the world, of having something in common which is not shared beyond the limits of the nation.[49]

It is Powell's search for, and expression of, these two aspects of national consciousness – 'the picture of its own nature, its past and future, its place among other nations in the world, which it carries in its imagination'[50] – that provides the essence of his approach to nationalism.

To Powell the search for this national consciousness must be undertaken from the standpoint of a new realism which must be in part objective – the rejection of harmful myths – and also in part subjective – the selection of good myths. Mythology is essential to national consciousness for Powell because the latter derives from history and history itself is nothing but myth.[51]

In Powell's view the expression of national consciousness must also concern itself with its two dimensions – unity and difference. First and foremost it must be expressed by delineating the limits of the nation in terms of its territory, membership and influence, and secondly by a definition of the distinctiveness of the nation in its internal aspects. The first of these might be taken as implying an objective search, the second a subjective one.

Powell's response to the four policy issues mentioned above clearly contains his view on the true limits of the nation. Powell's attitude to defence, for example, most clearly embodies his view of the limits of the nation in terms of influence. Underlying his volte-face from being an adamant supporter of east of Suez and colonial defence policy to the perspective of Britain as a European power lies one of the major re-orientations in his thought. As Utley has said:

The starting point of Powell's thinking about defence is his conviction that, to all intents and purposes, the limits of the British nation and therefore of the responsibilities of the British government were fundamentally changed by the loss of India . . . With the ending of the Indian Empire . . . British defence policy must be directed exclusively to the defence of these islands.[52]

Powell's retreat from imperialism was painful not least because one, if not the prime, motivation of his entry into politics was to secure the retention of India within the British Empire. But once begun the retreat was total; so total that Powell eventually reached the position in which he denied the very existence of an Empire in British history. This conclusion was advanced in a remarkable speech given at Trinity College Dublin on 13 November 1964 in which he sought to destory the 'harmful myth' within the national consciousness that 'Britain was once a great imperial power, which built up a mighty empire over generations and then, in the lifetime of most of us, lost or gave it up'.[53] Powell points to the fact that the imagined empire found no expression in British life prior to 1890, and that although British rule of India approached an objective definition of empire, subjectively it was not regarded as such during that period but rather as an embarrassment and a burden. It is only after that date that imperialism emerges – as a political invention primarily of Joseph Chamberlain, an invention the 'British people came to believe, instinctively, implicitly'.[54] To Powell, the myth of imperialism has haunted British political history since that time, not least in recent years when it has resulted in the national disease of self-deprecation in the face of the supposed retreat from empire, and considerable errors of judgement in policy.

His gradual rejection of imperialism is paralleled by an increasing opposition towards first the concept and then the reality of the Commonwealth, which he suggests needs to be re-examined in order to recognise the true limits of the nation.

His opposition to the concept of the Commonwealth can be traced to one of the most famous of his parliamentary speeches, that in opposition to the 1952 Royal Titles Bill which sought to introduce new nomenclature for the monarchy and thereby in Powell's view, heralded the breakdown of the unity of the Empire based on a common allegiance to one sovereign.

This links in with the immigration question because from the late 1950s onwards Powell campaigned for the laws of citizenship to be rewritten. This can be seen as an attempt to delineate the limits of the nation, in this instance, in terms of membership. As he has stated: 'The purpose of a law of citizenship is to define those who belong to the nation whose law it is'.[55]

His attitude to the law of citizenship pivots round the 1948 British Nationality Act. In the early 1950s, his opposition to the Act was based on an appeal for a return to the old conception of a common imperial citizenship. By 1968, as part of his campaign against further Commonwealth immigration, he was advocating that the law be rewritten to the effect that citizenship be restricted to those who belonged to the United Kingdom (and as he has made clear in his statements on Ulster, that would include treating citizens of the Republic of Ireland as aliens).

As for his questioning of the reality of the Commonwealth:

> I believe . . . that the great majority of people in this country see no reality or substance in the proposition that they belong to a Common-wealth . . . a number of these countries are antipathetic to one another . . . antipathy towards Britain is a marked feature of the visible, public behaviour of some of these countries . . . none of them appears to recognise any common interest with Britain where it would override or conflict with its own . . . the manner in which the internal affairs of some of these countries are conducted . . . are repugnant to their own basic ideas about liberty and democracy.[56]

For Powell the failure to recognise this reality has involved Britain in at least three situations which are contrary to the national interest: aid to the Commonwealth, involvement in Rhodesia, and Commonwealth immigration. Of the latter he has stated that it has 'entailed upon ourselves a fearful and wholly unnecessary problem, one which has brought no compensatory benefit to any other country, and one with the consequences of which our children and their children will still be coping'.[57]

The need for a realistic appraisal of the true territorial limits of the British nation also lies behind his attitude towards Ulster. The true cause of civil violence in that province in Powell's view cannot be traced to questions of discrimination and the withholding of civil rights to a minority. It rests rather on a failure of national consciousness:

> To live with a state of law and a form of government which half denies the fact that the Irish Republic is an independent foreign state, and half denies the fact that the six counties are an integral part of the United Kingdom is a standing invitation to violence to try to drive home the wedge these ambiguities represent. The question is one of belonging or not belonging, nothing else.[58]

For Powell, then, that part of the national consciousness which is based on a recognition of the limits of nation is clear. Both in terms of territory, member-ship and influence the limits of the British nation are no more and no less than the United Kingdom itself. A recognition of this involves the rejection of the myth of imperialism and also an understanding that the Commonwealth completely lacks the ingredients of unity necessary for it to be included in the national consciousness. A reassessment of national consciousness in these terms will free the State from the errors of an overstretched defence policy based on an illusion of imperial influence; the 'folly' of Commonwealth immigration based on an outmoded concept of national membership; and the civil violence in Ulster based on a failure to fundamentally acknowledge the sanctity of the territory of the nation.

But while Powell defines the unity dimension of his nationalism in the objective terms of territory, membership and influence, his portrayal of the differential dimension is expressed as a subjective glorification of the character and institutions of the British nation.

With regard to the character of the nation he is at his vaguest. The only aspects that he particularly specifies are those of solidarity and homogeneity: 'The homogeneity of England, so profound and embracing that the counties and the regions make it a hobby to discover their differences and assert their peculiarities'.[59] But though he finds it difficult to define the national character in more specific terms he has no doubt that it exists and the certainty of its existence leads him to make those statements on immigration that have earned him the title of racist. He talks of areas of immigrant settlement as 'foreign areas'[60] and 'alien territory',[61] and the process of immigration itself as an 'invasion'.[62] But of all such statements it is the following that has aroused greatest comment: 'The West Indian or Asian does not, by being born in England, become an Englishman. In law he becomes a United Kingdom citizen by birth, in fact he is a West Indian or an Asian still'.[63] And he has also made clear by his repeated assertion that 'numbers are of the essence' that there is an optimum level of immigration beyond which there will result a dilution of the national character.

Powell is somewhat more specific concerning the institutional aspects by which, in his view, the British nation is made distinct. Throughout his writings and speeches there is constantly purveyed a total commitment to, and glorification of, two particular British institutions – the monarchy and Parliament. Of the monarchy he has written:

> Symbol, yet source of power; person of flesh and blood, yet incarnation of an idea; the kingship . . . seems to us to embrace and express the qualities that are peculiarly English . . . this continuous and continuing life of England is symbolised and expressed, as by nothing else, by the English kingship.[64]

The importance of the British Parliament to the national consciousness is brought out most fully in a speech on the Common Market which he delivered in Lyons in February 1971. In that speech he emphasised that his opposition to British entry to the Common Market was based not essentially on economic but on political grounds: 'In a word, it is nationalist'.[65] And the lynchpin of his nationalist response was that British membership would involve the eventual destruction of the British Parliament, a step of far more consequence to Britain than to other European states:

> The British parliament in its paramount authority occupies a position in relation to the British nation which no other elective assembly in Europe possesses. Take Parliament out of the history of England and that history itself becomes meaningless. Whole lifetimes of study cannot exhaust the reason why this fact has come to be; but fact it is, so that the British nation could not imagine itself except with and through its parliament.[66]

The nature of the nationalism that Powell seeks to portray and re-establish in Britain lies, then, upon two foundations: a recognition that its limits are now restricted to the United Kingdom alone, and also that its contents are based on a recognition of the homogeneity of its people and the uniqueness of their political institutions. What links and sanctifies both of these foundations is their historical origin:

> So we today at the heart of a vanished empire, amid the fragments of demolished glory, seem to find, like one of her own oak trees, standing and growing, the sap still rising from her ancient roots to meet the spring, England herself.[67]

It is to an appreciation of England's past that the nationalist must turn in order to find the essential ingredients of his creed and the solution to contemporary problems.

From the above analysis of Powell's position on a number of policy issues, three underlying dimensions of his political thought have been distinguished. Two of these – corporate philanthropy and economic liberalism – are concerned with the fundamental question of the role of the State: the first with regard to social welfare, the second with regard to economic decisions. The third dimension – nationalism – is concerned with the nature of the State, its characteristics and its relationship to society.

The significance of Powell's political ideas, it has been suggested, can be assessed from the three perspectives which have emerged from the various ways in which the term Powellism has been used. Firstly, it is possible to question from an ideological perspective whether Powell's political ideas, and particularly the three major themes within them, provide a more or less universal guide to poltical conduct in the sense of their application to current political issues and the degree of internal consistency between them.

That the dimensions of Powell's thought are applicable to the major political concerns of contemporary politics in Britain is evident from the above analysis. A wide number of such concerns, from the provision of pensions to entry into the Common Market, from housing to Ulster, have come within the purview of Powell's politics and for each of them the three dimensions, either singularly or in combination, provide a key to relevant policy stances. It is the element of internal consistency between the three dimensions that has yet to be demonstrated.

Between the two dimensions concerned with the role of the State – those of corporate philanthropy and economic liberalism – such a consistency clearly exists. This is achieved both by the articulation of principles to demarcate the fields in which the two dimensions are applicable, and also by the solution Powell offers to cover the problem of areas of public concern in which the two fields overlap. As we have seen, by his definition of economic decisions, Powell clearly demarcates the area of policy in which his economic liberalism is applicable. We have also seen that his corporate philanthropy excludes from state involvement all those areas of social welfare to which economic criteria apply. But Powell is equally aware that many issues concerning the role of the State straddle the boundary between issues that are purely economic and to which economic liberalism is applicable, and those that are purely social and to which corporate philanthropic considerations apply. He offers a principle to cover such issues: issues may be identified which are non-economic in their intent but which affect the economic field in their implementation. With regard to such issues, Powell distinguishes two alternative responses for the State: general prescription and particular instruction. An example of 'general prescription' might be a decision, on health grounds, to control conditions of employment, or, on welfare grounds, to give financial assistance to the unemployed. To Powell, such decisions are general because the implications and consequences for the economic field that result from them are allowed to occur freely and without limitation. Examples of 'particular instruction' might be, on community grounds, the direction of industry to a particular location, or, on welfare grounds, the enforcement of a minimum wage. Such decisions are distinguished from general prescriptions because they displace economic criteria and completely deny free action to the individuals concerned.

From this distinction between general and particular non-economic decisions, Powell lays down the following principles:

Of non-economic decisions [the Conservative] rejects those which are particular in character and tend to abolish the economic field, and he is critical of those which are general in character and tend to limit it.[68]

The consistency between Powell's dimension of corporate philanthropy and nationalism lies in the interconnection between his portrayal of society as a community and of the nation as an organic entity:

Society is much more than a collection of individuals acting together, even through the complex and subtle mechanisms of the free economy, for material advantage. It has an existence of its own; it thinks and feels; it looks inward, as a community, to its members; it looks outward, as a nation, into a world populated by other societies, like or unlike itself.[69]

Corporate philanthropy is the expression of the national community's care and compassion for its members; nationalism is the psychological and cultural component that weds a society to its political form, the nation.

Of the three interconnections between the dimensions of Powell's thought, that between economic liberalism and nationalism might be seen as the hardest to demonstrate, not least because the first flows from a clear logic and the second from a heady sentimentalism. There are conflicts between them as, for example, in the nationalist call for immigration controls which can be seen as stemming the free flow of labour market forces. But despite such conflicts, Powell achieves an ultimate consistency by portraying capitalism as one of the foremost ingredients of his nationalism:

It is not for the sake of a dry-as-dust theory, or because of the academic beauty and precision of a market economy, or from materialist calculation . . . that we are called upon to commend the test of competition to the nation, and to submit our policies and actions to that test first. The demand comes passionate and direct from the heart of national pride itself. Britain today needs desperately for its own sake, for the sake of self-respect, to regain the confidence and the conviction that it can hold up its head in competition with all comers in the world. It can never have that distinction unless it is first willing to face the test of competition at home.[70]

For Powell, not only is nationalism dependent upon capitalism, but the opposite is equally the case. As Harris has pointed out, it is Powell's view that 'The sole creative force was not the State but the nation, and only insofar as the nation decided to act could there be any economic advance'.[71]

Corporate philanthropy, economic liberalism, and nationalism are thus no mere potpourri of ideas. It is therefore not unreasonable that some commentators, from an ideological perspective, have graced his ideas with the term Powellism.

Having established the existence of ideological Powellism, it is also necessary to ascertain whether Powell's political ideas are distinguishable and distinct within the party political context.

One point is clear: the political party within which Powell's thought is located is the Conservative Party. Powell himself is in no doubt of this. As he so forthrightly stated after his famous 'Enemies Within' speech: 'I was born a Tory. I have lived a Tory. I will die a Tory'.[72] And although he is at present not a member of that party in Parliament, there is no doubt in the minds of the majority of party members and the electorate at large that it is the Conservative Party which is his true home.

In order to locate his political thought within the Conservative Party two further facets of it need to be recognised: an appeal to political principle and the expression of a conspiratorial thesis of political power.

To some observers Powell's thought is outside the mainstream of conservatism because his ideas are seen as being derived not pragmatically in response to political practice, but logically from fixed and universal political principles.

That Powell asserts the importance of establishing principles to govern political practice is undeniable, and their importance is expressed by him as essential both to the performance of governments and to the electoral success of a party. With regard to their importance to government, he has stated:

> If government decisions are to be more than a series of unconnected expedients and party policies, more than an anthology of electoral bribes, those decisions have to be taken, and those policies framed, with some reference to some general notions of what Government ought, and ought not, to do.[73]

With regard to the importance of principles to the electoral fortunes of a political party, this was stated most clearly in a *Political Quarterly* article where Powell pointed to the lessons to be learned from Labour's period in opposition between 1951 and 1959:

> An opposition must have a categorical imperative: 'do this and this alone, if you would be saved'. There must be a great, simple, central theme, branching into all fields and subjects of debate, but in itself easily grasped, which runs through the words and actions of a successful opposition.[74]

Powell is his own best student of political affairs, since this precept upon opposition parties can be seen as a major factor in the emergence of Powellism as so far defined. His economic liberalism and his nationalist stance on such policy questions as defence, immigration, Ulster and the Common Market most clearly emerged as cohesive and interrelated principles during the years of Conservative opposition between 1964 and 1970. No doubt other factors were at work – the gradual recognition of the end of imperialism, the search for personal power, and the emergence of new political issues – but there is much evidence that these years of opposition were of major significance in the evolution of his political thought.

His frequent exhortations for the identification of political principles to govern political practice do not place him outside conservatism itself. Although conservatism often identifies itself as non-ideological, rather a persuasion based on the importance of tradition and political practice, it is clear that the history of conservatism in fact displays numerous statements of principle.

The other facet of Powell's political thought is his frequent appeal to what might be described as a 'conspiratorial thesis' of political power. The targets of this thesis are numerous: the mass media is lampooned both for mis-representation – playing down the true facts – and also perversion – the increasing practice of intermingling the reporting of facts with editorial comment;[75] governments are attacked, among other reasons, for their underhand attempt to substitute corporatist collaboration for the rule of law; and also for their refusal to take responsibility for inflation; within the government the Home Office is singled out for manipulating propaganda with regard to the number of immigrants that have settled here.[76]

For Powell, these are symptomatic of a wider conspiracy by a minority to defraud and hoodwink the majority. The nature of this conspiracy was clearly alluded to in a speech before the 1970 election, a speech which has since become known as 'The Enemy Within'. Powell stated that Britain was under attack from forces aiming at its actual destruction, and that these forces were not an external enemy but invisible forces within. This enemy had already achieved notable advances through creating disorder in the universities, demonstrations in the streets and civil violence in Ulster. While the enemy is not defined, its tactics are made clear:

The power of the minority, which, though still in its infancy, we have watched being exerted here and elsewhere during the last few years, derives from its hold over men's minds. The majority are rendered passive and helpless by a devilishly simple, but devilishyly subtle, technique. This is to assert manifest absurdities as if they were self-evident truths. By dint of repetition of the absurdities, echoed, re-echoed and amplified by all the organs of communication, the majority are reduced to a condition in which they finally mistrust their own senses and their own reason, and surrender their will to the manipulator. Our danger is that the enemy has mastered the art of establishing a moral ascendency over his victims and destroying their good conscience.[77]

This conspiratorial thesis of political power with its appeal to the majority, to denounce an all-powerful but undefined minority exhibits what might be called a populist facet to Powell's political thought. And it is this aspect which unambiguously places Powell to the Right within the Conservative Party.

The same conclusion is reached by recognising what is a minor theme in Powell's conspiratorial thesis, but a major part of his political platform: the denunciation of consensus politics. In his view the majority have been, to all intents and purposes, disenfranchised by the failure of political parties to offer them clear alternatives. For Powell, 'there comes always a time "when the kissing has to stop".'[78] And what has specifically to be stopped is the failure of the Conservative Party to denounce or disengage itself from collectivism. As Utley has stressed: 'Powell now plainly thinks that an important part of his mission in politics is to challenge and destroy the collectivist assumptions which marked the end of the Macmillan era'.[79]

Powell's political thought therefore includes, in addition to the three dimensions already defined, two further facets. The first, an appeal to political principles, does not disqualify his thought from being securely located within the Conservative Party. The second, support for a conspiratorial thesis of political power, has been described, at one level, as approaching populism and, at another, as an expression of opposition to consensus politics. Both aspects of the conspiratorial thesis place him unambiguously on the right wing of the Conservative Party.

This right wing largely consists of those members of the Party who hold to an essentially libertarian as opposed to a collectivist political view. But, as Greenleaf has recently emphasised, there are two groups within the libertarian strand in conservatism:

> The adherents of a more or less orthodox laissez faire and free trade doctrine; and the supporters of a modified position which draws a distinction between social and economic intervention, the former being permissible and the latter, generally, not.[80]

As has been demonstrated above, the dimensions of Powell's thought that we have called corporate philanthropy and economic liberalism clearly place him within the second of these two libertarian traditions. Greenleaf also comes to this conclusion:

> It is wrong . . . to see Powell simply as an old fashioned classical liberal. He is prepared to have government play a significant role in the affairs of the community, especially in matters which concern the quality of its life.[81]

What distinguishes Powell's thought within this spectrum of opinion is its

120

comprehensiveness and its coherence compared to other advocates of modified libertarianism in the Conservative Party.

It is also the case that modified libertarianism is in itself a broad definition which on the question of application to contemporary political issues contains the seeds for numerous contradictory conclusions. From this view there is much in Powell's application of his ideas that separates him from other supporters of modified libertarianism. With regard to education, for example, Powell has opposed the introduction of education vouchers and loans to post-graduate students – two policies closely associated with the New Right in the Conservative Party. And while he has called for a revision of trade union law, he does not share with many right wing colleagues the call for the outlawing of unofficial strikes and the state enforcement of compulsory 'cooling-off' periods in the national interest. There are also examples of personal idiosyncrasies which identify Powell more with the progressive wing of the Conservative Party than the New Right. One of these is his attitude towards capital punishment. From 1955, he has consistently been in favour of its abolition. This can perhaps be seen as indicative of his general lack of emphasis on the law and order question, the backbone of much New Right thinking. Another example is his attitude towards homosexuality. In May 1965, he was co-sponsor of the Leo Abse's Bill to legalise homosexuality between consenting male adults. This is likewise indicative of his general non-involvement in the right wing attack on permissiveness.

Powell's application of nationalism, the third dimension of his thought, to various policy issues also separates him from any clear grouping within the Conservative Party. While an appeal to the nation is a theme common to all strands in the Conservative Party, and in its more extreme version of particular appeal to the right wing, the policy conclusions that Powell draws from his nationalism do not find universal support either within the Party generally or on the right in particular. The progressive wing of the Party is at odds with most of his conclusions and especially those regarding the Common Market and Ulster, as well as opposing his approach to the question of immigration. And within the New Right there are many who would oppose his 'little Englander' conclusions on defence.

Powell's thought is then clearly located within the right wing of the Conservative Party, and amongst advocates of modified libertarianism in particular. But because of both the comprehensiveness and cohesion of his thought, and his interpretation of it as policy conclusions, it is both distinguishable and distinct from other constellations of ideas within the Conservative Party.

There is a third possible definition of Powellism – that of an electoral force.

Powellism so defined can be seen as encompassing not only a body of ideas aimed to gain wide support from the electorate but also 'an alternative leadership to carry them through'.[82]

Many believe that Powell's political tactics can be explained by a belief that he is offering the electorate an alternative leadership. His frequent rebellions against the leadership of the Conservative Party, the populist aspect of his political thought, his avoidance of factions, and his successful use of the mass media are all seen as indicative of his search for personal power, which most commentators take to mean the leadership of the Conservative Party.

That he has succeeded in imprinting his personality upon the electorate is beyond doubt. This has been shown by numerous surveys and opinion polls. The following figures illustrate the public's attitude to Powell before and after his rise to prominence:

Gallup Poll findings on public response to Enoch Powell 1964–69[83]

'If you were making up a new Conservative Government who are the first three people you would put in for Prime Minister and other jobs?'

	Dec. 1964 %	Nov. 1965 % Rank	Jan. 1967 % Rank	Jan. 1969 % Rank	Oct. 1969 % Rank
Powell	0	6 6	13 6	33 2	36 1

From a position of not being mentioned as a possible leading member of a Conservative government in December 1964, he had become first choice by October 1969.

In February 1970 a Harris Poll found that he was the first choice of 18 per cent of a sample asked about their preference for Prime Minister.[84] Another survey, undertaken by Marplan for the *Birmingham Evening Mail*, indicates that four years later he was still a prominent personality in the eyes of the electorate. The Marplan survey covered three Birimingham constituencies and respondents were asked to name which of six politicians – Heath, Wilson, Powell, Thorpe, Whitelaw and Jenkins – would make the best Prime Minister. Powell was the choice of 22 per cent of the Birmingham Perry Barr sample and ranked second, of 19 per cent in Walsall South (ranked third), and of 17 per cent in Bromsgrove and Redditch (again ranked third).[85] It may thus be true as Harrington has suggested that Powell is 'a politician with more proved vote-getting ability than any other'.[86]

Powellism as an electoral force based on the appeal of Powell's political ideas involves an argument of a different order, namely that the various dimensions and facets of Powell's political thought can be distinguished as an attempt to offer an electoral programme of universal appeal. As Utley has put it: 'Like the Young Disraeli, Powell is attempting nothing less than a drastic re-alignment of the classes, a new version of Tory Decmocracy'.[87]

Seen in this light, the dimensions and facets of Powell's thought that we have described take on a different character. The dimension of economic liberalism can be seen as an appeal to the middle-class, and the small entrepreneur in particular, with its opposition to high taxation and government planning: and as an appeal to the working-class with its opposition to restrictions on free collective bargaining. The dimension of corporate philanthropy can likewise be seen as an appeal to the middle-class with its championship of independent welfare provision, and to the working-class with its support for state action to ensure a tolerable standard of living for all, and the dimension of nationalism can be seen as an appeal to both classes to unite for the higher interests of the nation itself.

Such a view of Powell's thought can be subjected to two forms of criticism. The first is to question the viability of his thought as an electoral programme, the second is to question its actual success. Nairn's critique of Powell, for example, concerns the first. With regard to Powell's position on immigration – which we have suggested is an important aspect of his nationalism – Nairn has argued that Powell has chosen an inappropriate vehicle for mobilising popular sentiment because England's black population:

> is, in fact, almost entirely proletarian in character, and unlikely to be anything else for some time to come – hence it is impossible to pretend plausibly . . . that it is the oppressive 'tiny minority', or at least in league with it. England's Indians and West Indians can scarcely be identified with 'the system' by which the majority feels obscurely oppressed. They do not measure up to the task of re-defining England's destiny, as it were. In addition, they present the defect of being geographically concentrated in a few areas . . . Above all, it should not be overlooked how vital immigrant labour has become for the British economy.[88]

Nairn also argues that Powell's thought includes a 'too overt identification with capitalism' which will never appeal to a large 'area of the national soul'.[89]

While these are matters of opinion, it is possible to test empirically the success of Powell's thought as an electoral programme of universal appeal. As has been shown elsewhere,[90] Powell has succeeded in attracting support from all classes and also from different party supporters. But, and this is really the central point, that support has not been gained as a result of the appeal of the full range of his political ideas that from an ideological and political perspective we have called Powellism. Rather, his support is based upon identification with only one narrow aspect of that body of thought: his attitude towards immigration.

Two of the major findings that support this conclusion are summarised by Studler:

> Although Powell has established himself as a conspicuous dissenter on a number of issues, his views on these issues have not taken hold among the public as have his views on immigration. In a September 1968 survey of public opinion on issues raised by Powell other than immigration, NOP found that although a substantial minority supported Powell's position on decentralisation and a prices and incomes policy, support for these positions themselves was not very strongly related to support for Powell as a political leader. [NOP *Bulletin*, September 1968, pp. 4, 7–9]. In another analysis covering several issues, including the Common Market, Franklin and Inglehart found that concern about immigration was the only issue strongly related to support for Powell.[91]

King and Wood come to a similar conclusion based on their analysis of the 1974 Marplan survey in Birmingham:

> It is worth pointing out that at the time of the survey Powell's admirers were only marginally more likely to regard the Common Market issue as an important issue in the election, and their pattern of concern generally reflected that of the sample as a whole, with full employment and inflation having the most importance.[92]

Finally, Steed has attempted to explain the high swing to Labour in the West Midlands constituencies between the 1970 general election and the February 1974 election as a result, not of the influence of Powell with his call to vote Labour and his appeal on the question of the Common Market, but as a result of 1970 Labour defectors returning to their party following the defusing of immigration as a political issue.[93]

Powellism as an electoral force is thus a different order to Powellism perceived from ideological and political perspectives. While the latter refer to the whole body of Powell's thought, electoral Powellism is more simply stated as a conjunction between the person of Powell himself and his attitude towards immigration. And of the two it is the latter which is dominant because it was the issue of immigration that brought him to the fore in the minds of the electorate – it was the April 1968 'Rivers of Blood' speech that resulted in his meteoric rise to fame. In a Gallup Poll conducted just before this speech only 1 per cent of a sample survey mentioned Powell as a replacement for Heath. In the month following he was the choice of 24 per cent of another sample and was ranked first. During the Ugandan Asians conflict in

1973 he was once again the prime ministerial choice of about a quarter of the electorate.

The foregoing analysis of Powell's political thought goes a long way to explaining the public attention he has received in recent years. Few other politicians in Britain have presented so clearly and unequivocally such a coherent and concise body of ideas. Within recent conservative history, his personal interpretation of modified libertarianism in terms of its application to current political issues is unique. And few can claim to wield so much personal influence over the electoral behaviour of the general public.

But Powellism is more than an intellectual exercise in political thought and in order to assess its total significance it is necessary to search beneath its outward verbal form to discover its underlying strategies and motivation. Such a search does of course entail considerable speculation, but it is suggested here that Powellism embodies a three-fold strategy involving nation, party and self. In terms of nation, Powellism represents, as we have seen, a vigorous attempt to foster a new, emboldened spirit of national consciousness. For party, Powellism involves a concern to provide the Conservatives with a set of political principles upon which to base a challenging electoral programme and to provide the imperatives of government. Finally, Powellism must also be recognised as a vehicle for personal ambition.

These interwoven strategies have met with contrasting and limited success. At the present time the only semblance of a national consciousness that Powell has succeeded in awakening is to impart a degree of respectability to what might otherwise be considered as prejudiced and misdirected antagonism towards the immigrant population. His other nationalistic platforms – opposition to the Common Market and to devolution, and a veneration of our political institutions, as well as capitalism itself – appear not to have aroused the same reverberations among the electorate.

In contrast, the recent policy document of the Conservative Party under its new leader – The Right Approach – would seem to suggest greater success for the second prong of the Powell strategy. On social welfare, the Conservative Party has moved even closer to his plea for a limited and selective Welfare State. Even more significantly, the Party's apparent acceptance of monetarism as opposed to an incomes policy heralds a major movement towards economic liberalism.

But it is the nationalistic issues of Powellism that still divide the Party politically and ideologically from Powell. Although 'The Right Approach' suggests an acceptance of the need for greater controls on the entry of immigrants, including dependants, the Party's attitude towards immigration, as expressed at its 1976 Conference, remains far short of Powell's escalating demands which now include the allocation of public funds to financially encourage repatriation. An even greater and apparently unbridgeable divide also separates Powell from the Conservative Party on such issues as Northern Ireland and the Common Market.

Of the three strategies, that of personal ambition appears to be the furthest from fulfilment. If that ambition is to be achieved through the Conservative Party then its success seems highly unlikely. Not only will the Party find it difficult to forgive Powell's public defection to the side of the Labour Party in the 1974 elections, they will also find little encouragement in his recent out-pourings of scorn for Mrs Thatcher and other leading Tories. Additionally, he has continually rejected suggestions for the formation of an organised base either inside or outside the Party from which to launch an attack on the leadership. He has been content, so it seems, to use the vehicle of the small Ulster Unionist group in Parliament, with whom he has many differences, in order to retain a political platform.

To conclude from this that the strategies embodied in Powellism are unlikely to succeed and are therefore misguided is to assume that they derive from a conventional view of the future of British politics. An alternative conclusion suggests itself. In many of his speeches, not only those on immigration, Powell alludes to increasing national decay and degeneration and points to the likelihood of a future crisis both in State and society. It is for such a situation that Powellism might be seen as being ultimately motivated, for in the face of national crisis it is designed to provide a renewed national identity, clear principles and policies, and an untarnished leadership. As Powell himself has written: 'To pull down, upon its own head, the structure which it spent its life and lost its soul to rear and to dominate, is the only ending which can suit ambition'.[94]

Notes

[1] J. E. Powell, 'Conservatives and the Social Services' *Political Quarterly*, vol. 24, no. 2, April 1953, p. 164.
[2] J. E. Powell, 'The Welfare State', CPC no. 245, October 1961.
[3] Ibid., p. 12.
[4] J. Wood (ed.), *A Nation Not Afraid*, Batsford, London 1965, p. 58.
[5] J. Wood (ed.), *Freedom and Reality*, Batsford, London 1965, p. 69.
[6] Powell, 'The Welfare State', p. 13.
[7] Ibid., p. 14.
[8] J. Wood (ed.), *Still to Decide*, Batsford, London 1972, p. 13.

[9]   Ibid., p. 18.

[10]   Wood, *Freedom and Reality*, p. 55.

[11]   J. E. Powell, 'The social services', *The Spectator*, 12 June 1964.

[12]   I. Macleod and J. E. Powell, 'Social services: needs and means', CPC, 2nd edition, June 1954, p. 11.

[13]   Ibid., p. 36.

[14]   Ibid., p. 40.

[15]   T. Utley, *Enoch Powell. The Man and His Thinking*, Kimber, London 1968, p. 161.

[16]   Powell, 'The social services'.

[17]   Powell, 'Conservatives and the social services', p. 165.

[18]   Wood, *Still to Decide*, p. 4.

[19]   Ibid., p. 122.

[20]   Wood, *Still to Decide*, p. 120.

[21]   Wood, *A Nation Not Afraid*, p. 40.

[22]   Ibid., p. 49.

[23]   Ibid., p. 51.

[24]   Wood, *Still to Decide*, p. 120.

[25]   Ibid., p. 119.

[26]   Wood, *A Nation Not Afraid*, p. 28.

[27]   Powell uses the term 'philanthropic considerations' in his article 'The limits of laissez-faire', *Crossbow*, vol. 11, 1960, p. 26.

[28]   Ibid., pp. 25–8.

[29]   6 February 1968 (abridged in Utley, op. cit., pp. 117 *et seq.*)

[30]   Powell, 'The limits of laissez-faire', p. 28.

[31]   Ibid., p. 25.

[32]   Quoted in Utley, op. cit., p. 122.

[33]   Quoted in ibid., p. 114.

[34]   J. E. Powell, 'Savings in a free society', Institute of Economic Affairs, London 1966.

[35]   J. E. Powell, 'Is it politically practicable', in A. Seldon (ed.), *Rebirth of Britain*, Pan Books, London 1964, p. 266.

[36]   Wood, *A Nation Not Afraid*, p. 27.

[37]   Wood, *Still to Decide*, p. 68.

[38]   Powell, 'Is it politically practicable', p. 266.

[39]   Wood, *Still to Decide*, pp.5 and 80.

[40]   Wood, *Freedom and Reality*, p. 122.

[41]   Ibid., p. 144.

[42]   J. Wood (ed.), *Powell and the 1970 Election*, Elliot Rightway, London 1970, pp. 95–6.

[43]   Wood, *A Nation Not Afraid*, p. 102.

[44] Ibid., p. 75.
[45] Ibid., p. 7.
[46] Ibid., p. 135.
[47] Wood, *Still to Decide*, p. 164.
[48] Ibid., p. 168.
[49] A Maude and J. E. Powell, *Biography of a Nation. A Short History of Britain*, John Barker, London 1955, pp. 7–8.
[50] Wood, *A Nation Not Afraid*, p. 136.
[51] Wood, *Freedom and Reality*, pp. 136–7.
[52] Utley, op. cit., pp. 102–3.
[53] Wood, *A Nation Not Afraid*, p. 137.
[54] Ibid., p. 139.
[55] Wood, *Still to Decide*, p. 190.
[56] Ibid., p. 188.
[57] Wood, *Freedom and Reality*, p. 189.
[58] Wood, *Still to Decide*, p. 188.
[59] Wood, *A Nation Not Afraid*, p. 145.
[60] Wood, *Freedom and Reality*, p. 226.
[61] Ibid., p. 234.
[62] Wood, *Still to Decide*, p. 185.
[63] Wood, *Freedom and Reality*, p. 232.
[64] Wood, *A Nation Not Afraid*, pp. 145–6.
[65] Wood, *Still to Decide*, p. 212.
[66] Ibid., p. 216.
[67] Wood, *A Nation Not Afraid*, p. 144.
[68] Powell 'The limits of laissez-faire', p. 28.
[69] Wood, *A Nation Not Afraid*, pp. 4–5.
[70] Wood, *Freedom and Reality*, p. 16.
[71] N. Harris, *Competition and the Corporate Society*, Methuen 1972, p. 245.
[72] *The Guardian*, 9 June 1973.
[73] Powell, 'The limits of laissez-faire', p. 25.
[74] J. E. Powell, '1951–9. Labour in opposition', *Political Quarterly*, vol. 30, no. 1, Jan.–Mar. 1959, pp. 340–1.
[75] Wood, *Still to Decide*, ch. 2.
[76] Ibid., pp. 187–96.
[77] Wood, *Powell and the 1970 Election*, p. 108.
[78] Wood, *Freedom and Reality*, p. 190.
[79] Utley, op. cit., p. 75.
[80] W. H. Greenleaf, 'The character of modern British conservatism' in R. Benewick, R. N. Berki and B. Parekh (eds.), *Knowledge and Belief in Politics*, Allen and Unwin, London 1973, pp. 194–5.

128

[81] Ibid., pp. 205–6.

[82] A Gamble, *The Conservative Nation*, Routledge and Kegan Paul, London 1974, p. 115.

[83] Based on table compiled in D. Studler, 'British public opinion, colour issue and Enoch Powell. A longitudinal analysis', *British Journal of Political Science*, June 1974, p. 379.

[84] Quoted in M. N. Franklin and R. Inglehart, 'The British electorate and Enoch Powell', unpublished paper, Strathclyde University, undated.

[85] Quoted in R. King and M. Wood, 'The support for Enoch Powell', in I. Crewe (ed.), *British Political Sociology Yearbook 1975*, Croom Helm, London 1975, p. 256.

[86] M. Harrington, 'Swallowing the pill', in *The Spectator*, 4 May 1974.

[87] Utley, op. cit., p. 173.

[88] T. Nairn, 'Enoch Powell. The New Right', *New Left Review*, vol. 61, 1971, pp. 18–19.

[89] Ibid., p. 22.

[90] See, for example, King and Wood, op. cit.

[91] Studler, op. cit., p. 379.

[92] King and Wood, op. cit., p. 258.

[93] M. Steed, 'The Results Analysed', Appendix II of D. Butler and D. Kavanagh, *The British General Election of February 1974*, Macmillan, London 1974. For a detailed criticism of this conclusion, and for a new analysis of Powell's impact in the 1970 general election see R. W. Johnson and D. Schoen, 'The "Powell Effect": or how one man can win', *New Society*, 22 July 1976.

[94] Quoted in Johnson and Schoen, op. cit., p. 172.

PART III

THE EXTREME RIGHT

6 The ideas of the British Union of Fascists*

N. NUGENT

Although the British Union of Fascists has attracted the interest of a number of observers relatively little attention has been given to their ideas and no completely adequate account exists.[1]

I believe a detailed consideration is justified on at least four grounds. Firstly, the BUF elite genuinely believed in many of the ideas they propagated and would have attempted to implement them had they achieved power. The view that they, and Mosley in particular, were purely opportunistic is an oversimplification. Certainly there were manipulations of policy in attempts to increase support, but for the most part there appears to have been a deep commitment to many of the central ideas.

Secondly, many of the ideas, or aspects of them, have subsequently become conventional wisdom. This is not to say that one necessarily agrees with Skidelsky, in his biography of Mosley, that the social and economic policies advanced were broadly right for the time. Skidelesky's belief that there was a set of 'right' answers is almost breathtaking given the enormous complexities of the situation and also the subsequent failure of interventionism to solve basic economic problems. The politicians of the 1920s and 1930s may not have been brilliantly inventive but it is just not true, as Skidelsky argues with regard to the immediate pre-Fascist period, that the rejection of Mosleyite solutions is attributable simply to the intellectual bankruptcy of the Labour government, its lack of understanding of his ideas, and its dislike of an arrogant young man with an aristocratic background. On the contrary most politicians realised, as perhaps Mosley did not, that any sudden movement towards radical policies involving large scale government intervention and budget deficiting, let alone reforms of the institutions of state, would inevitably bring, in a period when the main need was investment, a crisis of confidence and a run on the pound.

Nor is a recognition of the subsequent adoption of many BUF policies to suggest that there is a cause and effect relationship, for even in the year of the

* I would like to thank Jeffrey Hamm and Robert Rowe of the Union Movement for allowing me access to their collection of BUF pamphlets and newspapers. I am also grateful to Michael Moran and John McHugh for their comments on the article.

BUF's formation, 1932, they were not alone in their condemnation of economic orthodoxy or in their calls for greater government activity. The Conservative and Labour Parties were already beginning to move away from non-interventionism, and the unemployment policy of the Lloyd George Liberals, deeply influenced by Keynes and a number of other economists, had from the late 1920s onwards been concerned with the need for direct government action to stimulate purchasing power. Further, Mosley himself in May 1930, had found sympathy and support in the Parliamentary Labour Party for his memorandum, and at the Party Conference at Llandudno in October 1930 he received considerable backing, only narrowly failing to defeat the executive.

But what should be recognised is that the BUF took their proposals regarding the need for direct government action and greater centralisation much further, and on a far broader front, than any of the leading politicians of the day. Yet much of what they stated and advocated now seems neither distant nor outrageous. Given the central role of the corporate State in BUF policy it is of particular interest to note the current discussion on corporatism and the suggestion that for a number of reasons – Labour's nationalisations, incremental advances in socio-economic planning, the crisis of capitalism, etc. – Britain is today becoming a neo-corporatist State.

Thirdly, it is important, given that the term 'fascism' has become almost as much abused as 'democracy', to establish exactly what individuals and movements generally characterised as being fascist were saying. Studies such as this should lead to a greater understanding of the general phenomenon.

Finally, an understanding of the ideas assists analysis of other aspects of the BUF, for example, public attitudes towards it, recruitment, the violence and disorderly behaviour which accompanied many of its activities, etc.

A major initial problem is one of classification. A great number of ideas were expressed during the period by Fascists or people having Fascist connections; which ones are we to consider and more particularly which ones are we to regard as authoritative? They can, I think, be placed in the following hierarchical order: First, Mosley's speeches and writings. His personality dominated the movement, it was his personal creation, and only the briefest survey of BUF literature is necessary to appreciate his dominance of policy formulation and expression. He was by far the most prolific in terms of official policy statements (in the sense of material published by BUF, later Greater Britain, Publications, speeches at major BUF rallies, etc.) and his activities and pronouncements assumed a central place in the Fascist press. Secondly, the speeches and writings of an inner core which formed around

Mosley. The membership of this group is open to dispute but at various times it certainly included Alexander Raven Thomson, Neil Francis-Hawkins, William Joyce, A. K. Chesterton, John Beckett, and W. E. D. Allen. This group is not to be equated with the Policy Directorate for there were, as Benewick has pointed out, influential members of the BUF who were not on that body. Thirdly, the periodic publications of the Fascist press, notably the weeklies, *Blackshirt* and *Action*, and the quarterly, *Fascist Quarterly*, later *British Union Quarterly*. Fourthly, the speeches and writings of a number of Fascists who were on the fringes of power, e.g. the eighty prospective parliamentary candidates who were named in the period 1936–38. Finally, all other pronouncements.

While all these groups are worthy of consideration I propose to focus primarily, although not exclusively, on the first two categories, i.e. those which can be regarded as expounding authoritative BUF ideas. Cross in fact states that Mosley was the 'sole policy-maker and only source of authority' but this goes too far. It is true that the contributions of people such as Joyce and Raven Thomson were not outstandingly original, but they were often more than simple restatements of Mosley's position; they expanded ideas and filled gaps in a number of areas where Mosley had sketched only broad outlines. Indeed Mosley himself refers us to them: 'Books and pamphlets by my colleagues, whose range of abilities now covers every sphere of national life, will meet any inquiry . . .'.[2] As regards the latter three categories it is clear that in a movement where authority and leadership were so strongly emphasised there was no question of the elite being committed to, or bound by, ideas expressed at these levels.

This distinction between 'authoritative' and 'non-authoritative' is not merely a convenient analytical device for limiting the scope of this study. Although it is true that the agents at the lower levels did in the main confine themselves to reiterating the authoritative position and seldom advanced radically different policies some differences can be detected, particularly as regards approach and emphasis. The argument that the leadership must have agreed with the non-authoritative views, otherwise they would have been suppressed, does not hold up. It may well have been felt that their expression was a useful aid in the bid for power, or that censure would be internally dangerous. Neither of these possible explanations, however, implies a commitment by the elite.

The main area of concern is then the authoritative ideas. Consideration will be given to the other sources only insofar as differences are significant.

The analysis of the authoritative ideas must begin with an outline of those expressed in the early Mosley policy statements, i.e. of the 1932–34 period.[3]

The theme which dominates is summarised in the first page statement of *The Greater Britain*: 'The object of this book is to prove, by analysis of the present situation and by constructive policy, that the necessity for a fundamental change exists.' As we shall see, the analysis was to hinge on the fact that 'economic life has outgrown our political institutions' and the constructive policy on the need 'to reconcile the revolutionary change of science with our system of government, and to harmonise individual initiative with the wider interests of the nation'.[4]

To take the analysis first, Britain was seen to be facing a crisis. Although its nature was never precisely identified it was clearly primarily economic in nature and manifested itself most clearly in terms of under-utilisation of resources, particularly labour. This had serious implications both for the individual, who was degraded and unable to be truly free, and for the nation, which lost prestige and was hampered in playing its true role as a major world power. But economics as well as being the fundamental basis of the trouble were also a symptom of a more general malaise. Accordingly the analysis and critique extended beyond economics, in the narrow sense, into the political and social spheres.

Restricting the analysis for the moment to the economic, the problem was seen as essentially one of under-consumption; too little purchasing power in relation to the productive capacity of industry. Since the nineteenth century, science and technology had 'rationalised' the economy, thus increasing productive capacity. However, because purchasing power had not increased proportionately this rationalisation had only been able to express itself in terms of unemployment. 'Because the demand for goods does not increase at the same rate as the power to produce goods the labour displaced by rationalisation is not re-absorbed in industry.'[5] There was accordingly a vicious circle of rationalisation, unemployment, lower purchasing power, more unemployment.

There were two reasons why purchasing power had not increased proportionately. In the domestic market there was no one body able to exercise overall control over wages, the main source of internal consumption; accordingly, the competition which capitalism demands ensured wages were low. In the external market, and it was continually emphasised that 30 per cent of our manufactured goods went there, every nation was attempting to produce as large a proportion as possible of the goods it consumed, i.e. to be as near as possible a self-contained economic unit. Britain was consequently faced with 'the artificial closing of our former markets'.[6] In addition to tariff barriers a whole host of new devices such as quotas, embargoes and vetoes now had to be surmounted.

Lack of purchasing power was thus at the centre of the economic analysis. There was discussion of the role of finance in '. . . supporting speculation, and short term lending abroad, rather than assisting in the constructive work for which the financial system is primarily intended',[7] but this was seen very much as a contributory factor. Basically the problem arose from the new and permanent characteristics of the modern age: 'Today we have passed from the economics of poverty to the economics of plenty. Our problem is no longer how to produce enough to live; our problem is how to consume what is produced.'[8] The old system of distribution was no longer capable of coping with the increased capacity of industry; it could not provide the necessary level of effective demand. Deterioration into a crisis was inevitable if appropriate action was not taken. In the absence of any apparent response on the part of the government to this clear need for radical policies, an attack on politicians and the structure of British parliamentary democracy itself was a logical step. So, in contrast to continental fascism where the authority of the State was the first concern, in the BUF the attack on the political system was an outgrowth of an economic analysis.

While industry had rationalised '. . . our machinery of distribution' (which the politicians controlled) 'and of government has remained practically unchanged . . .'.[9] The hostility was not then primarily based on the assertion that politicians were pursuing the wrong policies, although there were elements of this, as for instance in references to an excessive reliance on international trade and a failure to be 'tough' with financiers. It was more concerned with the broader issue that the whole structure of government and philosophy of the politicians were so outdated as to be unable to cope with the problems. Even had the will existed to tackle the problems in the 'right' way the political environment and framework of government precluded effective measures: 'The sphere of government has widened and the complications of government have increased. It is hardly surprising that the political system of 1832 is wholly out of date today.'[10] In an age when dynamic and effective action were the primary requirements the whole machinery of government was designed to prevent things being done.

On a more specific level Parliament was singled out for having its time 'mainly taken up with matters of which the nation neither knows nor cares. It is absurd to suppose that anybody is the better for interminable discussion of the host of minor measures which the Departments and local interests bring before Parliament to the exclusion of major issues'.[11] As for the political parties, their ideologies resulted in the two essentials of government, 'stability and progress', being seen as contradictory rather than complementary; the Right seeking stability but denying 'the power of adaptation which makes stability an active force', and the Left seeking progress but

137

rejecting 'all effective instruments and robbing authority of the power to make decisions'.[12] The Conservatives were irrelevant to the situation, their policies, especially protection, being no solution, for they merely protected industry from foreign competition, not British employers paying low wages. As for the Labour Party it was torn between the evolution of socialism (which Mosley saw as futile) and revolution (which the Party feared); as a consequence '. . . in practice they squat impotent in front of the problems of the day like a hypnotised rabbit in front of a snake'.[13]

There were also references, especially in *The Greater Britain*, to the political organs and agents being under the influence of finance – '. . . the weak surrender of all parties to the power of finance . . .' – but again, as in the economic analysis, the role of finance at this stage was seen more as a contributory factor rather than being the essence of the problem. The focus of attention was the 'Old Gangs' who, by their inaction and incompetence, were betraying Britain.

What then was the programme of action; what were the BUF policies to meet this 'crisis of the twentieth century'? The central feature was, inevitably, a fundamental economic reform. The economy had to be on a firm basis for only then could the nation be strong and exert its true influence and only then could the individual be truly free – the only true form of liberty being the economic liberty which was achieved by measures such as shorter working hours and higher wages. With the prime necessity being the need for higher purchasing power, two related problems had to be tackled: (a) how to re-organise the industrial life of the country so as to build up a home market which could absorb current production, without the dislocation and chaos which would result if such a process were attempted under the existing system; and (b) the adjustment of any solution to the world economy.

As regards the first problem the BUF solution was the corporate State; It was indeed the crux of their 'constructive' thinking: 'The main object of a modern and Fascist movement is to establish the Corporate State.'[14] It was described in a number of ways: 'In psychology it is based on team work; in organisation it is the rationalised State';[15] '. . . it means a nation organised as the human body, with each organ performing its individual function, but working in harmony with the whole, and co-related with the general purpose by a directive and controlling intelligence . . .'.[16] It was basically a structure providing for central management of all aspects of the economy; it was to provide the framework and limits within which private interests would work for the public, as opposed to sectional, good. It involved a clear rejection of naked laissez faire economics; as Raven Thomson (who amplified Mosley's writings on the corporate State, and who, Mosley stated, could be regarded as authoritative) wrote, 'Whatever the advantages of economic liberty in

138

solving the problem of scarcity . . . it has become a positive menace to social welfare in a dawning age of plenty.'[17] It was continually emphasised, especially by Raven Thomson, that an economic system must consider more than the individual (which the existing system was seen to exalt), and more than the social group (which socialists and communists were held to over-emphasise). Rather it must look to a wider interest, that of the nation, and to that interest all lesser interests and sectional concerns must be subordinate. Fascism '. . . insists upon treating the community as a single organised corporate state, controlled and planned by a central government empowered with sufficient authority over individual and group to protect the general welfare of the whole, and advance the national purpose'.[18]

Raven Thomson gives the best account of the machinery envisaged.[19] (Mosley himself, although laying down the broad principles, was vague on the actual structure.) The main feature would be the division of the economy into twenty corporations each embracing an area of connected and inter-dependent industries (e.g. agriculture, iron and steel) on which employers, workers and consumers (the latter appointed by the government) were all to be equally represented. Though nominally self-governing bodies they were to work within the limits laid down by the Fascist government and the National Corporation, the latter supposedly being the synthesis of all the corporations.

The functions of the corporations, whose decisions were to be binding, were to include planning, rationalisation of industry, social welfare, etc. Of most importance, however, was the aim 'to raise wages and salaries over the whole field of industry as science, rationalisation and industrial technique increase the power to produce. Consumption will be adjusted to production, and a Home Market will be provided by the higher purchasing power of our own people'.[20] This was the main device for tackling the basic problem of unemployment, of the inability of the people to buy and consume the goods produced by industry. The corporations, through their control of wages, salaries, production, etc., would themselves adjust consumption to production; wages and salaries would be compulsorily increased in proportion to the increase in productive power. Only by this regulated order of the corporate system, by control over the whole sphere of industry, could the problem of raising wages and salaries be tackled without chaos ensuing. (One might add that temporary measures, including the use of credit facilities, were in hand to bridge the gap between the raising of wages and the consequent increase in production.)

The functions of the National Corporation were vague. Mosley said its function 'would be to plan, to regulate and to direct the whole national economy, under the guidance of the Minister, who himself would have to account for his work in Parliament'.[21] Raven Thomson was somewhat more specific and stated that apart from settling disputes between the corporations, it would also have the power of 'industrial planning on a national scale', which apparently referred to the adjustments between consumption and production, and 'all broad economic issues' would come before it, although, and this is a significant point, it would only sit as an advisory council to the Minister of Corporations.[22]

It was also to exercise direct control over a number of corporate institutions, of which a National Investment Board should perhaps be singled out. As we have seen, the analysis regarded misuse of finance as a contributory cause to the economic troubles of the country; accordingly Mosley proposed, within the corporate structure, to set up a National Board which, '. . . working in conjunction with the National Corporation of Industry, would at last succeed in relating the activities of British finance to the needs of British Industry', and would further perform the vital task of 'holding a proper balance between consumption and saving'.[23]

Two things need to be noted at this point. Firstly, whatever the specific functions of the National Corporation were to be, it is clear that it would have had considerable powers of 'interference' in the individual corporations. Secondly, and this will become clearer later, the government was to have wide directive powers in respect of the National Corporation. The economic structure would be a long way from self-governing.

The corporate State was, then, the BUF's answer to the problem of balancing productive power with consumption, and reconstructing the economy on a social basis and in Britain's interests. Clearly it involved a fundamental reordering of the whole system and for this reason it is necessary to question Mosley's claim at the time, and subsequently, that they were building on and using the existing system rather than destroying it. Certainly private enterprise was to be retained and institutions such as trade unions were to remain, but both in such an emasculated form as to amount to a fundamental revision of the whole socio-economic order. This is obvious when one places the proposals for the various sectors of the economy in the Fascist context of all-embracing national direction: 'There will be no room in Britain for those who do not accept the principle "All for the State and the State for all".'[24] Despite Mosley's claim that the government would set merely the 'limits' within which activity would take place, such statements unmistakably implied the closest central control and effectively a non-toleration of autonomous group activity, be it private enterprise or employee organisations. In short the policies involved a completely planned economy in which the participating units would have been forced to co-operate.

As we have seen, the second main economic problem was that of relating the corporate economy with its high wage structure to the world economy.

The solution advocated, in the age of plenty when most countries had the potential capacity to produce virtually everything they needed (a clearly nonsensical belief), was to insulate domestic economies, and the British economy in particular, from 'world chaos'. International trade, based on the 'poverty economics' of the nineteenth century, was merely disruptive since science had now transformed the problem. Specifically, three things were advocated. Firstly, the exclusion from Britain of foreign goods which were capable of being produced at home. This would be more than the ordinary protection of the type practised by the Tories; it would be 'scientific protection' since the 'standard of life' would also be protected from 'the competition of British employers who pay low wages'. In the transitional period Britain would not be uncompetitive abroad because the cost of production was determined more by the rate of production than by the rate of wages. (A dubious argument if wages increase greatly.) The increase in demand at home, following higher wages, would increase production, thus lowering prices and benefiting Britain in the export markets. Corporate organisation would enable the country to move and act as one trading bloc since buying and selling would now be consolidated instead of as 'a thousand incoherent and struggling voices'. Britain would thus be in a position, with respect to her trading partners, to drive '. . . hard bargains in pursuit of our simple policy of "Britain First" '.[25] Secondly, a particular emphasis on domestic agriculture, which, it was felt, could double its output over a three-year period. Thirdly, the final aim was, 'The building of a Britain as nearly as possible self-contained, and an Empire entirely self-contained . . .'.[26] This was what Mosley called autarchy, a completely self-contained Empire, resting on the fact that the Dominions were primarily food producers and Britain was an industrial nation. The Empire would proceed according to a predetermined plan; 'the Dominions should constitute with us a permanently functioning machinery of economic consultation and planning in place of haphazard and occasional conferences'.[27] (This was perhaps the most fanciful aspect of the ideas advocated for it rested on the assumption that the democratic countries involved, in particular Canada, Australia and South Africa, would follow Britain in going fascist and would therefore naturally wish to participate. As for the Crown Colonies who 'owe everything to Britain', they would be forced to co-operate.)

These then were the economic policies to meet the crisis. In the interests of clarity, however, an artificial division has been made here between these and the political proposals, for the implementation and running of the new economic structures was very much dependent on the new political system that would also emerge. It is now necessary to turn our attention to this.

It will be recalled that a key point in the analysis of the existing situation was that neither of the major political parties was able to reconcile the pre-requisites of good government. Accordingly, it is not surprising to find that '. . . our Fascist Movement seeks on the one hand, Stability, which envisages order and authority as a basis of all solid achievement; we seek, on the other hand, Progress, which can be achieved only by the executive instrument that order, authority and decision alone can give'.[28]

There emerged from this need a political system which, if not totalitarian, can most certainly be described as authoritarian. Again the claim was made that BUF proposals involved building on rather than destroying the old system, and again many institutions and processes remained in name, but once more roles and functions were so drastically altered as to make them virtually unrecognisable.

What particular form did the political system envisaged take? Two main themes run through the proposals. First, it was a rigidly hierarchical system in which the highest level was to be absolutely dominant. All 'zones' of authority had to operate within the guidelines and limits demarcated by the government. There was thus the same intolerance of opposition that was noted with reference to the economic structures. Secondly, within each zone of authority there was an emphasis on the leadership principle. (In the 1932 edition of *The Greater Britain* this appears to have meant a small group taking the decisions but in the 1934 edition Mosley stated that one man dominance would be the best solution.) This principle involved personal responsibility for decisions, authority in the last analysis being based on a direct bond between the leaders and the electorate, and the restriction of the powers of intermediary bodies, e.g. Parliament and local councils, in their control of executives. The application of these principles would open the way for those in authority to take action in an orderly and stable context, to make decisions unhampered by the waverings and indecisiveness of committees.

The key role on achieving power was to rest with the government. It was to be the driving force defining the overall goals for society and specifying the limits within which individuals, groups and institutions could work (these limits being 'the welfare of the nation'). Although there was no definite commitment as to the size of the government, Mosley's position in the movement, the emphasis on the leadership function, and the clear hint noted above all suggest his personal direction.

To provide the necessary freedom of manoeuvre the Fascist parliamentary majority would 'be used to confer upon government complete power of action by order'. Parliament, though called at regular intervals, would have only limited powers, the principal one being to 'review the work of the Government'. It should be emphasised that this position was a substantial and important move away from the position advanced in the 1932 edition of

The Greater Britain and in *Fascism Explained*, where Parliament was explicitly given the power to dismiss the government by a vote of censure.

At the end of the first Fascist Parliament elections would be held on an occupational franchise. This would have two advantages over the existing system: (a) it would be more truly representative than a system in which 'Electors vote on general consideration of policy, which they cannot understand, since the facts are not fully before them';[29] and (b) it would be more efficient in that it would bring to parliament 'technicians' and 'experts' to deal with the technical and complicated affairs of government. Men with constructive ideas (rather than amateurs whose sole claim to power was an ability to be obstructive and destructive) would emerge and gain positions of authority.

In addition to this occupational vote the nation would also exercise a direct control over the government in that 'the life of the government will be dependent on a direct vote of the whole people held at regular intervals which in any case will not exceed the life-time of a present Parliament'.[30]

These moves were aimed at removing the obstructive and dilatory nature of party politics, what Mosley frequently referred to as the nonsense of electing a majority to take action and then electing an opposition to stop it. An authoritarian one-party state was clearly intended. Mosley denied this, claiming he was constructing the 'Rationalised State', a dictatorship only in the modern sense of the word, '. . . which implies Government armed by the people with power to solve problems which the people are determined to overcome'.[31] He preferred in fact to avoid the term dictatorship altogether and referred to leadership, arguing that for the first time the British people would be able to elect a government and actually see it carry out its declared aims.

Despite these euphemisms, however, it is difficult to avoid the conclusion that the BUF was seeking to construct a 'conventional' dictatorship. Indeed Mosley's own words confirm it, the end of party politics being plainly foreseen in his statement: 'Party warfare will come to an end in a technical and non-political Parliament which will be concerned not with the Party game of obstruction, but with the national interest of construction'.[32] The most illustrative point of all is perhaps a response to a question at an Oxford University Fascist Association meeting as to whether after ten years he would allow the nation to change its mind. Mosley replied that no fascist nation ever changed its mind.[33]

Thus although the Crown would have the power to call for new ministers in the event of the government being defeated by the direct vote, it is difficult to imagine how anyone other than Fascists could be called. Furthermore, Fascists were to dominate other authoritative institutions. Certainly their will would not be frustrated by a reformed second chamber, which was to consist of the representatives of 'every major interest in the modern state'. In local government there were to be major reforms so as to abolish the system whereby different levels of government could pull in different directions, and lower levels could frustrate the national will. Executive officers, with some assistance from locally elected councils, would have power and these would be the local Fascist MPs.

So although Mosley attempted to soften his policies in respect of the structure of government by using phrases such as 'the Rationalised State', 'leadership', 'dictatorship in the modern sense', etc., his position was fundamentally the same as that of William Joyce, who, though, like Mosley, made comforting statements about the wishes of the people etc., could still assert that, 'Fascism, in its very essence cannot conceive of the sovereignty as resident in the people'.[34]

To conclude this section on the ideas expressed in the early policy statements it is necessary to consider a number of general themes which were built around the specific policies.

It was strongly emphasised that the BUF was part of a general movement, 'the modern movement', which had come to resolve the crisis of the twentieth century, to provide a salvation from unbridled individualism and political and economic chaos. Fascism was an inevitable universal phenomenon which 'comes to all the great countries in turn as their hour of crisis approaches'.[35]

The question as to whether the various fascist organisations between the two World Wars were part of a common movement is of course something which has long interested historians and political scientists. Without wishing to get involved in that debate here it is worth noting that the BUF did indeed display many of the traits common to the European movements: the antagonism towards liberal democracy with its alleged muddling through and lack of direction; the emphasis on action and the demand for immediate revolutionary changes in political, social, and economic structures; the aggressive patriotism; the rigidly hierarchical nature of the internal organisation and the supreme position of the leader.

At the same time, however, as this claim to universality, fascism, it was held, also assumed a form peculiar to each nation. The BUF specifically rejected the widely expressed view that their ideas were merely imports from the continent of Europe. The basis of the claim to distinctiveness was unclear but apparently rested on the movement's patriotism which undoubtedly was intense and which often took the form of an insistence that of the many political forces in British politics only the BUF continually backed Britain and put her needs before all else. The other parties were accused of being over-committed to international arrangements and organisations. Important though this patriotism may have been, however, it cannot as such be regarded as a distinguishing feature of British fascism since the only difference with the equally patriotic European movements was the focus of the patriotism.

There are, however, other grounds for arguing that there was a distinctiveness about the ideas we have considered. As compared with the general, often vague, sometimes philosophical, ideas of most European fascist parties, the BUF was highly programmatic. If not always highly detailed, its ideas were by comparison extremely thorough, well-developed, and logical. It is true that the BUF did claim that by coming to power and implementing their plans they would be ushering in not only a superior material era but also a more spiritual one. A number of the texts opened with the idea that a civilisation based on individualism was ending and that a new era, based on service and commitment to the nation, was about to begin: 'Fascism is a thing of the spirit. It is acceptance of new values and of a new morality in a higher and nobler conception of the universe'.[36] Taking the ideas as a whole, however, there was little attempt to put the specific policies in such a philosophical context. The main concerns were clear and specific, and certainly the Italians, with whom the comparison was, and is, most often made, never attempted so rigorous an economic analysis, or advanced such detailed programmes.

Furthermore, while it is beyond the scope of this chapter to attempt to trace the source of each of the many aspects of BUF thought, it nevertheless can be noted that many of their ideas had their roots firmly embedded in British soil. While not wishing to deny the influence of Italian fascists or American economists,[37] it is quite clear that there were a number of very important British influences upon Mosley: in particular, the interventionist State of 1914–18; Keynes; associates in the Independent Labour Party; and the Lloyd George Liberals.

Perhaps of most interest is the very clear similarity with many of the central ideas of British social imperialism, the movement which spanned a number of political organisations and which reached its height in the early years of this century. It is particularly noticeable with regard to Joseph Chamberlain and those associated with him in the Tariff Reform League.

Semmel in his study of social imperialism goes as far as to state:

> Lest it be thought that the support of these social-imperialists of the turn of the century was given upon false or inadequate grounds, we need only turn to the many speeches and writings of Sir Oswald Mosley, who can be said to have combined virtually all of the salient views of virtually all of the social-imperialists whom we have discussed, and to have welded them into a British fascism. . . .

Mosley was a compound of Joseph Chamberlain and Robert Blatchford, primarily, with healthy mixtures of Karl Pearson, and with somewhat lesser contributions from others we have discussed . . . Mosley did not publicly acknowledge his debt to Chamberlain and to Blatchford, despite his obvious paraphrasings from their writings and speeches.[38]

In being so categorical Semmel has in mind such features of the Tariff League as its intense patriotism; its advocacy of a self-contained Empire; the protection of Britain against unfair foreign competition provided by low wages and long hours; the suspicion of finance capital; and the stress on the common interest of employer and employed. The parallels are clear. It should be stressed, however, that important differences also existed; this being so, Semmel's statements require qualification. Thus although the social policies of the Tariff Reform League programme clearly demanded a greater role for government, there was nevertheless a firm commitment to free enterprise and a corresponding absence of corporatism. In addition, apart from Blatchford, who did talk in terms of the need for stronger and more centralised government, there was little concern with radical reform of British political institutions.

Further, Mosley himself specifically denies being much influenced by Chamberlain, Blatchford, or Pearson.[39] If we accept this the resemblances are, ironically, all the more striking and Mosley appears even more clearly as being in the British political tradition. For the explanation now becomes not one of overt influence but of similar historical situations – a general decline in Britain's world position and a specific threat to her economy from foreign competition – bringing forth similar responses.

In concluding the discussion on the political and economic analysis it must be emphasised that although, from 1935 onwards, the BUF began to be identified in terms of its anti-semitism, the ideas just outlined, for Mosley at least, remained to the fore throughout the 1930s. Indeed, I would argue that until the autumn of 1938 when foreign policy became the main concern, they were for him the *raison d'être*. I say this for a number of reasons. Firstly, even when the anti-semitic campaign was at its height, 'serious' political and economic ideas continued to form the major part of policy statements. It is true that the critique came to be conducted also on a second level, the anti-semitic, but that always appears to be supplementary to the first level of explanation. Secondly, insofar as the anti-semitic campaign was propagandist, and for Mosley I think in part it was, then it follows that any diminution in the space or time devoted to the 'serious' ideas in no way represented a repudiation of them, or a weakening of a resolve to attempt their implementation on achieving power. Thirdly, and most important of all, an examination of Mosley's political career reveals the above ideas to be the culmination of a process, the extension of a pattern, rather than a collection of policies opportunistically devised, to be discarded in the event of not bringing forth support. From the mid-1920s he had had no doubts as to the nature of the problem – lack of demand – or the remedy needed – a controlled increase in purchasing power. A comprehensive programme of reform was formulated as early as 1925, in the so-called Birmingham proposals, when he called for, amongst other measures, the 'socialisation' of the banks (so as to control credit and the currency), the planned raising of wages and welfare benefits, and the establishment of an Economic Council to plan the expansion of production and to ensure that prices did not rise as a result of either demand exceeding supply or 'capitalistic exploitation'. In the years following he developed his theme, that Britain's economic situation had fundamentally and permanently changed, until by 1930 (when he resigned from the government because of its economic policies), he was suggesting that the remedy to the central problem of deficiency of demand was not only direct government intervention but major reforms of the political structure itself. The publication of *The Greater Britain* was thus merely another step, albeit an important one, along a straight road.

Mosley's commitment to the ideas outlined above cannot then be doubted and as we now proceed to consider other BUF ideas it should be borne in mind that the analysis and programme of the early years remained to constitute a fundamental aspect of BUF policy throughout the 1930s.

In respect of the post-1934 developments there are three areas which need to be examined. Firstly, there was some development of the ideas already examined. As, however, they tended to be clarifications rather than modifications they will be discussed only briefly.

Many of these clarifications took the form, especially in the middle years, of specific appeals to particular social and economic groups. Among those singled out for special attention were women (whose position would be 'elevated'); farmers (agriculture would be expanded in the corporate State); Lancashire cotton workers (who would be protected against 'oriental coolie competition which is ruining the industry'); miners (a national minimum wage for miners and the exclusion of foreign oil, petrol etc. was proposed); shipyard workers and seamen (the scrapping of old ships and the building of new, Empire-only crews for Empire ships was advocated).[40]

This more propagandist approach was in many ways a development of a difference in emphasis which was already perceptible between those groups earlier identified as 'authoritative' and 'non-authoritative'. The latter had from 1932 onwards launched a number of direct appeals to clearly identifiable and vulnerable sections of the population (vulnerable in the sense of offering potential support bases). Attention was especially focused on occupations where trade unionism was weak or where the threat from foreign competition was particularly fierce and where the promise of guaranteed and higher wages in the corporate State was thus likely to be most attractive. Sustained campaigns, based essentially on the traditional extreme right wing attempt to exploit fears, were aimed at the farmers, the Lancashire cotton workers, shopkeepers (on the basis of the alleged domination of Jewish chainstores), and, above all, the unemployed.

This tendency of the 'non-authoritative' to operate on a rather more mundane level, even during the early period when Mosley was so concerned to explain the theoretical nature of his ideas, was further apparent in their reluctance at any stage to examine at length the 'serious' economic and political argument. The main concern was to convey general impressions of the BUF as the new dynamic movement, headed by a great leader with a panacea for the nation's ills.[41] There was a much greater indulgence in polemics, in personalised attacks on individuals engaged in various forms of political activity. Two particular targets were the so called 'Old Gangs' (a not untypical headline was 'Labour runs away again – the mothers' meeting at Hastings',[42] referring to the annual conference), and the communists. In respect of the latter great efforts were made to play on public fears by emphasising the alleged influence and power of the communists – usually by portraying them as waiting in the wings for the existing system to collapse. Only Fascism lay between the Reds and power.

Another development of the early ideas lay in a greater emphasis by the elite on the 'classless system' which was implied by BUF policies. This was not to be in the socialist sense, however, but rather rested on the idea of a meritocratic egalitarianism (something which was to become very fashionable in the Labour Party in the post-war years). Merit itself was never defined – it was merely assumed that the naturally gifted would 'emerge'. Property was to be inherited only when 'deserved'; the educational system was to be orientated towards talent and away from privilege. In short, 'in place of class and privilege shall arise the Brotherhood of the British to give equal opportunity to all in service and possession of their native land'.[43]

The only modification of any substance was a reversal back to the original position in respect of parliamentary powers. This involved an increasing emphasis on controls over the government and was probably explained by the common belief that the BUF was dictatorial.

The second main area identifiable in BUF ideas was anti-semitism. As has already been intimated, this issue did not replace the earlier ideas but rather was built onto and around them. Increasingly the discussion, and the analysis and critique in particular, was pursued not only in serious intellectual terms, but also on a second level. This involved an attempt to expose the power of 'finance', which after 1934, if not before, became synonymous with the Jews.

The starting point of the anti-semitic campaign is open to debate, since it is questionable whether the attacks on the power of finance in 1932 and 1933 were really attacks on the Jews. Certainly there are reasons for thinking they perhaps were. In the 1932 edition of *The Greater Britain* Mosley wrote: '. . . we have within the nation a power, largely controlled by alien elements, which arrogates to itself a power above the State, and has used that influence to drive flaccid governments of all political parties along the high road to national disaster'. Again one might quote him referring at the Memorial Hall, London on 25 October 1932 to 'three warriors of class war – all from Jerusalem',[44] and in reply to another question stating that Fascist hostility to Jews was directed against those who financed communists or who were pursuing an anti-British policy.

These might however be dismissed as isolated incidents if put in the context of the considerable written and spoken output of Mosley and his senior associates at that time. Further, in 1933 Mosley stated his belief that anti-semitism was Hitler's greatest mistake. Nevertheless, the fact remains that in the autumn of 1933 Jews were barred from BUF membership.

But whether these early remarks amounted to an anti-semitic campaign or not, there is no doubt that from the autumn of 1934 onwards anti-semitism certainly did become an important part of official BUF thinking (anti-semitism being used here in the sense of the Jews being identified as a group and attacked on that group basis). It first appeared at a meeting at Belle Vue, Manchester on 29 September when an apparently incensed Mosley stated amongst other things that 'The mention of the Empire makes the alien mob yell louder than ever. It will take something more than the yelping of a Yiddish mob to destroy the British Empire'; and again, 'What they call today the will of the people is nothing but the organised corruption of Press, cinema and Parliament, which is called democracy but is ruled by alien Jewish finance . . .'.[45]

These attacks were put into a more coherent form and formally launched as an issue in a speech at the Albert Hall on 28 October.[46] Mosley opened his remarks on the subject of the Jews by referring to the fact that he had encountered forces which he had not believed existed in Britain; in particular, the power of organised Jewry mobilised against Fascism. Of those convicted in the courts of attacks on Fascists or Fascist meetings since June, 50 per cent were Jews, yet Jews made up only 6 per cent of the whole population (this was later shown to be inaccurate). Further, he had evidence of victimisation of Fascists by Jewish employers. Accordingly Fascism in Britain took up the challenge which had been thrown down by the Jews. He went on to claim that there were businessmen who sympathised with the BUF but who dared not come out openly in support of it for then the Jews would ruin their business. It was these big, unseen Jews who were the real menace for they had a grip on the nation. An organised community within the State owing allegiance not to Britain but to foreign countries could not be tolerated, all the more since that community was striving to arouse feelings and passions of war with a peaceful nation. The Fascist answer was clear: 'We fought Germany once in a British quarrel; we shall not fight Germany again in a Jewish quarrel'.

Contained in this speech were what were to be the five main aspects of official BUF anti-semitism:

(1)   The persecution theory. On evidence as flimsy as that noted above the BUF claimed that it was being persecuted by the Jews and was in consequence forced to defend itself. The alleged reason for the campaign was that both British and continental fascism were aiming to bring to an end international usury, the system by which the Jews lived.

Skidelsky is sympathetic to this claim and documents further examples of Jewish participation in anti-Fascist activities.[47] But this is hardly convincing, particularly as most of the Jewish organisations counselled non-involvement. Given the inevitable identification of British Fascism with its continental counterparts it would have been surprising if Jews had not been reluctant to support newspapers which backed the Fascists, or if a number had not been arrested for going too far in their opposition to the BUF. It cannot, however, be regarded as evidence of a persecution.

(2)   The conspiracy theory. This was the central tenet of the anti-semitism of the middle years. Increasingly, the major institutions of State together with the mass media were accused of being controlled by Jewry, either directly or by virtue of money power. British democracy and government was increasingly described as 'financial democracy'. The following examples illustrate the appeal: Mosley speaking on the forces destroying Lancashire; 'It is a force which is served by the Conservative Party, the Liberal Party and the Socialist Party alike, the force that has dominated Britain ever since the war, the force of international Jewish finance';[48] Mosley addressing a rally at the Royal Albert Hall on 24 March 1935; 'We see at last the enemy and foe, sweating the East to ruin the West, destroying the Indians to fill the unemployment queues of Lancashire, grasping British Governments and Parliaments, grasping the puppets of Westminster – that is the enemy that Fascism challenges, Jewish international finance';[49] Mosley writing in

Blackshirt: 'How can a few Jews dominate so much of the life of this nation by their money power except by the consent and connivance of the political parties?'[50] and Raven Thomson in a series of articles, significantly entitled 'Our financial masters', referring to the 'incompetence and greed of our financial masters . . . the alien financial oligarchy that dominates our so called democracy'.[51]

In terms of analysis and critique there thus emerged a curious combination of the arguments we examined earlier and this second level of blaming all on the Jews. The mixture is best illustrated in *Tomorrow We Live*, where the rational argument is punctuated with what appear to be enraged outbursts against the financier or the Jew; 'Thousands of Britons may walk the street in unemployment because some big rogue of finance on the other side of the world has gambled in the raw materials of industry'.[52]

The essence of the conspiracy theory then was that the Jews were successfully engaged in propagating a system of international finance and trade from which the world, and Britain in particular, lost, but from which they, the Jews, derived profit. Power in Britain and abroad was dominated by international finance (a term often preferred to 'the Jews').

(3)   The charge that the Jews were trying to drag Britain into a war in which she had no interest. A crucial argument in the Fascist peace campaign, which was run from 1935, was that it was international finance alone which wanted war, the motive being to defeat the challenge posed to it by Germany and Italy. This was the conspiracy theory reformulated. Although most vigorously asserted between 1938 and 1940 the claim was first advanced in 1935. In a speech at the Manchester Free Trade Hall in September of that year Mosley attacked the Jewish-controlled press for being anti-German and anti-Italian, 'because they have challenged and overthrown those corrupt financial interests which dominate the older parties of the state'.[53] The campaigns and slogans of the middle and later periods – 'Britons first', 'Britons fight for Britain only', etc. – all had this financial interest aspect very much in mind. Events abroad did not concern the British – it was alien elements, especially the international financiers, who were warmongering: 'A million Britons shall not die in your Jews' quarrel';[54] and after the war had broken out, 'This is no quarrel of the British people; this is the quarrel of Jewish finance'.[55]

(4)   The Jews had set themselves up as a 'State within a State'. Again concrete evidence to support the charge was weak but it apparently referred to Jewish use of finance in interests other than those of Britain plus the Jewish role in pushing for war with Germany. In short they had '. . . set the interests of their co-racialists at home and abroad above the interests of the British State'.[56]

(5)   The BUF response to these alleged Jewish activities. This was of

secondary importance to the business of exposing the power of the Jew and warning against his mischief. That the BUF would tackle the problem was of course understood, but exactly how was not made clear. Rather it was assumed that a BUF government would curtail Jewish control; indeed this was the reason the BUF was being persecuted. There were many generalisations but few specifics. Thus Mosley at the Albert Hall on 22 March 1936 asserted that it was the intention of British Fascism to challenge and break for ever the power of the Jew in Britain. Some of the 'inner core' were more prosaic. Raven Thomson stated: 'Our problem must be to get the Jewish genii back into the bottle of the ghetto in which our forefathers in their wisdom kept him before his money power strangled the world'.[57]

Not that those policy responses which did emerge are to be ignored. In 1936 Mosley proposed stopping all immigration because, 'Britain for the British, is our motto, and all of Britain is required for the British'.[58] In addition, 'Those who have been guilty of anti-British conduct will be deported. Those against whom no such charge rests will be treated as foreigners, but in accordance with the traditional British treatment of foreigners within these shores, will not be ill-treated or molested'.[59] This position was reasserted in *Tomorrow We Live* with the addition that the final solution could only be the creation of a Jewish national home (but not in Palestine which belonged to the Arabs).

From the autumn of 1934 onwards the campaign built up and there can be little doubt that between 1935 and 1938 the movement was principally identified in terms of its anti-semitism. Not only were there the constant references in policy documents, the press, and speeches but there was also the notorious campaign in the areas of Jewish settlement in East London where marches, demonstrations, election campaigns and street corner meetings all served to raise the tension.

There are a number of possible explanations of the role of anti-semitism in BUF thought.

(1) A common view is that Mosley used it purely opportunistically. This is Benewick's position; Skidelsky leans heavily towards it; Cross and Mandle believe it to be a partial explanation.

By the autumn of 1934 what initial success there had been was tapering off, the crisis was looking less likely, membership was not increasing as rapidly as before, the movement was making virtually no inroads in the most depressed areas, and Rothermere had withdrawn his support. Mosley therefore perhaps needed a rationale for the failure and an issue to stimulate interest. This could be achieved by moving away from an abstract enemy and focusing on a more identifiable one. The projection of these troubles on to the Jews may have appeared an attractive and obvious option – after all anti-semitism had apparently gained considerable political advantage for the Nazis in Germany.

There is some evidence to support this interpretation. Firstly, there are comments from intimates of Mosley at the time. According to Baroness Ravensdale, his sister-in-law, Mosley 'argued . . . that a dynamic creed such as Fascism cannot flourish unless it has a scapegoat to hit out at such as Jewry'.[60] John Strachey stated that Mosley's anti-semitism 'was 100 per cent insincere', and claimed he had used it only to hold the allegiance of his followers and as a result of the influence of National Socialism.[61] Further, it has been suggested by BUF participants that Mosley only decided to take up anti-semitism on hearing that the biggest crowds at East End meetings were where there were anti-semitic speakers. Secondly, there is the suddeness with which the issue was taken up after a career in which there was no trace of anti-semitism. Thirdly, Mosley's use of the issue was, as we have seen, mainly in respect of analysis and critique; there was little concern with specific policy proposals. Fourthly, in his speeches and writings he never dwelt on it at length: Cross says that he rarely allowed the issue to fill more than ten minutes of a speech lasting an hour;[62] Skidelsky observes that Mosley's most extensive treatment of the question (in *Tomorrow We Live*) covered only three pages.[63] Finally, there was no attempt to racially identify the Jews or to categorise them as being a lower form of being, i.e. there was no biological racialism.

But these five points do not constitute conclusive proof. The last three in particular are weak. As important as what was said is what was not said and in this context the reluctance to condemn what was happening in Germany in the 1930s is marked. Nor should too much be made of the rather vague nature of Mosley's policies. After all, Hitler too in the early stages was unspecific in his attack and directed most of his energies towards raising fears rather than spelling out a detailed programme for solving the Jewish problem.

In any event even if Mosley was completely opportunistic in his use of the issue, that constitutes no reason for a softening of criticism. On the contrary, to calculatingly use anti-semitism as a political tool is in some respects to be deplored even more than the activities of genuine anti-semites.

(2) The anti-semitism may have been genuine. For many in Mosley's immediate entourage this undoubtedly was the case. Joyce, Chesterton, Beckett, Raven Thomson and others constantly referred to the subject and while they did not attempt to construct a racial theory their language was often horrific. Chesterton prophesied thus:

The day of the great reckoning is at hand; the day when there is another flash swallowing up the Yiddish St. George with all his foul values of profit, exploitation and decay; the day when the people of England regain possession of England and assert once more their ancient values of patriotism, and service, and square dealing among men.[64]

Joyce referred to Jews who had physically attacked Fascists:

These little sub-men are a nuisance to be eliminated, but their wealthy instigators and controllers, well known to us, are, in sum, a criminal monstrosity, for which not all the gold of Jewry can pay the just compensation which we will demand and obtain.[65]

As for Mosley, the case is not so clear cut. In addition to those points suggesting an 'opportunist' interpretation we can note that his pronouncements were usually more restrained than those of his immediate followers and also that, according to police records of 1936, he gave a definite warning to BUF speakers to refrain from attacking Jews at public meetings, albeit on the grounds that it was likely to lose them support.[66]

Mosley himself claims that he was not anti-semitic, arguing that he never attacked any man on account of race or religion. Be that as it may, we have seen some of the extremely nasty remarks he did make. As he gradually came to believe in the pervasiveness of Jewish power, so his theme became more constant and his language stronger. There was even discussion of the necessity of racial purity.[67] All this at a time when it must have been apparent even to Mosley that anti-semitism was not winning popular support, except perhaps in the East End of London.

Nor can the vehemence of the Fascist press be ignored. Although I have not categorised the press as an authoritative agent this does not mean that it was beyond Mosley's control. The claim that he was too busy travelling around the country to exercise an effective influence will not do. He may not have read every line but his dominance of the movement was such that a general restraint could certainly have been effected had he found the material over-offensive.[68]

Neither must it be forgotten that despite an initial determination to avoid it, Mosley was again to raise the question of Jewish power after the war. Given that in the post-war period it was, more than ever, politically unproductive to be tarnished with an anti-semitic brush, we are entitled to draw certain conclusions from Mosley's renewed interest.

(3) There is also the argument that Mosley was subjected to irresistible internal pressures to bring the issue of the Jews to the fore. As we have seen, many around him were confirmed anti-semites; to have offered them nothing would have caused immense problems, not least in terms of their continuing membership. Referring to the autumn of 1933, Cross writes, 'Now at every

level in the BUF there was pressure in favour of an anti-semitic line'.[69] This was increasingly so as the belief grew that Jews were greatly involved in anti-Fascist activities. Such restraining influence as Mosley attempted to exercise met with the disapproval of influential followers. The mood is indicated by a meeting called by Joyce in September 1936 for the principal BUF speakers. In Mosley's absence Joyce delivered a tirade against the Jews and, whilst advising the avoidance of personal abuse, urged his audience to face imprisonment rather than modify their attacks on Jewry. He went on to claim that large scale arrests would serve to intensify antagonism towards Jews.[70]

The evidence would therefore appear to suggest that Mosley attacked the Jews for a number of reasons. Opportunism and internal pressures probably explain the early development; a growing belief in Jewish power explains the increasing concern and hostility shown.

Before leaving the issue it is necessary to take some account of the views expressed by non-authoritative agents in the BUF.

Although the position of the Jews was at first claimed to be irrelevant – 'The Jewish question is no issue of Fascism, and the great cause of Fascism should not be obscured by sideline or irrelevance'[71] – it did emerge in the Fascist press in the autumn of 1933, i.e. a year before Mosley introduced it. An initial attempt to distinguish between good and bad Jews was soon replaced by general attacks highlighted by headlines such as 'Shall Jews drag Britain to war'; 'The Jewish world challenge'; and 'Too many aliens'.[72] The line was then dropped for about six months, apparently to avoid antagonising Rothermere and losing his support. When that support was withdrawn, the question of the Jews re-emerged to stay as the most constant issue until the end, reaching a peak between 1936 and 1937.

It would be wrong to suggest that it continuously and completely dominated to the exclusion of all else. For reasons of either personal disinterest or electoral gain it was sometimes played down. For example, the election addresses of BUF candidates at the Manchester municipal elections of 1938 contained no reference to the Jews. In this instance the approach tended towards populism with the emphasis on patriotism, improving social welfare, guarding against corruption, and bringing forth men of action: 'Now is the opportunity to elect real live men to your Council who will for a change put the interests of the people first'.[73]

But whilst recognising such exceptions, and always bearing in mind the attitudes of Joyce, Beckett, Chesterton et al., it is still a fact that the non-authoritative agents raised the issue earlier, pressed it harder, and in their treatment became generally more offensive. In *Blackshirt* a particularly unpleasant weekly column written for the most part by Angus McNab appeared in 1935. At first entitled 'The Jews again' it was later called 'Jolly Judah – I sketch their world'.

As Jewish influence came to be seen everywhere so the claims of the Fascist press became more hysterical to the point that virtually all the major anti-fascist countries were accused of being run directly or indirectly by the Jews. There was even a 'Jewish world plot' based on Moscow and New York.[74]

German action against the Jews was not only condoned but actually justified. Shortly after the night of horror of 9–10 November 1938, when Jewish shops and businesses were set alight throughout Germany and several Jews were killed, *Action* spoke of the provocation that Germany had received and of the anti-German Jewish world plot. It gave as evidence: 'World economic boycott of German goods by Jews. Individual attacks upon prominent Germans by Jews. And finally a world Jewish Press that deliberately inflamed the world at the time of the crisis'.[75]

The non-authoritative agents were also more prone to label the Jews with undesirable racial characteristics. Major J. F. C. Fuller wrote: 'The predominant characteristic of the Jew is his materialism which endows him with a destructive social force when he is placed in a spiritually ordered society'.[76] Such an approach was apparently not at all uncommon amongst street corner speakers, the most notorious being the known anti-semites in the East End of London.

The third area to be discussed, foreign policy, did not become an important issue until 1935. As however many of the important guidelines had already been established by then, a brief examination of the early policy documents is necessary.

The 1932 edition of *The Greater Britain* stated that 'We should be less prone to anxious interference in everybody else's affairs and more concentrated on the resources of our own country and Empire'. In addition, Britain's role should be to work for peace through a League of Nations so reorganised as to allow the large powers to have the decisive voice. In this body, 'we should call a halt to the flabby surrender of every British interest which has characterised the past decade, and has reduced this nation to the position of a meddlesome old lady holding the baby for the world'. On the arms question Britain should work towards universal disarmament but in the meantime should radically overhaul her present system of defence, especially the air force. Overall, 'Our main policy, quite frankly, is a policy of "Britain first", but our very pre-occupation with internal reconstruction is some guarantee that at least we shall never pursue the folly of an aggressive Imperialism.'[77]

These policies were elaborated and clarified in other statements. Mosley emphasised that it was international economic competition that caused wars and that in consequence the only sure way of guaranteeing peace was the existence of fascist governments in all the major countries. (Such a claim is of course questionable on a number of counts, not least the highly nationalistic nature of fascism as well as the enormous difference between the various fascist movements in terms of background, interests, and ideology.)

This belief in the overriding importance of international economic competition for the maintenance of peace was further reflected in the 1934 edition of *The Greater Britain* where a rather ominous addition was that, 'It will be necessary to revise at least economic boundaries which have constituted uneconomic units in Europe with a constant tendency to disturb the peace'.

Other statements emphasised the need to concentrate on the Empire.[78] India in particular was singled out for attention, both Mosley and Joyce claiming that it was not only Britain's right but her duty to stay there. There should be an end to the policy which rested on the idea that a continent of people speaking 250 languages and having many divisions of religion, race and class could in a short time become a nation.[79]

So when foreign policy became an important issue, as it did in 1935 with the Italian intervention in Abyssinia, the broad guidelines of a BUF foreign policy were already formulated. The peace campaign 'Mind Britain's business', which emerged as a result of the crisis, was entirely consistent with the early statements. If Britain's interests were not involved, that is, if the Empire was not threatened, she should keep out.

This policy remained constant throughout the period; it governed the BUF's attitude towards the Italian–Abyssinian war, the Spanish revolution, Japanese expansion, and Germany. Continually, the slogans were heard: 'Britain first', 'Mind Britain's business', 'Briton's fight for Britain only'. Constantly Mosley repeated and argued the case, 'Not one drop of British Blood shall be spent except in defence of Britain and our Empire'.[80]

The continuance of world tension and the emergence of Germany as an apparent threat to national security naturally resulted in some reformulation of policy but only in one area could it be described as a change in direction.

By 1936 the BUF no longer saw the League of Nations as being capable of reform. It was merely perpetuating the balance of power which it was designed to eliminate and to which Mosley was so strongly opposed. In the League an alliance had emerged of 'decaying democratic systems, with the bloodstained Soviet against the renaissant Fascist countries'.[81] The BUF alternative was a formal union between fascist governments in Germany, Italy, France and Great Britain.

There was also a major clarification of relations with Germany. This rested on the argument that Britain and Germany had different 'missions' in the world. Germany's lay in 'the union of the Germanic peoples of Europe in a consolidated rather than diffused economic system which permits her with security to pursue her racial ideals . . .'. Britain's lay in 'the maintenance and development of the heritage of Empire . . .'. Accordingly, far from Germany's interests clashing with Britain's they were complementary: 'British power throughout the world and German power in Europe together can become two of the main pillars of world order and civilisation'.[82]

As the war appeared more likely so the international situation came to dominate policy pronouncements. Great nations such as Germany had to have room to expand but this expansion did not challenge British interests for they lay elsewhere. Austria, Czechoslovakia, and Poland were outside the British sphere of influence and hence none of Britain's concern. A speech given at St Pancras on 15 March 1939 is illustrative. Mosley argued that by means of sane and realistic policy we could establish a manly relationship with nations such as Germany on the basis of live and let live. To this end we should: (a) renounce all Eastern European commitments; (b) return the mandated colonies; (c) ask in return a measure of European disarmament; and (d) concentrate on the development of our own Empire, which, so long shamefully neglected, was being abandoned to alien exploitation.[83] At the 'Britain first' rally at Earls Court in July 1939 he went on to say that it seemed as natural to him that Germany should have a Monroe doctrine in Eastern Europe as America had on the American continent.[84]

It should be emphasised, however, that BUF policy with regard to Germany was not completely based on appeasement and the unrestrained pursuit of mutually exclusive interests. British Fascism, like its continental counterparts, had a militarist streak. In any case it did not wish to be accused of opening the door to Nazism. The concern with conciliation was thus complemented with demands that security be strengthened. The government was bitterly criticised for neglecting to build up defences.

Skidelsky suggests that Mosley in his relations with Germany made two assumptions and that both were reasonable. Firstly, that Hitler's expansionist aims were confined to Central and Eastern Europe. Secondly, that an Anglo-German settlement could have been concluded at almost any time during the 1930s. However, the 'reasonableness' of the first of these assumptions is questionable. That being so, the usefulness of the second is also a matter of doubt. It is, for example, true that Hitler, in *Mein Kampf*, reserves expansionist talk for Eastern Europe but he also discusses at some length Jewish influence in the West. He speaks of Britain as displaying a cleavage '. . . between the official, or, better expressed, the traditional, British statesmanship and the controlling Jewish stock exchange powers . . . '. France is described as '. . . the inexorable mortal enemy of the German people'.[85] These are hardly the words and sentiments of someone who could be trusted not to interfere in the West.

There was also a third assumption in the BUF's German policy. This was that even if Hitler did attack, a properly re-armed Britain could successfully resist. But, as Bogdanor has argued in his interesting review of Skidelsky's biography, this was a quite unrealistic belief.[86] A Germany that had achieved its aims in the East would have had at its disposal greatly increased human and physical resources and an isolated Britain would surely have been stretched beyond her capacities.

Until 1938 two arguments were presented as to why the 'old parties' and 'financial democracy' wanted the war. The first was that they had misled the people with lies about the home economic situation which was now under greater stress than ever; every boom was getting shorter, every depression longer – war was thus the only way out.[87] The second was that Germany had struck a blow at the forces which they served. By 1939 this second argument almost completely dominated and increasingly hysterical charges were being made by Mosley against the alleged alien influence: 'We have no interest in what happens in Eastern Europe. For the merits of that dispute I care not one sop. British Empire is our concern; not the Balkans, or the oriental usurers who possess them. We enter this dispute because we are determined that a million British lives shall not be spent in a moneylender's quarrel'; 'Save Britain from the Plots of Money Power'; 'It is only the Money Power that is not prepared to negotiate'.[88] Foreign policy was thus increasingly an outgrowth of the anti-semitic campaign.

The attack continued after the war had started: 'This is not only a capitalist war but a war which serves some of the vilest interests that even Financial capitalism has produced'.[89] A new slogan appeared: 'Join the British Union and work for peace'. Three new points were emphasised in *Action* and at public meetings. Firstly, it was made clear that though they might disagree with the war, and though they believed peace was possible, nothing would be done by the BUF to hinder the war effort. Secondly, it was argued that if war was justified with Germany then it was ten times more justified with Russia. Thirdly, the demand was made that the British people be allowed to vote on the war. They had not been consulted and given the choice they would voice their dissent. (In fact, in by-elections contested by BUF candidates and peace candidates in 1939 and 1940 a derisory number of votes was received.)[90]

As to the general importance of foreign policy, there can be no doubt that many in the elite passionately believed in the ideas they advanced. The consistency of the policies has been demonstrated. 'We should be less prone to anxious interference in everybody's else's affairs and more concentrated on the resources of our own country and Empire'.[91] This statement of 1932 was to apply as much to not attacking the Soviet Union and not helping France as it was to not being hostile to Italian or German expansionism. In addition, if it was not obvious in 1936 that supporting Germany and Italy was counter-productive as regards recruitment and appeal, it most certainly was by 1939.

Part of the explanation for the commitment may well lie in Mosley's 1914–18 experience which apparently resulted in a fierce determination to resist another war. In his autobiography he states: 'I had seen enough in the air and in the trenches to be left with one resolve, some may say obsession: war must never happen again'.[92] There seems no reason to doubt this. From his early days in Parliament he had devoted particular attention to the problems of ex-servicemen, Ireland, and the League of Nations. The latter he saw as the best chance of world peace and in the early 1920s he spent much time actively supporting it. But it was a support which was always conditional on Britain not becoming militarily involved. For example, speaking during the Ruhr crisis of 1923, Mosley expressed a view which was little changed fifteen years later: 'Statesmanship should lay down in advance, and be careful to observe, one fundamental maxim, that not another drop of British blood is to be spent in the European quarrel. We should proceed thus far and stop short of any appeal to arms'.[93]

Not that everything can be put down to Mosley's war experience. His flexibility in defining what were Britain's interests in Europe, and his willingness to believe that Hitler would not invade, necessitates some weight being given to a genuine sympathy in the movement for Nazism. The wane of the Italian star and the rise of the German was indeed signalled by the introduction of a number of Nazi trappings and by a change of name for the movement in 1936, to the British Union of Fascists and National Socialists. Further, although Mosley now plays this down, one cannot ignore the fact that in October 1936 he married in Germany and that Hitler attended the wedding luncheon. (Joyce of course operated from Germany during the war as the notorious Lord Haw Haw.)

In conclusion a number of general points need to be made.

Sir Oswald Mosley has dominated this study. Nevertheless it is justifiable to claim that an examination of BUF ideas has been presented here. Reference has been made to other 'authoritative 'sources when they did have a useful contribution to make; that such contributions were limited is a result of the structure of the movement and the personality of Mosley. Further, there has been discussion of the 'non-authoritative' agents insofar as they differed in approach and emphasis from the 'authoritative'.

It has been shown that three main issues or areas concerned the BUF: the institutional crisis, anti-semitism, and foreign policy. This does not, however, necessarily justify categorising BUF policy, as Benewick does, into three phases. It is true that these issues received different prominence at different periods in time, but is equally true that the early ideas remained, at least on the authoritative level, central, and indeed the *raison d'etre*, until 1938. For Mosley anti-semitism was built-on; it was a supplement to analysis and critique, rather than a replacement. In addition, foreign policy was partially an outgrowth of anti-semitism, in many ways the issue reformulated. So while it is justifiable to speak of changes in emphasis it is doubtful if we can refer to 'phases'.

Finally, it should be emphasised that the widely-held view of Mosley and the BUF as merely a collection of anti-semites and opportunists is too simple. Naturally they wanted power and were prepared to make policy manoeuvres in attempting to achieve this. The enticements offered to vulnerable sections of the population are an example of this, as doubtless anti-semitism was for some. But one must also bear in mind the evidence that suggests a deep belief in many policies: the constancy of position, the continual advance of views which were manifestly not popular, and the sheer intensity of much of the language used.

Notes

[1] The BUF existed in Britain between October 1932 and May 1940 under the leadership of Sir Oswald Mosley. The main secondary sources on the movement as a whole are: C. Cross, *The Fascists in Britain*, Barrie and Rockliff, London 1961; W. F. Mandle, *Anti-Semitism and the British Union of Fascists*, Longman, London 1968; and R. Benewick, *Political Violence and Public Order*, Penguin, London 1969. Of these only Benewick, in a fairly short chapter, attempts a systematic analysis of the ideas of the movement.

There is also the recently published biography of Mosley: R. Skidelsky, *Oswald Mosley*, Macmillan, London 1975. Thoroughly researched though this book is, it does not make reference to all the material available on the ideas. In addition Skidelsky's interpretation has been widely criticised for what many see to be an over-sympathetic treatment of Mosley. Although I am not engaged here in a critique of Skidelsky I shall refer to a number of points of departure in my interpretation.

[2] O. Mosley, *Tomorrow We Live*, 3rd ed., Greater Britain Publications, London 1938, Foreword.

[3] O. Mosley, *The Greater Britain*, BUF Publications, London (reference

here will be to the more detailed 1934 edition except where otherwise stated); *Blackshirt Policy*, BUF Publications, London (no date but almost certainly 1933); *Fascism in Britain* (no date but almost certainly 1933); and *Fascism Explained. 10 Points of Fascist Policy*, 1933.

[4]   Mosley, *The Greater Britain*, pp. 17, 17 and 18 respectively.
[5]   Mosley, *Fascism in Britain*, p. 4.
[6]   Mosley, *The Greater Britain*, p. 62.
[7]   Ibid., p. 160.
[8]   Mosley, *Blackshirt Policy*, p. 39.
[9]   Mosley, *The Greater Britain*, p. 61.
[10] Ibid., p. 18.
[11] Ibid., p. 28.
[12] Ibid., p. 24.
[13] Mosley, *Fascism in Britain*, p. 8.
[14] Mosley, *The Greater Britain*, p. 34.
[15] Ibid., p. 34.
[16] Mosley, *Blackshirt Policy*, p. 25.
[17] A. Raven Thomson, 'Corporate Economics', *Fascist Quarterly*, vol. 1, no. 1, January 1935, p. 21.
[18] Ibid., p. 23.
[19] Especially in *The Coming Corporate State*, Greater Britain Publications, London. Although it was not published until 1937 it is best to discuss this work at this point.
[20] Mosley, *Fascism Explained*, p. 5.
[21] Mosley, *The Greater Britain*, p. 114.
[22] Raven Thomson, *The Coming Corporate State*.
[23] Mosley, *The Greater Britain*, p. 167.
[24] Ibid., p. 168.
[25] Mosley, *Blackshirt Policy*, p. 32.
[26] Ibid.
[27] Mosley, *The Greater Britain*, p. 137.
[28] Ibid., p. 26.
[29] Ibid., p. 44.
[30] Ibid., p. 43.
[31] Ibid., p. 26.
[32] Ibid.
[33] Quoted in Benewick, op. cit., p. 149.
[34] W. Joyce, *Dictatorship*, BUF Publications, London 1933, p. 8.
[35] Mosley, *The Greater Britain*, p. 19.
[36] Ibid., Preface to the 1934 edition.
[37] See O. Mosley, *My Life*, Nelson, London 1968, p. 207.

[38] B. Semmel, *Imperialism and Social Reform*, Allen and Unwin, London 1960, p. 251.
[39] Correspondence dated 18 September 1974.
[40] In addition to references in the major policy booklets a number of unsigned documents and leaflets were issued in specific policy areas, e.g. *The Miners' Only Hope*, undated; *Fascism and Agriculture*, 1936.
[41] I am referring here particularly to the 'independent' contribution of the press as opposed to articles therein by the 'elite'. Excluded here, however, is the *Fascist Quarterly*, later the *British Union Quarterly*, which was the most philosophical and discursive of all BUF agents.
[42] *Blackshirt*, 14 October 1933.
[43] Mosley, *Tomorrow We Live*, p. 62.
[44] *The Times*, 25 October 1932.
[45] *Blackshirt*, 5 October 1934.
[46] An extensive report of this speech appeared in *The Times*, 29 October 1934. My outline here is largely drawn from this source.
[47] Skidelsky, op. cit., ch. 20.
[48] *Blackshirt*, 30 November 1934.
[49] *The Times*, 25 March 1935.
[50] *Blackshirt*, 3 October 1936.
[51] *Action*, 23 December 1937.
[52] Mosley, *Tomorrow We Live*, p. 35.
[53] *Blackshirt*, 6 September 1935.
[54] *The Times*, 17 July 1939 (report of a Mosley speech at a 'Britain First' rally at Earls Court).
[55] Mosley, *The British Peace – How to Get It*, Greater Britain Publications (no date but definitely late 1939).
[56] Mosley, *Tomorrow We Live*, p. 63.
[57] Raven Thomson, *Our Financial Masters*, Abbey Supplies, London, no date. Quoted in Benewick, op. cit., p. 158.
[58] Mosley, *Fascism: 100 Questions*, Q. 94.
[59] Ibid., Q. 97.
[60] Baroness Ravensdale (M. I. Curzon), *In Many Rhythms*, Weidenfeld and Nicolson, London 1953, p. 144.
[61] Reported in Benewick, op. cit., p. 151.
[62] Cross, op. cit., p. 153.
[63] Skidelsky, op. cit., p. 390.
[64] A. K. Chesterton, 'The Apotheosis of the Jew', *British Union Quarterly*, vol. 1, no. 1, Jan–April 1937, p. 54.
[65] Joyce, *Fascism and Jewry*, BUF Publications, London 1936, p. 8.
[66] Quoted in Skidelsky, op. cit., p. 537

[67]   Mosley, *Fascism: 100 Questions*, Q. 93.

[68]   Two editors have in fact claimed that he did exercise scrutiny. See Skidelsky, op. cit., p. 536.

[69]   Cross, op. cit., p. 123.

[70]   Police reports quoted in Skidelsky, op. cit., pp. 537–8.

[71]   *Blackshirt*, 1 April 1933.

[72]   *Blackshirt*, 4 and 18 November, and 2 December 1933 respectively.

[73]   British Union Candidates' Election Addresses, Manchester 1938. Available in Manchester Central Reference Library.

[74]   See, for example, *Action*, 20 August 1938; and 'The Judaic–Communist Movement in the United States' (by 'Americanus'), *Fascist Quarterly*, vol. 11, no. 1, January 1936.

[75]   *Action*, 26 November 1938.

[76]   J. F. C. Fuller, 'The Cancer of Europe', *Fascist Quarterly*, vol. 1, no. 1, January 1935. Fuller, who is often thought of as having been on the fringes of the inner group, wrote a number of articles in this vein.

[77]   Mosley, *The Greater Britain*, 1932 ed., pp. 143, 144 and 145 respectively.

[78]   See, for example, W. Joyce, 'Britain's Empire Shall Live', *Fascist Quarterly*, vol. 1, no. 1, January 1935. He advances a mixture of an organic vision of the Empire, a fervent nationalism (the humiliation of Southern Ireland and India), and an insistence on the political and economic necessities of the Empire.

[79]   See W. Joyce, *Fascism and India*, BUF Publications, London 1933. Also *The Times*, 25 March 1935 for Mosley's position.

[80]   *Blackshirt*, 6 September 1935 (Mosley addressing a meeting at the Manchester Free Trade Hall).

[81]   Mosley, *Fascism: 100 Questions*, Q. 92.

[82]   O. Mosley, 'The World Alternative', *Fascist Quarterly*, vol. 11, no. 3, July 1936, pp. 384–5.

[83]   *The Times*, 16 March 1939.

[84]   *The Times*, 17 July 1939.

[85]   A. Hitler, *Mein Kampf*, Hutchinson, London 1969, pp. 567–8 and 565 respectively.

[86]   V. Bogdanor, 'A Deeply Flawed Hero', *Encounter*, June 1975.

[87]   See, for instance, an article by Mosley in *Action*, 3 September 1938.

[88]   *Action*, 25 March, 8 April and 2 September 1939 respectively.

[89]   Mosley, *The British Peace*, p. 4.

[90]   See A. Calder, *The People's War*, Panther, London 1971, p. 91.

[91]   Mosley, *The Greater Britain*, 1932 ed., p. 143.

[92]   Mosley, *My Life*, p. 70.

[93]   House of Commons Debates, vol. 161, col. 1365.

7 The political parties of the extreme Right

N. NUGENT

The National Front totally rejects laissez faire economics and advances a range of highly interventionist social and economic policies. Aims for Freedom and Enterprise, on the other hand, stands firmly in support of a free enterprise economy. Yet while few would argue with the placing of the former on the extreme Right of the political spectrum there would be no such consensus as regards the latter. Thus, as in other chapters of this book, the problem of definition is again highlighted.

The problem is in part one of identifying the relevant criteria for classification and deciding how these criteria should be weighted. In part it is also one of interpretation of terms. Thus if we focus on the word 'extreme', there are a number of possible points of reference – extreme by comparison with dominant values, by comparison with current government policies, even perhaps by comparison with some absolute moral standards. If we were to use the first, we might conclude that only small minorities, possibly only those who openly embrace the extremist label, are indeed truly extreme. If however we were to use the second, we may well feel obliged to include in our categorisation organisations as diverse as racialist societies, middle-class associations, private armies, even Conservative pressure groups, despite the fact that all of these, with perhaps the exception of the first, are at pains to emphasise their moderation.

Given these difficulties, it is clear that it is just not possible to draw a hard and fast line that clearly and exclusively identifies the extreme Right in Britain. All that can be said with any certainty is that, even on a narrow definition, a comprehensive account of their activities would require a book in itself.

It is for this reason that I am restricting myself here to a consideration of the most publicised and potentially explosive section of the extreme Right: the political parties. These are characterised by their rejection of the established parties and by their decidedly right of Tory position on a number of important issues.

By far the largest and best known of them is the National Front. Formed in 1967 it brought together a number of small groups, the most important of which were the League of Empire Loyalists and the British National Party.

The first of these, the LEL, had been founded in 1954 by the former BUF figure A. K. Chesterton and for a while its policies, which included total opposition to 'anti-national' organisations such as the United Nations and the EEC, preservation of the Empire, opposition to coloured immigration, and revision of the monetary system, resulted in it attracting a large and disparate support: from reactionary and disaffected Tories to embittered racists. Success however was short lived and from 1958, when membership was numbered in thousands, there was a gradual decline. Many sympathisers became unhappy with the League's tactics (the attempt, for example, in 1958 to disrupt Macmillan's speech to the Conservative Party Conference made it extremely difficult for Tories to remain), while others were disturbed at the increasing emphasis in the literature on Jewish power and influence. Accordingly many switched their allegiance to the much less controversial Freedom Group of Edward Martell.[1] With the death in Chile in 1961 of the League's chief benefactor, R. K. Jeffrey, resources as well as recruitment became scarce and gradually the movement faded from the public eye. Three seats were contested at the 1964 general election but without any success. (Standing as Independent Loyalists the candidates polled 1·3 per cent, 0·7 per cent, and 0·7 per cent respectively – even worse than the 4 per cent they had received at the 1957 Lewisham North by-election, the only other seat they fought.) By the time of the 1967 merger it seems unlikely that the LEL membership numbered much more than 200.

As for the other main partner in the 1967 merger, the British National Party, one sees in its history that whole range of tendencies commonly associated with extremist politics: groups appearing, merging, disbanding; ideological disputes, leadership struggles, personality conflicts; takeovers, splinter groups, factionalism, etc.

The Party was itself the result of a merger, in 1960, between two groups that had appeared and achieved some notoriety during the racial disturbances in Notting Hill in the summer and autumn of 1958: the White Defence League led by Colin Jordan and the National Labour Party led by Andrew Fountaine (now deputy chairman of the National Front) and John Bean. Many of their supporters had in turn come from the LEL, a fact which doubtless contributed to the total opposition of both the WDL and the NLP to Jewish power, communism, and, above all, coloured immigration.

In outlining its version of the conspiracy theory the NLP paper *Combat* made clear who were the enemies: 'This long-standing Judaeo–Communist–Masonic plot for the enslavement of the world is the final horror prepared for all the nations of the earth'.[2] At a Trafalgar Square meeting in May

1959 Fountaine said that, as a result of coloured immigration, European civilisation was facing the greatest peril since the sack of Rome and that it was all the fault of the Jews.[3]

For its part the WDL's news-sheet stated:

> The National Assistance Board pays the children's allowances to the blacks for the coffee coloured monstrosities they father, regardless of whether they are legitimate or illegitimate . . . Thus material rewards are given to enable semi-savages to mate with the women of one of the leading civilised nations of the world.[4]

On the formation of the BNP Fountaine became president, Mrs Arnold Leese vice-president,[5] Jordan national organiser and 'leader', and Bean deputy national organiser. Policy was almost entirely concerned with the racial question. A Racial–Nationalist Folk State was advocated which would exclude Jews and coloured immigrants. North East Europe and the white Commonwealth should establish a confederation of white solidarity.

But internal differences created strains. Bean and Fountaine apparently became increasingly concerned about the National Socialist sympaties of Jordan and John Tyndall. Jordan's creation of 'Spearhead', a uniformed para-military elite corps, was also a source of disquiet as were his increasing demands that anti-semitism assume a more important place in BNP propaganda. Consequently, in 1962 a further split took place. Bean and Fountaine took the name, the newspaper and most of the membership; Jordan and Tyndall went off to found the National Socialist Movement.

The political activity of the new BNP focused on the usual themes: the international financial conspiracy and the need to defend the British race and its civilisation from the destruction which coloured immigration would inevitably bring. Areas with a high coloured population were particular targets and some limited electoral success was gained – 27 per cent of the vote and second place in one Southall ward in 1963; 9·1 per cent for Bean in Southall in the 1964 general election; and an average 5·3 per cent for three candidates in the 1966 general election. There was no suggestion, however, of a significant breakthrough and this more than anything seems to have stimulated the merger negotiations. Indeed active membership at its maximum appears to have been no more than around 500, most of this being concentrated in South London.[6] As for the nature of that membership, one hesitates, without access to records, to say anything very definite but the impression is of a predominantly unskilled working-class movement.

Other associations that participated in the founding of the Front, or quickly joined it, included the Patriotic Party, the True Tories, branches of the Anglo-Rhodesian Society, and a section of the Racial Preservation

Society. In the long term, however, the most influential of the 'second tier' of participating bodies has proved to be the Greater Britain Movement, despite the fact that it numbered probably no more than 150 at the time of the merger.

The GBM was set up by John Tyndall and Martin Webster in 1964 after Tyndall and Jordan had expelled one another from the National Socialist Movement (Jordan had been leader and Tyndall national secretary). The basis of the dispute appears to have been personal differences between the two, although doubtless the desire of Tyndall and his followers to make National Socialism 'more British' was also a factor.

Certainly the NSM had never disguised its nature:

> The National Socialist Movement declares that the greatest treasure of the British people – the basis of their greatness in the past, and the only basis for it in the future – is their Aryan, predominantly Nordic blood; and that it is the first duty of the state to protect and improve this Island.[7]

That some should wish to tone down the Nazi influence by dressing National Socialism in a Union Jack is understandable. Whether the GBM actually did this is however questionable. Certainly the following extracts from the official programme of the GBM suggest a basic continuity of outlook and objectives:

> We aim for an authoritarian system of government in Britain, based on personal leadership as opposed to the democratic principle of rule by conflicting committees and factions . . .

> It will be the first duty of the State to recognise Race as being the primary factor in our nationhood . . .

> We hold it to be the Jewish influence, in politics and commerce, in morals and culture, that is perhaps more than any other single factor responsible for the organised filth and corruption that has infected the body of our society. The removal of the Jews from Britain must be a cardinal aim of the new order . . .

> For the protection of British blood, racial laws will be enacted forbidding marriage between Britons and non-Aryans. Medical measures will be taken to prevent procreation on the part of all those who have hereditary defects, either racial, mental, or physical.[8]

The influence of the GBM on the National Front has been twofold. Firstly,

168

within a short time of the 1967 merger many of its supporters were beginning to take up key positions within the movement, including seats on the Front's key policy-making body, the Directorate. Secondly, the internal power struggles, which have been an almost continual feature of the Front since its formation, can, in recent years, be explained to some extent in terms of a conflict between former GBM adherents, or at least sympathisers of their radical and authoritarian approach, and those who can best be described as militant nationalists. This is not of course to suggest that the latter are merely populists. As Kingsley Read, the former chairman and 'leader' of the nationalists has said, people like himself, Roy Painter, and Richard Lawson also take a very tough line on matters such as immigration, corporal punishment and international finance capital.

As for those internal struggles, they began almost as soon as the Front was founded with Fountaine, who had been appointed executive director, and Chesterton, the policy director, engaging in what appears to have been a non-issue related struggle for power. Apparently resolved at the 1968 annual general meeting when there was an overwhelming vote in favour of Chesterton, it proceeded to drag out into a court action with Fountaine claiming that his expulsion from the party was invalid. However, no sooner had his victory been won than Chesterton found his exercise of power being circumscribed by the designs and ambitions of others. Webster's appointment in 1969 as activities organiser – a position he still holds – was particularly important. His forceful personality and his definite ideas (he is reported to have said, 'It was necessary to kick our way into the headlines'[9])quickly made him a key figure. The fact that Chesterton spent much of the year in South Africa and hence could not give the Front his full attention added to the feeling that he should step down. Almost inevitably, then, at the end of 1971, he resigned and left the party. The parting of the ways was, to say the least, not amicable. Chesterton stated:

I had had more than enough, after four years of stamping out nonsense such as plots to set fire to synagogues. Two per cent of the members of the National Front are really evil men – so evil that I placed intelligence agents to work exploring their backgrounds, with results so appalling that I felt obliged to entrust the documents to the vaults of a bank. Some of these men are at present placed close to the centre of things.[10]

Surprisingly, after this, and up to Chesterton's death in 1973, the two sides continued to support one another publicly, each advertising the other's activities in their respective publications.

The new chairman was John O'Brien, a former Conservative who had resigned from the party in 1968 to form a 'Powell for Premier' group.

Generally seen as a moderate, in Front terms, he in turn left in mid-1972, again in an atmosphere of some bitterness. On leaving he made much the same sort of comments as had Chesterton: 'There is a small caucus working within the National Front attracted by the trappings and ideologies of foreign nationalisms from the past. These persons see Britain's future best served by her becoming a rigidly administered, authoritarian police state. They sought to use me as a docile puppet behind whose respectability they could operate from the shadows'.[11] He stated that he was referring to people 'now in the leadership of the National Front' and that he also knew that some members were taking part in reunions in Germany with ex-Nazis and ex-members of the SS.

With O'Brien being followed as chairman by John Tyndall the two most important positions within the Front thus came into the hands of former GBM adherents. Naturally this was seized on by the Front's opponents and during the 1974 election campaigns in particular taunts over the political background of Tyndall and Webster were common.

The Front's 1974 election performance did not live up to expectations and it was perhaps inevitable that some supporters should come to argue that a major advance would have to be preceded by the removal of those who barred the way to the attaining of respectability. By all accounts the entry into the Front of a number of Conservatives, disillusioned at their party's performance in office, and in particular at the 'soft line' on the Ugandan Asians, added to the friction. Not, it should be emphasised, that the struggle which ensued was solely over the Front's image. Other factors were also important: personality differences, questions concerning the administrative competence of certain individuals, and a general unease on the part of many as to the direction in which Tyndall wished to take the Front.

The first round of the battle resulted, in October 1974, in Tyndall's replacement as chairman by Kingsley Read, formerly a prominent member of the Conservative Party in Blackburn.

The arguments, only thinly veiled, were carried to the NF press. Richard Lawson, the editor of *Britain First*, in December 1974 lumped together fascism and communism as both having 'sought to replace the existing capitalist oligarchy with another tyrannical ruling class'. He continued: 'We are irrevocably committed to a belief in democratic nationalism and reject all forms of authoritarianism'. In what could only be seen as a reply to such views Tyndall wrote in the February 1975 edition of *Spearhead*, the journal that he personally controls, that there is a clear need in a democracy for an identifiable and responsible leadership.

Behind the scenes Tyndall started appealing directly to the membership for support and documents were apparently circulated in his name bitterly attacking other members of the Directorate. According to a report in *The Guardian*, one of these documents referred to Directorate member Roy Painter as 'a vain, bumptious and insufferably conceited little man'.[12]

There then followed what was perhaps the most dramatic move of the whole saga with the appearance in the May edition of *Spearhead* of a number of detailed proposals by Tyndall for changes in the NF constitution. In essence they called for a more authoritarian structure with an executive council to be elected by the membership as a whole; this body, and in particular the chairman, should enjoy genuine executive authority independent of the Directorate.

That this was a response to his ousting from the chairmanship was made clear in accompanying comments:

> Another fact that arises out of our experience with this system is that the authority of the Chairman is seriously undermined when it comes to exercising his responsibilities as Leader of the party. Sometimes, inevitably, the chairman has to take a firm stand against a Directorate colleague who has acted wrongly – that is what he is there for; that is what leadership is about. However, the will of the Chairman to face this responsibility is liable to be inhibited by the knowledge that he has only to take such a strong line with two or three colleagues during the year for their votes to be decisive at the end of the year in getting him thrown out! The Chairman is therefore always faced with this dilemma: whether to always take the line of least resistance in inter-Directorate disputes, never facing an issue squarely, never reprimanding the recalcitrant, being a constant opposer – never in fact giving a real **lead**.[13]

Such activities left the Directorate with little option if it was to retain credibility as a collective body. A motion of no confidence in Tyndall was passed and he was gradually stripped of his remaining positions of influence. Even *Spearhead* came under threat with the offending sections of the May edition being removed from copies distributed from NF headquarters. Some branches indeed became reluctant to sell it at all and Tyndall was forced to admit to a substantial loss of sales and had to appeal for cash to keep the journal running.

Events then became increasingly bizarre. At the 1975 annual conference, held in October, Tyndall was re-elected to the Directorate but his proposals for changing the constitution were defeated. The press was excluded from the meeting but according to one report the voting on the decisive resolution 8, which sought to permit constitutional changes by a simple majority of the annual conference rather than the required two-thirds, was defeated by a vote of about 580 to 508.[14] Following this the party's Croydon offices were occupied by supporters of Tyndall, apparently in an attempt to gain access to membership lists. In November Kingsley Read expelled ten members, including Tyndall, by then policy chairman, and Andrew Fountaine, deputy chairman, from the twenty-man Directorate. The purpose of this move, according to Mr Justice Goulding in the High Court on 19 December, was to get round a decision of the Directorate to take no disciplinary action over the occupation. He ordered that they be reinstated.

With this Read and his supporters withdrew from the Front and proceeded to establish a new party, the National Party of the United Kingdom. It would be a party, so it was claimed, that would be distinguished from the Front by being more democratic and 'less authoritarian and cultist'.

The struggle for power having revolved principally around questions of style and personality, it is not surprising to find few policy differences between the NF and the NP. Both naturally claim to be taking the tougher positions – the Front saying that they have got rid of 'left wing influences' and the National Party proclaiming a continuity of policy except insofar as they now 'take a much harder line against immigration, international finance, and Irish Republicanism' – but in fact there appear to be no major differences of substance between them.

On the economy there is a striking similarity to the corporatist, insulationist, and autarchic ideas advanced by Mosley in the 1930s. This is seen in both the defence of free enterprise (as long as it works within 'clearly defined limits . . . determined by the national and public good') and also in the determination to protect the domestic economy from the dual threat of international finance capital and international communism.

Finance capital is held to be an evil for two reasons. Firstly, by creating credit which is not related to increases in real national wealth it is the prime cause of inflation. Any attack on inflation must then begin with state control of credit. Secondly, international finance, through bodies such as the International Monetary Fund and the World Bank, is held to exercise excessive control over the nation state. This, it is argued, could be avoided by bold new policies: cancelling those parts of the National Debt which have been incurred through inflationary credit created by international banks; striving for maximum self-sufficiency through restriction of foreign investments, protection of the home market, and expansion of agriculture; and finally by attempting to integrate economically with a reformed white Commonwealth.

Protection must also be sought against international communism because it is part of the same conspiracy that seeks to undermine national sovereignties. The left wing class conception of society is deplored; it is a device designed

172

in reality to achieve the same end as its apparent opponent, international finance. That end is national divisiveness and ultimately world tyranny. In consequence the 'treasonous', anti-British Reds are continually attacked, and their influence in world politics (especially in Southern Africa), in the Labour Party, in the trade union movement, and in the IRA is constantly discussed and analysed.

The apparently curious belief that international finance and international communism are really allies is explained by the traditional ultra-Right belief that both are inextricably linked to international Zionism. Although there is in both parties a careful avoidance of anti-semitism, the Front in particular spares little effort in its attempts to expose Jewish influence. Thus the Bolshevik revolution is seen as having been part of the world conspiracy – the number of Jews involved frequently being quoted. The influence of Jews in the Parliamentary Labour Party is presented as further evidence of Zionist-socialist links. As for those who seek to oppose and discredit the Front – whether they be councillors (who frequently deny them premises), the media, or the various anti-fascist organisations – they are generally held to have some links, knowingly or not, with the Zionist conspiracy.

Another issue on which passions run high in both the NF and the NP is Britain's membership of the EEC. Given their nationalist stance and their dreams of linking up with the white areas of the former Empire this is hardly surprising. Nor is it surprising that their main objection to the EEC is political rather than economic for any hint of federalism is totally alien to parties which put such a high premium on national sovereignty.

On other policies too the NF and the NP are in accord. They call for an improved welfare state which involves, amongst other things, the social services putting 'true' Britons first in housing, jobs, education and welfare. In education retention of the selective system is advocated but there must be an increased emphasis in the curriculum on patriotism, left wing influences must be eradicated, and 'pseudo-scientific' subjects such as sociology must be restricted. Another major priority of both parties is the strengthening of Britain's defences; this to be achieved primarily by increased spending and by withdrawal from those international alliances in which British forces are placed under foreign control. On law and order a much tougher line with thugs and criminals is demanded. Only on Northern Ireland is there any discernible difference between the two; both support the Loyalist cause but the NP appears to be much more firmly committed to a separately elected local parliament.

Despite this wide arrange of policies, however, it is of course with their opposition to coloured immigration that the two parties are publicly identi-fied. For both this is absolutely central, not only as an issue in itself but also as an underlying factor in problems associated with education, housing, social services, etc. Even when demonstrations have been ostensibly concerned with other issues – as, for example, in 1973 when the theme of the main annual NF London march was 'Clean up Britain' (by ending official corruption, banning pornography and controlling permissiveness) – most of the banners and chants have referred to immigration.

Whether it is because of a reasoned analysis of the problems caused by immigration, or because of a rationalisation of a lack of personal success, or because of straightforward racialism, there is no doubt that the majority of NF and NP supporters feel more strongly about this issue than any other. A substantial number, perhaps a majority, believe that Britain's social and economic ills can be explained primarily in terms of the presence of the coloured population.

The NF and the NP attempt to exploit racial tensions in a number of ways. They focus on grievances, many of which in themselves are perfectly genuine and understandable, but present them in a rather special light – the little man, defenceless against the 'race-mixers' of the establishment, is a favourite ploy. They seek to raise fears. This may take a variety of forms: elections are contested and rallies held in areas with a large coloured population. Leaflets, the factual accuracy of some of which is open to question, are distributed on a mass basis. (To take a recent National Party leaflet 'Do you care about Britain?': it asks the reader if he does not feel angry 'that Britain is being swamped by millions upon millions of coloured immigrants?'.) Their publications, *Spearhead* and *National Front News* in the case of the NF, and *Britain First* in the case of the NP, contain deliberately provocative material. By way of example here is a sample of the headlines from the August 1976 edition of *National Front News*: 'Government puts no limit on black invasion – official'; 'Let them all in – Jenkins'; 'Relf defeats Race Board'; ' "Meek and peaceful" Asians terrorise white families'; 'Rabid Asian bites nurse'.[15]

Each party presents itself as the sole defender of true Britons; it alone has the guts to stand up and accuse officialdom of complacency and the establishment of a cover-up. Who else has the courage to say 'enough is already more than enough'? With their spokesmen often proudly proclaiming their racism – or more often in the case of the National Party their 'racial nationalism' – their common message is that British people have been made second-class citizens in their own country.

A total ban on further immigration and an immediate start to repatriation is put forward as the only solution to the immigration problem. Without such policies Britain's racial identity will, it is claimed, gradually be destroyed. In words reminiscent of Racial Preservation Society publications *Spearhead* recently claimed:

Britain is simply committing genetic suicide. As we continually bale out a bottomless sea of inferior genes from the Third World and import them into our land, we are simultaneously spilling out a constant flow of our own white British racial stock that will increase as the situation worsens. That may balance the books for the Office of Population Censuses and Surveys, but in reality it means a rapid slide towards racial extinction for the indigenous people of this country.[16]

On the question of the form repatriation should take, spokesmen concede that if 'voluntary' repatriation proved to be ineffective stiffer measures would have to be used. Many describe their methods as a mixture of 'stick and carrot' tactics. As the chairman of the Front in the East Midlands has stated:

If the Asians will not take the initial incentive offered them we shall have to start removing progressively their rights. If bloodshed and racial strife is the result then all I can say is that it is an acceptable price to pay for clearing out the immigrants.[17]

In the light of the expression of sentiments such as these (and many are far more virulent) a rather surprising aspect of the anti-immigration campaign of the two parties is that there have not been more prosecutions under the Race Relations Act. It is true that an injunction was granted to the Race Relations Board against Kingsley Read in March 1976 restraining him from repeating his action of 1974 in which he distributed letters to householders in Blackburn urging them not to sell their homes to coloured immigrants. In addition, in August 1976, after the failure of all attempts at conciliation, two NF officials in Yorkshire were reported to the Race Relations Board for allegedly discriminating against a black reporter by refusing him admission to two meetings organised by the Front. But apart from these two examples, the law has been little used. Doubtless this is partly explained by weaknesses in the provisions of the law relating to incitement to racial hatred. In part, however, it also appears to be a result of a deliberately low key policy on the part of the authorities who are anxious not to create martyrs.

To turn now towards support, both parties have undeniably enjoyed some success. At the time of the break between them there were probably around 9,000 paid up members, this being perhaps 5,000 lower than the Front's peak of 1973. (This peak had followed closely on the Ugandan Asians affair.) Exact figures are a closely guarded and well kept secret however, as witnessed by the wildly differing estimates that appear in the national press from time to time. A good example of this was seen in July 1976. On 3 July in *The Guardian*, Martin Walker, who has long been an observer of the NF, stated that the number of currently fully paid up and committed workers was about 2,000. The very next day in the *Sunday Times* an estimate appeared putting current membership at 12,500. Clearly part of the explanation for this wide disparity was that the two papers were working on different bases, the *Sunday Times* not using the phrase 'fully paid up'. As many former activists had dropped out of political activity altogether in the previous twelve months there is little doubt that the *Sunday Times'* figures represented a gross overestimate. Incidentally, this article also stated that only 100 NF members left the party with Read – in my view a gross underestimate. (Read himself claims that in Blackburn alone all but five of a 100-plus strong branch came over to the NP.)

The exact distribution of former NF members and the size of current membership must therefore remain a matter of some doubt. Certainly no useful conclusions can be drawn from the number of local organisations, for though both claim to have over a hundred branches and groups, sizes can vary from a handful to a hundred and upwards. The tendency of extremist organisations to have a high turnover, and to experience waves and slumps in membership, makes estimates doubly speculative. In suggesting then that at the time of writing (September 1976), the National Front has a paid up membership of 4,000–5,000, and the National Party around 2,000, I am conscious of the fact that such figures are no more than an approximation. What is not in doubt, however, is that these figures represent a growth in support since the split. The publication of the Hawley Report, the 'immigrant racket' angle given by most of the popular press to the '£600 a week Malawi Asians', the unrest in Southall, the Robert Relf affair (Relf received national publicity early in 1976 for displaying a sign outside his house indicating that it was for sale to an English family only), and parliamentary by-elections, have all resulted in them gaining considerable publicity. In consequence, claims by Front spokesmen that June and July were record recruiting months, that many new groups are being set up, and that by the end of 1976 5,000 new members will have joined, seem in no way exaggerated.

As for the nature and distribution of the membership of the two parties, the main areas of strength are those where there is a higher than average coloured population: London, the Midlands and Lancashire. In terms of social composition both appear to be predominantly lower middle- or working-class. This is not of course to say that all local groupings contain such a mix. As Hanna observed in 1974, NF branches such as Camden and Brent are mainly middle-class and professional; south coast branches such as Worthing mainly middle-class and retired; others, such as many in Lancashire, mainly working-class.[18]

But whilst recognising local variations such as these, generalisations are still valid and useful. In this context one's overall impression of local branches is close to the picture painted by Scott in his interesting study of the NF organisation in 'Fettlerbridge', 'a medium sized industrial town north of London'. Scott identified two distinct elements amongst Fettlerbridge local activists: a middle-class group numbering five or six who were mainly responsible for directing branch activities, and a working-class group who 'appear to have come from above the lowest skill areas – just that group where social and economic tensions might be greatest'.[19] The latter carried out a substantial proportion of the work of the branch.

This picture would also tend to be confirmed by the fact that, in terms of political background, most members appear to be either former Labour Party supporters or, and this applies particularly to the younger members, non-political. Spokesmen, whilst at pains to stress the breadth of the Front's appeal, do in fact usually confirm this. F. Cribbenn, an NF election agent at a local by-election in Bolton in 1974, thought half his local branch were former Labour voters; M. Lobb, the NF candidate in the 1974 Newham by-election, maintained that of the estimated 300 NF cardholders in Newham two-thirds were trade unionists; Kingsley Read in conversation with the author in mid-1975, at which time he was still NF chairman, estimated that over 60 per cent of NF members were former Labour Party supporters.

An additional indication of the socio-economic make-up of the Front is provided by a breakdown of the background of their candidates at the October 1974 general election. While, as in all parties, the professional/business categories were overrepresented (with a total of 42 per cent), the proportion of workers (40 per cent) was second only to that of the Communist Party. In addition, the number of candidates who had had a university education (11 per cent) was lower than in all other parties, again with the single exception of the Communist Party.[20]

Reasons for joining the NF or the NP, as in any political organisation, naturally vary and are a complex mixture of the political, the social, and the psychological. It may well be, however, that these parties attract a higher than average proportion of those who might be described as non-political. There is an extensive body of literature suggesting that members of extremist organisations are motivated primarily by reasons other than those of rational political choice. This is the theme of Scott's article. He argues that for many Front activists satisfaction is achieved not via the normal indicators of political success – election victories, the capture of power and the implementation of policies – but through membership itself and activities such as marches, demonstrations, and heckling.[21]

At the polls the number of seats contested at both parliamentary and local levels has been impressive and sizeable votes have been obtained. Such indeed has been their success at local elections, and at a number of parliamentary by-elections too, that the major parties have increasingly had to alter their strategies to take account of the challenge. Although the Front themselves have not as yet won any seats, in local elections they have frequently won over 20 per cent of the total vote; the North East is indeed now the only region of England where no vote of over 15 per cent has been recorded in their favour. Equally significantly they are, on an increasing number of occasions, pushing the Liberals out of third place.

In 1976, with more candidates standing than ever before (the Front put up 176 and the NP around 50), their share of the vote increased in virtually every seat that had previously been contested. In all, almost half the Front's candidates polled over 10 per cent. Their best results were at Leicester where, for the first time, a full complement of three candidates was put up in each of the city's sixteen wards: over 20 per cent was obtained in six wards and the overall average was 18·5 per cent, roughly double the percentage of the previous elections in 1973. Other good results included those in Bradford, where the twenty-two candidates averaged 10 per cent, and in the West Midlands where nine votes of over 15 per cent were gained (four at Sandwell, four at Warley, and one at Wolverhampton). In addition, it should be borne in mind that there were no elections in London where, to judge from past performances, good results could reasonably have been expected. Overall, National Party results were lower but in Kingsley Read's home town of Blackburn two of their candidates were elected – Kingsley Read himself and John Frankman. It is worth noting that in neither seat did the Conservatives put up a full complement of candidates. Following on from this success, at a remarkable by-election at Deptford in July 1976, the NP, with 26 per cent of the poll, came second to Labour; with the NF coming in third the two extreme Right parties obtained a combined vote of 44·5 per cent as compared with the successful Labour candidate's 43 per cent.

Impressive though these votes are, they must however be kept in perspective. Firstly, and this applies to many of their better results at parliamentary by-elections also, they are usually achieved on low polls and hence the absolute number of votes involved is small. Secondly, it is reasonable to assume that the extreme Right, unlike the major parties, is polling near its maximum vote, i.e. its potential voters are more likely to turn out. Thirdly, successes of this order have not been achieved at general elections. In 1970 the ten NF candidates averaged 3·6 per cent; in February 1974 fifty-four averaged 3·1 per cent and in October ninety again averaged 3·1 per cent. The highest individual votes were, respectively, 5·4 per cent, 7·8 per cent, and 9·4 per cent. In short, in 1974, as in 1970, the Front did little more than

178

drain that pool of 3–4 per cent of the electorate which appears since the war to have been permanently available to most right wing protest groups.

What explains these comparatively poor general election results? Certainly they were nowhere near as good as supporters might reasonably have expected given earlier local election results, and more especially the 16·0 per cent achieved by Martin Webster at a parliamentary by-election at West Bromwich in 1973. Furthermore, despite difficulties of hiring premises, great energy was put into the campaigns and a considerable amount of money spent – £21,000 in lost deposits alone, £100,000 in all during the year.[22] On a number of important issues – immigration, left wing extremism, law enforcement, capital punishment, and perhaps also the EEC – their policies closely accorded with majority opinion. On top of all this they had received, or managed to create, considerable publicity in the preceding months.

The main explanation for the moderate election results must be sought not, as some have suggested, in features of the Front itself, but in a wider context. In particular we must look to the importance of tradition in determining voting habits, to the social pressures to conform, and to the fear of the wasted vote. In established liberal democracies such as Britain where there are no major problems of national identity, extreme right wing parties are likely to attract wide support only in periods of severe social and economic disloca-tion, when the interests of the upper working-class and middle-class are fundamentally threatened. It is in these circumstances, when the existing forces and institutions are not seen as being able to provide the required stability, that simple explanations and panaceas, including those of the scapegoat variety, are most attractive.

It is for this reason that the continuation of high levels of inflation and unemployment can do nothing but assist the cause of the far Right. Certainly the experiences of the 1930s and the failure of the British Union of Fascists to capture mass support should not be taken as evidence of Britons having an unbreakable resistance to extremism. At that time Britain had not suffered the sustained decline in national prestige that it has experienced since the Second World War, nor, in socio-economic terms, was the demo-cratic loyalty of the 'vulnerable' upper working-class/lower middle-class tested to the extent that it was on the Continent.

At the same time scepticism is called for with regard to those rather com-fortable interpretations of British political culture which have emphasised the stability of the political base. People such as Rose, Nordlinger, and Eckstein have all suggested a congruence between attitudes and beliefs about political life and the major features of the political system.[23] Almond and Verba in their five nation study indeed coined the term 'civic culture' to describe what they saw to be a desirable balance between parochial, subject, and participant attitudes towards politics in Britain.[24] It may be, however, that beliefs such as these concerning the fairness and competence of political institutions and political decision-makers, the ability of the individual to affect policies, and the extent of deference have all been exaggerated. Evidence is now coming forward of widespread disaffection, even hostility, towards politics and politicians.[25] Political stability may be based as much on apathy as on a supportive political culture.

The increased electoral volatility of recent years, and the dramatic decline in the support for the two major parties, is perhaps evidence of this increasing disillusionment. Up to the present the benefits have been reaped primarily by the Liberals and the Scottish and Welsh Nationalists, the first respectable and established, the second respectable and tapping a source of discontent not available to English-based right wing parties. It should not, however, be assumed that this pattern will inevitably continue. If the extreme right can improve its image, and if social and economic circumstances continued to favour them, they could well continue to increase their support.

Not that an improvement in their image will be an easy task. The taunts of 'Nazis' and 'Fascists', the violence that has accompanied many activities, both of which may have attracted a few but which doubtless have scared off many more, will continue. Indeed as the anti-fascist and anti-racist movement in the country broadens to include not just the extreme Left but a whole variety of people and organisations – the Liberal and Labour Parties, immigrant associations, and religious groups amongst others – the extreme Right will find itself increasingly under criticism and attack. Whereas previously most people in the anti-fascist movement have argued that the most effective means of preventing the extreme Right establishing itself is to ignore it and thus deny it publicity, recent electoral advances have convinced many that the tactic should now be to discredit the Right and to deny it respectability.

Nor will the National Party, which as we have seen was partly set up because of the Front's image, be immune from the campaign. Already it has given its opponents firm grounds on which to launch their attack. Firstly, despite Kingsley Read's claim to have eliminated from the party any taint of neo-Nazism and fascism, there has not been a complete break with those individuals who were associated with Tyndall in the Greater Britain Movement: both Gordon Brown and Dennis Pirie were welcomed into the new party; the latter indeed is a member of the National Executive. Secondly, two leading NP members in Blackburn, John Frankman and Robert Horman, have been involved in a much publicised disturbance when, at a meeting at Blackburn Town Hall concerned with race relations, they were involved in incidents during which the chairman of the town's housing committee was floored. Thirdly, and more seriously, John Frankman has had to resign from the Blackburn council because under electoral law he was ineligible, having previously been given a six-month prison sentence, suspended for twelve months, for a motoring offence. Further to this, Robert Horman, chosen by the National Party to contest the vacant seat, was committed for trial at Preston Crown Court, shortly before the election, accused of carrying a firearm in a public place. (He was subsequently fined £10 for this offence.)

As for those good results that the extreme Right has achieved, two sets of circumstances appear to explain most of their votes over the 3–4 per cent mark. The first, a lower turnout, has already been mentioned. The second is when the electorate 'indulges' itself by being influenced by factors other than the socio-economic issues which are normally the major determinants of general elections. Both of these are more likely to occur when the government of the day is not at stake, i.e. at local elections and parliamentary by-elections.

Two forms of 'indulgence' have been particularly helpful to the extreme Right.

Firstly, when immigration has become important. It would be inappropriate to become deeply involved here in the very complex question of the relationship between immigration and voting. A number of points do, however, need to be made of which the first is that although it is clear that a large part of the population displays varying degrees of colour prejudice,[26] it is by no means certain that at general elections immigration itself is a major issue. The evidence is open to different interpretations. On the one hand there are those surveys and opinion polls which suggest it has been of minor importance. When Butler and Stokes' respondents were asked what they thought were the most important problems facing the government, immigration was mentioned by only 2 per cent in 1963 and 8 per cent in 1970.[27] Surveys by Opinion Research Centre point the same way, the trendlines for immigration as an important priority for government action varying between 1973 and early 1976 from 9 per cent in August 1973 to 2 per cent in February 1974. It has tended to appear between twelfth and fifteenth place.[28] On the other hand it could be argued that feelings on the subject are expressed as much through anxieties about housing, education, and employment as by any specific reference. In addition, fears of being thought racist might result in the issue being deliberately not mentioned by respondents. Certainly in more structured surveys, when immigration is actually raised by the interviewer, it tends to assume a greater importance.[29]

In consequence there is no general agreement about the *national* effect of immigration on general elections, either in terms of turnout or swing between the parties. It would be fair to say that most observers have tended to play it down but inevitably, given the problems of measurement, such conclusions are speculative and subject to qualification. Thus Butler and Stokes have shown that 1966 Labour voters were much more likely to support the Conservatives in 1970 if they perceived a tougher Tory policy on immigration. They also point out, however, that a cause and effect relationship is not thereby proven since switchers tend to see virtues in their new party in areas which do not actually influence their change in allegiance.[30]

We are on much firmer ground when we look for immigration having exerted a local influence on general elections, for then we can look for differential turnouts and swings. That there has been some effect is undeniable. As early as 1964 an anti-immigrant vote directly resulted in the Labour Party losing three seats. The disproportionate swings in the West Midlands, in both 1970 and 1974, have generally been accredited by observers to Enoch Powell and his stand on immigration. Outside these instances, however, there is little else to support this. There has, for example, been no noticeable influence on the immigrant areas of London or Lancashire; nor have Powellite candidates attracted higher or lower swings than Conservatives in the country at large.

With the evidence thus tending to suggest that the influence of immigration, in terms of the performances of the major parties, has been limited, it is not altogether surprising to find that the relationship between the vote for the National Front at general elections and the presence or not of a coloured population is not as strong as might at first have been thought. Certainly there is a correlation, for, as Steed has shown for the February 1974 election, in the thirty-one constituencies where more than 5 per cent of the population had New Commonwealth roots the average NF vote was 3·9 per cent; in the twenty-three with fewer than 5 per cent the average was 2·1 per cent.[31] But the relationship is by no means consistent. If, for example, we look at the 'top ten' constituencies with populations with New Commonwealth roots only five were contested by the Front at the October election; in only one of these, Haringey Tottenham, did the Front poll over 4 per cent.

The conclusion would appear to be then that although the presence of a local immigrant population is a prerequisite for an above average extreme Right vote, other factors, some of which cannot be quantified, will determine its exact effect, e.g. the state of local community relations, the strength and skill of the local party branch, the size of the immigrant population in surrounding areas, and the level of unemployment. It should also be remembered that the larger the size of the local immigrant population, the smaller is the total potential support for the extreme Right; the immigrants themselves overwhelmingly vote Labour.

A much clearer relationship is seen at local elections for there virtually all the best results have been obtained in areas where the coloured population approaches, or is over, 10 per cent: at Blackburn, Bradford, Leicester, and Huddersfield in the provinces; at Newham, Haringey, Islington and Hounslow in London. Interestingly, though these are all *areas* of high immigration the highest returns are not always in the *wards* where the concentration is highest. As in general elections the explanation is partly that the immigrant communities themselves overwhelmingly vote Labour; but in part too there is the clear suggestion of a 'fear factor' in surrounding neighbourhoods.

The second 'indulgence' that benefits the Front is where there is a general protest vote. Traditionally regarded as a basic element of extremism its exact size is difficult to estimate, although there seems little doubt that it has constituted an important part of the recently increased support for the far Right. Certainly analysis of the 1974 elections gives more than a suggestion of this. In February the highest correlation with the NF vote was the presence or not of a Liberal; the seven Front candidates who did not have a Liberal opponent polled on average 6·2 per cent; the forty-seven who were competing with a Liberal averaged 2·7 per cent. In the forty-seven seats fought in both February and October the Front suffered an average decline of 11 per cent in its vote – only slightly more than the other parties, there being an overall decline in turnout. Of these forty-seven seats all had a Liberal candidate in October but only forty had in February. In the forty the decline was only 3 per cent; in the remaining seven it was a remarkable 34 per cent.[32] Now if the general interpretation of the increase in Liberal support in 1974 is accepted (that it was in large measure a result of disillusionment with the two main parties), then the relationship between that vote and the Front's vote, given the gulf between the two parties in virtually every area of policy, is indicative of the size of the protest element in the Front's support.

Attempts have also been made to correlate the extreme right wing vote with socio-economic variables. The fact that many of the better votes have been gained in traditional Labour areas has led many to conclude that the support is overwhelmingly working-class. One writer has gone so far as to suggest that in 1974 at least two sources of discontent were tapped – a middle-class anti-immigrant backlash in the Midlands, and a working-class social and economic malaise in East and North East London.[33] His analysis may be correct. Support for the Front probably is eclectic. But to come to such specific conclusions merely from census data and aggregate votes is hardly satisfactory.

The fact is that the general reluctance to admit publicly to supporting the extreme Right makes any accurate social and economic analysis of its support well nigh impossible. The numbers involved, at least in surveys conducted to date, are so small as to make them statistically meaningless.

To take just one example, in a Marplan survey conducted during the February 1974 campaign a sample of 1,500 voters was studied in three Midlands constituencies, including Perry Bar where there was an NF candidate. The number of declared Front supporters did not exceed single figures.

One further area of the far Right vote that should perhaps be examined, especially in view of the publicity the question has received, is its relationship to the vote of the major parties. A belief that it has been disproportionately losing votes was indeed the main reason behind the Labour Party's launching, in the autumn of 1976, a nationwide anti-fascist campaign.

Close analysis, however, reveals the issue to be by no means clearcut. It is true that in the last general election (October 1974) the best NF results were in London Labour strongholds. It is also true that in 1975 and 1976 the Labour Party has suffered more, most obviously at Blackburn where the two NP candidates elected in May 1976 were both at Labour's expense. But disproportionate losses for Labour after 1974 were to be expected, for not only did they become the government of the day, and hence more vulnerable to a protest vote, but in local elections they had to defend seats which were won in 1973 – a very good year for Labour. It should be noted that prior to the Conservatives being removed from office in 1974 Labour were by no means the certain losers; a study of the vote for the British Campaign to Stop Immigration in Bradford in 1971 has shown that votes were taken disproportionately from the Tories.[34] What is more, a significant part of the NF and NP support often comes not from the established parties but from potential abstainers. This is by no means a universal pattern but a good extreme right vote does often coincide with a turnout higher than might otherwise have been expected.

General election results too give some comfort to Labour, since the evidence from October 1974, when both the Liberals and the Front put up many more candidates than they had done in the February election, suggests that NF drew votes fairly equally from each of the three main parties.[35]

As has been indicated, the future of the NF and the NP will be determined mainly by factors outside their own control, in particular by the state of the economy and levels of unemployment and inflation. In so far, however, as they do have control over their own destiny it seems likely that the bitterness and antagonism that clearly exists between the two will do their cause no good. Since the split at the end of 1975 accusations have flown both ways as they have vied with one another for membership. In a memorable article in *Spearhead* Tyndall wrote of those dissident groups that have appeared in the Front from time to time. He identified distinct categories. One consisted of people of a 'decidedly unprepossessing racial type . . . The features are usually markedly unintelligent, although sometimes betokening a kind of low animal cunning . . . The sheer physical ugliness of the type singles it out as a poor specimen, not just of the British race, but any race'. Another category, he said, sought the soft option: 'In outward appearance its chief personality trait is one, not of racial inferiority, but sheer wetness. It is distinguished by the limp handshake and the sickly smile and otherwise vapid expression'.[36]

The main effort, however, has been the attempt of both to present the other as the true fascists while at the same time proclaiming itself as taking the tougher policy position. Tyndall and Kingsley Read in particular have exchanged insults in public. Kingsley Read was quoted in *The Times* as stating that he left the Front because of '. . . the autocratic style of the Fuehrer [John Tyndall] and the Nazi proclivities at the centre of the party . . . The democratic principle they now pretend to follow is simply a facade. If the Front ever got power they would never let it go, they would take over the country . . .'.[37] Tyndall for his part replied in an interview in *The Observer*, 'He's just been babbling to the Press again. He's reported things that were said in private conversation. He once said to me – and he's often said it privately to others – that he considers himself a much bigger Fascist than I am. So I don't know what he's talking about. I can tell you *he's* not in a position to attack me on the grounds of not being democratic'.[38]

To speculate about the prospects for the two parties in relation to one another, the National Front seems likely to remain the larger for not only does it have the label that is popularly associated with anti-immigration but it also apparently has the greater resources. For its part the National Party is not only operating from a smaller base but it has not yet solved the problem of differentiating itself from the Front. In addition it has now lost one of its two council seats at Blackburn. At the by-election in September 1976, caused by the resignation of Frankman, Robert Horman polled 21 per cent of the vote as against the successful Labour candidate's 44 per cent.

But though the National Front and the National Party are today the main groups on the far Right this has not always been the case. In the immediate post-war period Mosley's Union Movement was the most important although, almost inevitably, it made little impact. Despite attempts to break with the BUF tradition, in particular by shifting the focus of political life away from the nation state towards a united Europe, the recent past could not be easily forgotten, either by supporters, who became active again in the old stamping ground of East London, or by the public at large, who, more than ever, were now inclined to equate any extreme right wing politics with fascism and Nazism. With Britain enjoying, at the same time, full employment and a slowly rising standard of living it is hardly surprising that in local elections the movement averaged only 4 to 6 per cent of the vote.

The emergence of immigration as a political issue in 1958, following the disturbances in Nottingham and Notting Hill, was thus a lifeline, particularly since the UM had been, in 1952, the first organisation to call for controls. Mosley, whose political activity had been intermittent since he had left Britain in 1951, returned to the fray and contested North Kensington, which contains Notting Hill, at the 1959 general election. Although only obtaining 8 per cent of the vote his candidature seemed to invigorate the declining movement and the following four years saw increased activity. In addition to local elections, parliamentary by-elections were contested at Manchester Moss Side in 1961 (5·2 per cent) and Middlesbrough East in 1962 (1·7 per cent). Mosley himself attended many marches and meetings, and seven rallies were held in Trafalgar Square alone between 1959 and 1962. A consequence of these activities was that leftist and Jewish organisations, again stirred, determined that Mosley should not get a public hearing. Once more harrassment and violence were the order of the day. In July 1962 the Trafalgar Square meeting was broken up; Mosley was physically assaulted at Dalston; thirty were arrested at Bethnal Green and the meeting stopped by police before Mosley was able to speak. At Manchester, where there was an attempt to hold a procession through the streets, 250 police were involved as running fights took place and thirty-nine people were arrested. The upshot of all this was the curtailing by the authorities of UM activities. Marches, such as the one proposed through the East End in the autumn of 1962, were banned by the police; local authorities, sometimes as a result of pressure from anti-fascist organisations, refused to let public halls to them.

Thus deprived of their principal means of gaining publicity and increasingly suffering from the emergence of competitors the UM has been in decline since the mid-1960s. Their greatest attraction, Mosley himself, after years of intermittent activity finally withdrew in 1966 from involvement in their affairs. This was shortly after the four UM candidates at the 1966 general election averaged only 3·7 per cent of the vote; this included a miserable 4·6 per cent for Mosley himself at Shoreditch and Finsbury. Apart from the involvement of Directory member Dan Harmston in the organisation of the Smithfield Meat Porters' protests against immigration in 1968 and 1972, very little has been heard of them in recent years. Elections are contested very infrequently – perhaps because they illustrate only too starkly how the UM has now been almost totally eclipsed by others on the far Right.[39]

Activities today are mainly focused on the publication of the fortnightly newspaper *Action* and the circulation of broadsheets which Mosley periodi-

186

cally issues. There is little doubt that the audience receiving these is declining, for though, as in similar organisations, membership figures are not revealed, admirers from the pre-war period are obviously now dying off and the new young blood is going to organisations with which the UM has no formal contact. The UM cannot number more than about 300 today.

Other parties on the far Right include the National Party of St George, the United Democratic Party, the National Independence Party, and the British Movement. Only occasionally, however, do they attract attention. They may do so as a result of a respectable vote at an election; the 7·6 per cent obtained by the New Liberal Party at Islington East in 1964, or the 21·9 per cent gained by the National Democratic Party against the Speaker of the House of Commons at Southampton Itchen in 1970 are cases in point. The particularly idiosyncratic nature of a campaign may also stir interest. A recent example is the Campaign for a More Prosperous Britain, although admittedly it can hardly be described as a political party. Financed largely by Tom Keen, a property developer from Oldham, it fought, without any noticeable effect, twenty-five seats in the October 1974 election, with Keen himself standing in eleven and his associate Harold Smith in twelve. The appeal was solely not to vote Labour '. . . because of the stranglehold that certain Life-Long Communist Leaders such as Jack Jones, Hugh Scanlon, Lawrence Daly and their ilk have over the Labour Party . . .'.[40] One sketch prominently displayed in their leaflets showed a Trojan horse entering Parliament; on it was written 'Labour Party – 70 Communists in my belly'. Something else which may bring notice to these parties is merger negotiations. Thus in 1973 and 1974 the press gave publicity to discussions which took place between a number of small groups, some of which were well populated with former Conservatives. The outcome was the Independent Democratic Alliance, which fought six seats in February, and the United Democratic Party, which fought thirteen in October of that year.

In general, however, these organisations have made little impact. Their membership is low, their public appearances scarce, and while emphases may vary their interests are predictable.

The only one that merits brief discussion on its own is the British Movement. Formed by Colin Jordan in 1968, and now headed by Michael McLaughlin, it is the successor to the National Socialist Movement, the organisation which was formed by Jordan and Tyndall in 1962 and whose early activities are described above. Its distinctiveness stems not from its size or influence, its active membership probably numbering no more than one hundred today, but from its particular interest in Jewry and Zionism.

Jordan himself, who though having resigned the chairmanship is still a

187

member, has noticeably toned down his public statements in recent years. Internal propaganda, however, still devotes much attention to the old themes. Links are alleged to exist between Jewish organisations and centres of political and economic power. The claim is made that people of Jewish descent are not British. This is based on the grounds that they belong not to a faith but to a race and as such must always have dual loyalties – to their own racial kin and to the 'bandit state' of Israel. It is suggested that the history of Nazi Germany has been widely misrepresented. Mementoes of the Third Reich are advertised.

During the October 1974 election campaign McLaughlin was convicted at Bury in Lancashire for stirring up hatred against the Jewish race. He had produced and published stickers throughout Bury, where the Conservative candidate was Jewish, urging people not to vote. They had stated: 'The Jews have Israel – let the British have Britain'. McLaughlin told the court: 'We are anti-Zionist and anti-Communist. We stand for race and nation'.[41] More recently, in June 1976, Jordan, McLaughlin, and the London organiser of the British Movement were all fined for offences in connection with a demonstration they had held supporting Robert Relf.[42]

There are a number of possible criteria for evaluating the importance and influence of small political parties and organisations. Although there has been a special concern here with electoral performances, other equally relevant areas for investigation and consideration include effects on public opinion and influences on the policies of the major parties. The problem with these is that conclusions are inevitably speculative, it being virtually impossible to accurately identify the causal influences of changes in opinion on, say, immigration or capital punishment. Has the extreme Right actually added to racial tensions in Bradford, Blackburn, Leicester and elsewhere, or merely benefited from them? Similarly is the 'hardening' of the Labour and Conservative platform on immigration related to the extreme Right, to Powell, to public opinion, or to a combination of many factors?

As for the future, the prospects for the organisations that have been examined here will be determined, as has been indicated, only partly by their own efforts. Doubtless they will continue to bang their own drum – the Front is indeed talking of putting up over three hundred candidates at the next general election – but the effect this will have will be largely dependent on the social and economic climate of the day. Extreme right wing movements have normally been successful in Western Europe when severe economic problems have become associated with other socially dislocating factors. This lesson of history should not be forgotten.

188

Notes

[1]   From 1955 onwards, Edward Martell, a former Liberal, set up a number of right wing pressure groups, federating them in 1963 into the Freedom Group. By 1964 their total membership was probably around 160,000. Interests varied and ranged from offering printing facilities to the public during strikes to pressurising the Conservative Party, both by infiltration at local level and by openly offering assistance at elections. After the 1964 general election financial problems and bankruptcy petitions curtailed Martell's activity.

[2]   Quoted in R. Glass, *Newcomers*, Centre for Urban Studies, and Allen and Unwin, London 1960, p. 177.

[3]   *The Guardian*, 25 May 1959.

[4]   Quoted in Glass, op. cit., p. 178.

[5]   Mrs Leese was the widow of Arnold Leese, the leader of the pre-war anti-semitic Imperial Fascist League. She particularly favoured Colin Jordan's politics and was prepared to put property at the disposal of organisations with which he was associated.

[6]   According to Fountaine, in 1965 the BNP had 4,000 adherents. Bean put the active membership at 500 – see C. Cross, 'Britain's racialists', *New Society*, 3 June 1965. Foot estimated total membership at 500 to 700 – P. Foot, *Immigration and Race in British Politics*, Penguin, London 1965.

[7]   C. Jordan, *Britain Reborn. The Policy of the National Socialist Movement*, National Socialist Movement, n.d. (probably 1962).

[8]   *Official Programme of the Greater Britain Movement*, Albion Press Ltd, London, n.d. (probably 1964).

[9]   *The Listener*, 28 December 1972, p. 88.

[10]   Ibid.

[11]   Ibid.

[12]   *The Guardian*, 15 May 1975.

[13]   *Spearhead*, May 1975.

[14]   *The Guardian*, 13 October 1975.

[15]   *National Front News*, no. 3, August 1976.

[16]   *Spearhead*, June/July 1976.

[17]   *The Times*, 24 July 1976.

[18]   M. Hanna, 'The National Front and other right wing organisations', *New Community*, vol. 3, Winter–Spring 1974.

[19]   D. Scott, 'The National Front in local politics', *British Political Sociology Yearbook*, vol. 2, Croom Helm, London 1975, p. 224.

[20]   D. Butler and D. Kavanagh, *The British General Election of October 1974*, Macmillan, London 1975, p. 216.

[21] Scott, op. cit., p. 229.

[22] This last figure is that given by the treasurer to the 1974 Annual Conference (*Spearhead*, February 1975). Given that the average expenditure of candidates in February was £254 and in October £236, the overall sum is easy to believe. (On election expenses see Butler and Kavanagh, op. cit., p. 243.)

[23] R. Rose, *Politics in England*, Faber, London, 1965; E. A. Nordlinger, *The Working Class Tories*, MacGibbon and Kee, London 1967; and H. Eckstein, 'The British political system', in S. Beer and A. Ulaa (eds), *Patterns of Government*, Random House, New York 1963.

[24] G. Almond and S. Verba, *The Civic Culture*, Little Brown, Toronto, 1965.

[25] See the interesting article by C. W. Chamberlain and H. F. Moorhouse 'Lower class attitudes towards the British political culture', *Sociological Review*, vol. 22, November 1974.

[26] See, for example, Gallup Political Index, no. 192, July 1976.

[27] D. Butler and D. Stokes, *Political Change in Britain*, 2nd edition, Macmillan, London 1974, p. 297.

[28] I am grateful to Nick Spencer of ORC for these figures.

[29] See, for example, the Marplan surveys around the time of the 1970 election. *The Times*, 5 June 1970, reproduces one.

[30] The only piece of research, to my knowledge, that unequivocally ascribes a decisive national role to immigration – through Enoch Powell – is by R. W. Johnson and D. Schoen, 'The Powell effect: or how one man can win', *New Society*, 22 July 1976.

[31] M. Steed in D. Butler and D. Kavanagh, *The British General Election of February 1974*, Macmillan, London 1974, p. 336.

[32] For a more detailed analysis see C. T. Husbands, 'The National Front: a response to crisis?', *New Society*, 15 May 1975.

[33] Ibid.

[34] C. Richardson and J. Lethbridge, 'The anti-immigrant vote in Bradford', *Race Today*, April 1972. The BCSI still retains its separate identity though it now works very closely with the National Front.

[35] D. Butler and D. Kavanagh, *The British General Election of October 1974*, Macmillan, London 1975, p. 351.

[36] *Spearhead*, February 1976.

[37] *The Times*, 2 July 1976.

[38] *The Observer*, 4 July 1976.

[39] In parliamentary elections the UM has met head on with the NF only once: at the 1972 Uxbridge by-election when the UM got 2·5 per cent of the vote and the NF 8·2 per cent.

[40] Campaign for a More Prosperous Britain, election leaflet, 1974.
[41] For a report see the *Bury Times*, 29 March 1975.
[42] *The Guardian*, 16 June 1976.

8 Support for fascism and the radical Right: some explanations

R. KING

Introduction

In recent years interest in movements of the far Right has been reawakened and social scientists have renewed their attempts at laying bare the conditions conducive to the emergence of such groups. They have pointed to social, economic, political and psychological factors rooted deep in modern capitalism that are seen to facilitate the ability of extreme Right groups to attract popular support and political power. As many sociologists, and increasingly historians, conceive their task to be the elaboration of general relationships between ideology and the constraints of social structure, their explanations often have taken the form of 'tendency' statements. For example, so-called 'mass society' explanations suggest that the destruction of primary and intermediary groups in modern society makes more likely the availability of the masses for manipulation by extremist leaders of the Right.

Similarly, the developing concern by social scientists with the phenomenon of fascism has seen not only the employment of such concepts as anomie, status anxiety and social mobility, but also the introduction of theories which modify and extend earlier explanations and which seem better adapted to the changing ideological climate following the Second World War.

Three sets of theories have been and remain especially influential.

(1) 'Extremism of the centre' theories that see popular support for fascism as firmly based on the middle-classes, groups alienated by the structural tendencies of modern industrial society, often squeezed between the growing power of big business and the organised working-class.

(2) 'Mass society' explanations that seek to locate the wellsprings of support for fascist parties in the general availability of the masses for totalitarian and extremist organisations brought about by the 'isolation' of the modern individual from traditional associations.

(3) Marxist accounts of the relationship between advancing monopoly capitalism and fascism. These have normally viewed the latter as little more than the agent of large financial and industrial interests.

However, alongside this concern with European fascism, the Cold War years also saw increasing academic interest in movements and groups of the American radical Right, such as McCarthyism, which gained much of their political leverage from a virulent anti-communism. Lipset, Shils, Bell and others argued that radical rightism was a response by the socially mobile and the ill-educated to status problems in an affluent and fluid social structure as found in the United States.[1] Conversely, it is maintained that whilst Britain is less socially immobile than is often suspected, the hierarchical, deferential and aristocratic nature of British political culture insulates the political processes from populist and extremist pressures of both Left and Right. More especially, the susceptibility under certain conditions of the working-class to simple, often authoritarian political solutions is made less likely by the British political tradition of deference and civility, thus reducing the risk of the popular mass support for radical rightism found in the United States.

Like the explanations for fascism, these· accounts contain a number of suspect and vague assumptions that are difficult to substantiate. As with interpretations of fascism they are worth looking at in greater detail.

Interpretations of fascism

Lipset – Fascism and middle-class extremism

One of the more influential theories of fascism amongst sociologists in the 1960s was to be found in an essay by Lipset entitled 'Fascism – Left, Right and Center'.[2] In it Lipset claimed that fascism could only be 'truly understood' if attention was concentrated on its mass base. The social composition of National Socialism was as important as the actual behaviour of the fascist party in power if its real nature was to be comprehended. Lipset maintained that the three major classes of modern industrial society exhibit both democratic and extremist political ideologies, although each class expresses it in different form. In times of economic and political stability, the essentially democratic ideologies of social democracy, conservatism and liberalism, are primarily the political expressions of the working-class, the upper-class, and the middle-class respectively. There is 'a fairly logical relationship between ideology and social base'.[3] Social democratic parties are primarily supported by manual workers and pursue their interests; conservatism is sustained by large capitalists and landowners; and liberalism is backed by the middle-class – the small businessman and white-collar worker.

In times of crisis each group similarly displays specific extremist characteristics. Communism is the ugly face of the working-class, authoritarian dictatorships that of the upper-class, whilst fascism is the extremist expression of the middle-class or centre. Fascism is liberalism gone bad, launched on the disillusionment of the middle-class at its ineffectiveness in halting the inexorable slide to a society dominated by big business and organised trade unionism. Caught in the centre, the small businessman, the clerk, the rural farmer, all see in fascism and its appeal to the 'little man' the chance of preserving their status in the face of challenges from both above and below. Fascism may favour greater state intervention in society than is normally compatible with liberalism but nonetheless Lipset claims that it is similar to liberalism in its opposition to big business, socialism and the working-class.

Lipset's thesis, therefore, is that fascism is basically a middle-class movement protesting against ongoing social and economic trends and seeking to solve its problems by taking over the State and 'restoring the old middle classes' economic security and high standing in society'.[4] There is impressive evidence to support this claim and much of it is provided by Lipset himself. The social characteristics of Nazi voters resembled those of the liberals much more than did those of conservatives. As the liberal centre parties collapsed between 1928 and 1932, losing almost 80 per cent of the vote, traditional conservative parties retained most of their support and the total vote of the socialists and communists dropped only slightly. The Nazi party, as Lipset suggests, appealed predominantly to those sections of the middle-class – the entrepreneurs in rural areas or small towns especially – previously sympathetic to liberalism.[5]

Nonetheless, it is doubtful whether an analysis of fascism's social base without some account of the behaviour of fascist regimes in power is sufficient for the 'true understanding' of fascism that Lipset seeks. As many Marxists (and others) have clearly shown, there were clear identities of interest between fascism and big business that did not square with fascist ideology and its overt concern for the petit bourgeoisie. Even before National Socialism assumed power Hitler was trying to make the party appear 'respectable' in the eyes of the large industrialists, playing down 'socialist' ideas with the overriding aim of improving the chances of gaining power. That this largely succeeded is well illustrated by the increasing financial contributions made by the industrial elites to the National Socialists from 1930 onwards, their willingness at a time of crisis to see Hitler provide much needed stability, and the purging of the 'socialist' wing of the party in 1934. Contradictions between early fascist appeals and the party in power grew as policies clearly did not favour small or medium capital. Rearmament, moves to build up heavy industry, and the encouragement of monopolisation served to confirm the economic dominance of large capital over small.

Finally, Lipset's account tells us little about the conditions that bring fascism in one industrial country but not in others. If the middle-classes are rebelling against the trend towards big business and big labour, and these are structural traits typical of advancing capitalism, why did they not rebel in other countries to the same extent, and why did protests there take other forms? As Benewick suggests, the strength of class loyalties articulated in political and trade union organisations – a factor Lipset recognises as a major characteristic of modern industrial societies – may have been one reason why the British Union of Fascists was not successful in recruiting the mass base found in German and Italian fascism. Existing class links with the Labour, Conservative and Liberal parties were too strong.[6]

Fascism and mass society

As fascism became more entrenched in the 1930s with its accession to power in Germany and continuing hold in Italy, social scientists saw it as being more than a passing aberration based on the alleged historical peculiarities of certain nations: rather it was symptomatic of a general and pervasive malaise in the structure of modern industrial society. It was argued that far-developing processes affecting all the major western societies – the destruction of identifiable communities and traditional group loyalties, and especially the erosion of large primary family networks – provoked a sense of despair and resentment amongst 'masses' of anonymous and isolated individuals. They become susceptible to the integrative nationalistic appeals of parties like the Nazis which manipulated and 'politicised' such feelings.

Psychologists were particularly quick to see in the pathological tendencies of fascist behaviour the operation of deep-seated personality processes. Awareness of the part played by the middle-classes in fascist parties was seen as indicative of the psychological problems experienced by them in times of crisis and change, sandwiched as they were between the encroaching claims of the large capitalists and organised trade unionism. They were specifically anti-modern in their resentment.

For Fromm, perhaps the most widely acclaimed of the social psychologists in the interpretation of fascism and whose analysis of the dynamic relationship between personality and the structure of capitalist society owes much to Marx, the essential characteristics of modernisation are rationality and what he terms 'individuation'.[7] With the development of scientific knowledge and economic maturity individuals free themselves from their dependency on nature. However, Fromm maintains that alongside this freedom from nature goes a more transparent 'freedom' – an escape from the traditional social order and its moral constraints. It is an illusory liberty, because the dissolution of primary and close family ties also deprives the individual of emotional support and a sense of belonging. There is a growing sense of isolation and

195

powerlessness accentuated by the growth of capitalism and its concomitant bureaucratic organisations.

As a consequence of the decreasing importance of 'intermediate' associations individuals seek an 'escape' from rational impersonality into the security of either conformism or authoritarianism. This is typified by the middle-class which is particularly threatened and sees its status declining. Fascism, with its 'irrationalism' and appeal to community provides an ideological and integrative outlet for such groups.

Whilst the evidence for Fromm's claims often appears sketchy, based largely on his own clinical records and scarcely referring to the political and economic conditions under which his personality types become mobilised, as opposed to available for political action, his theories find a sociological echo in Kornhauser's *The Politics of Mass Society*.[8] As with social psychological theories Kornhauser agrees that the crucial transition from traditional to modern social structures produces a tendency for individual isolation, lack of identity, and general helplessness, although as a sociologist Kornhauser prefers to talk in terms of 'mass culture', 'anomie', and 'atomisation'.

More clearly than Fromm, Kornhauser is concerned with specifying the conditions under which 'mass society' – a society in which large numbers of individuals are no longer insulated in autonomous group life – becomes a 'totalitarian' one. Whilst he is never totally clear as to the characteristics of either totalitarian movements or totalitarian societies, and, as with other theorists who employ the term, the vagueness of the concept detracts from its utility, Kornhauser's use of the term totalitarian clearly applies to mass movements hierarchically organised and totally manipulated by an increasingly inaccessible elite.

The clue to the propensity of mass society to throw up such movements rests in the changing relationship in modern democracy between elites and masses. With the extension of the suffrage, traditional elites become unable to manage, through institutional change, the demands unleashed on them by the masses. Instead new elites – and these can be either of the Left or the Right – promising revolutionary social change and using the masses and the ideology of democracy as their weapon take their place, although always taking steps to insulate themselves from their mass support.

Kornhauser believes that authoritarian movements such as fascism are especially likely when mass societies experience crisis, when apathy and fatalism are replaced by the aggressiveness of individuals lacking the 'proximate' relations and ends previously provided by Church, family, and community groups. New elites exploit the increasingly direct relations between isolated individuals and the State and with the help of new media techniques the individual is connected to the overriding ideal of the ideology. These

196

processes become more probable when social change producing major discontinuities in social organisation which results in large scale displacement and fluidity is compounded by economic depression or defeat in war.

However, whilst various formulations on these themes have been propagated by a host of writers, the mass society theory is not sufficiently discriminatory to explain satisfactorily why fascism was powerful in certain countries but not in others. Britain and the United States, for example, were amongst the most advanced of industrial societies and might have been expected to display greater fascist tendencies in terms of the theory. The location of the bases for fascism in the general structural conditions of modern mass society takes little account of the more specific and ancillary factors that characterise the historical development of different societies. It remains at best a plausible metatheory.

A further problem lies in the difficulty of giving empirical expression to notions such as 'atomisation', 'mass society' or 'social integration' in a way that might provide for a more thoroughgoing comparative theorising. Similarly, if mass society theorists maintain that 'mass not class' is the crucial concept in understanding recruitment to fascist parties ('a totalitarian movement attracts socially isolated individuals from all classes' – Kornhauser), they not only overlook the differential class basis of different mass movements such as socialism and fascism, but also one possible reason for the relative lack of success of the latter in Britain: the strength of class-based party loyalties.

Marxist explanation of fascism

Although most recent Marxist interpretations point to the functional importance of the fascist regimes in Italy and Germany to the interests of monopoly capitalism, there has never been a definitive Marxist explanation of fascism. This was particularly noticeable during the rise of fascism in the 1920s and 1930s when 'official' interpretations of the phenomenon, debated at successive congresses of the Communist International, displayed numerous shifts and turns.

At the beginning, with the relatively early accession to power of Mussolini in 1922 and under the influence of Italian Communist leaders who stressed the rural wellsprings of fascist violence, the Comintern maintained that 'economic backwardness' was the basis for what was seen to be an essentially reactionary agricultural movement of big landowners. Fascism was symptomatic of economic weakness and could not be repeated in more advanced industrial societies like Germany which had a stronger working-class and a more sophisticated cultural tradition.

As Italian fascism hived off its bucolic associations and became more visibly associated with the large bourgeois and industrial interests this thesis was turned on its head. By 1924 the Comintern espoused a form of vulgar economic determinism which argued that, contrary to earlier belief, fascism occurred in the most advanced industrial societies, those where the productive forces of capitalism had run their full course and were 'ripe for revolution'. As it became established in Germany, and as it attracted support in other European countries too, so the thesis that fascism was a positive indication of an imminent revolutionary situation seemed to be confirmed. It was a sign of capitalism's weakness in the face of a working-class offensive; it was another form of bourgeois state that would soon pass with the inevitable decay in productive forces.

However, a recent Marxist work on fascism, by Poulantzas,[9] has strongly critised such mechanical interpretations of Marxism for their 'economic catastrophism'. Comintern explanations saw capitalist development as part of a linear economic evolution, and portrayals of inexorable moves to economic crisis and decay 'conveyed the idea of a revolution ready to break out no matter where or when'.[10] It suggested that working-class struggle to combat fascism was unnecessary and it ruled out, until too late, anti-fascist alliances with other working-class parties such as the German SPD. It led to the view that fascism's ideology of national unity was little more than the extremist form of social democracy's belief in class cooperation which, it was believed, undermined working-class revolutionary consciousness.

Not until the Nazi seizure of power and the subsequent terrorist destruction of trade union, social democratic and communist organisations alike were such views changed. By 1935 it was beginning to be accepted by the Comintern that fascism was not simply another form of bourgeois government, but a vicious dictatorship of the most reactionary parts of finance and monopoly capitalism which eliminated even bourgeois liberties and rights. National Socialism was the willing agent of big business.

Similarly, fascism was not interpreted by influential Marxists as the consequence of working-class revolutionary strength, but at best as the outcome of a temporary stalemate between the bourgeoisie and the proletariat. Thalheimer and Gramsci, for example, claimed that the fascist State had a 'relative autonomy' from the capitalist classes, the result of an equilibrium between the two main classes. Following Marx's account of Bonapartism, Thalheimer, for example, suggests that absolutist forms of state, of which fascism and Bonapartism are similar though not identical examples, occur when the dominant class exchanges political power for a 'saviour', to preserve its economic power.

Poulantzas goes a step further. He argues that the working-class had already been thoroughly defeated by the time fascism came to power in Germany and Italy. Monopoly capital in its reciprocal alliance ('non-identical identity') with fascism was attempting to create the conditions for a more successful capitalism. This is only fully understood by discarding the Comintern's vulgar, economic explanations for fascism, and having a clearer appraisal of the 'ensemble' of class relations, their political and ideological as well as economic characteristics, that occur in specific historical circumstances.

For Poulantzas fascism belongs to the imperialist stage of capitalism with its competitive links and uneven rates of development between countries. In the 1920s Germany and Italy were the weakest links in the industrial–imperialist chain after Russia, but not because they were the least advanced economically. As latecomers to capitalism neither had achieved a fully unified bourgeois state on the advent of fascism. The management of German capitalist development 'from above' – by a State that continued to be dominated by feudal landowners with political power wholly out of proportion to their weakening economic control – had meant that the German bourgoisie remained in constant debt to it. With an agricultural sector lagging behind industry, the weakness of the home market for the production of raw materials, and also as a market for finished goods, becomes accentuated in times of unemployment. This is compounded by the lack of a colonial empire, a consequence of late industrialisation, for commercial outlets and material imports.

State intervention within this framework, argues Poulantzas, is hardly sufficient to promote the growth of monopoly capitalism which is required to meet the challenges of other industrial and imperialist powers. This can occur only when monopoly capitalism attains the political hegemony within the ruling power bloc to match its growing economic strength. Fascism develops when this power bloc – the fractions of class who make up the ruling class – are disorientated by crisis and change, when no one fraction can impose its domination on the others. Fascism comes to power and establishes the political and ideological hegemony of big monopoly capitalism to correspond to its economic dominance.

Not that Poulantzas claims that fascism's mass base in the petit bourgeoisie does not give it some autonomy. But big business sees in fascism a weapon for the securement of conditions appropriate to monopoly capitalism on manageable terms. Once established, fascist regimes gradually shed their petit bourgeois characteristics and function in the long term interests of big business, although never with complete unanimity on both sides. The fascist party is not simply an agent of monopoly capitalism as many Marxists have claimed, for its mass base gives it some freedom of manoeuvre, particularly

199

when there is an internal power bloc crisis. In establishing the hegemony of big money capital National Socialism finds itself on occasions obliged to make concessions to the masses against the will of big capital. But its policies of price fixation, tariffs, rearmament, the encouragement of cartelisation, and the destruction of working-class opposition clearly show that heavy industry benefited from fascist actions in the same way that fascism gained support for its rule from monopoly capital.

Poulantzas's theory, which gives some importance to the mass base of fascist support, is more sophisticated than previous Marxist accounts which tend to see fascism as the dupe of large capital. The vulgar Marxism of the pre-war period viewed it as an inevitable accompaniment to advanced capitalism, ignoring the specific historical factors which were crucial to understanding the development of fascism in Germany and Italy. As with simple versions of mass society theory, they lack the discrimination to explain why fascism and extreme rightist movements have not been of more significance in Britain, a highly advanced industrial country. Poulantzas's account takes greater care to identify the duality of interests between capitalism and fascism whilst stressing the functional significance of fascism to big business, a point ignored by Lipset.

Deference and the radical Right

In the years that followed the McCarthy era a number of American social scientists were led to ask why movements of the far Right had enjoyed more popular support in the United States than in Britain. In this country challenges from the radical Right have traditionally been limited and have rarely succeeded in gathering support outside a narrow fringe. Even those organisations which stood to benefit most from the depression and unemployment of the 1930s, notably Mosley's British Union of Fascists, never gained the support of more than a tiny fraction of the population.

In the United States, on the other hand, a long line of radical right movements have enjoyed widespread popular support. Lipset and Raab have chronicled the continuous presence on the American political scene of such organisations, albeit often short-lived and attracting only temporary acclaim, but usually succeeded at a later date by similar movements.[11] The remarkable feature of the American situation is not so much the number of radical right groups but the ability of some of them to obtain popular support. More especially, there have been certain periods when particular individuals have rallied much support around nativist, patriotic and morally conservative appeals. Britain, by contrast, has never experienced the recurring tradition of popular acclaim accorded such figures as Coughlin, McCarthy or Wallace.

Of course it is easy to exaggerate the different propensities for radical rightism between the two countries, for differences in political institutions allow radical right opinion to manifest itself more immediately in the United States than in Britain. Newton has pointed out how the comparative fragmentation of American government, particularly city administration with its lack of strong party systems and multiplicity of power centres, has meant that pressure groups of all descriptions play a more direct and visible role in political life than is allowed by the centralised apparatus of British local politics.[12] Nonetheless, the contrast between the two countries in the levels of popular support normally given to the radical Right has remained sufficiently striking to attract the attention of many students of such movements. It has raised the question: are there a set of factors perhaps located in the cultural attitudes of certain groups in their view of social and class relationships that serve to hinder support for extremist groups?

Lipset gained a certain notoriety in the early 1960s with a claim that whilst all social groups could display tendencies to extremism the working-classes were especially prone, because of their life situation, to embrace authoritarian solutions to political problems. Lipset's 'working-class authoritarianism' thesis was interpreted as stating that working-class styles of life – the emphasis on discipline in family relationships, economic insecurity, the low priority given to education, and the low participation in political or voluntary organisations – gave lower status groups a special purchase on intolerance. In consequence they were more likely to support intolerant movements of either the Left or the Right.[13]

Such assertions drew much hostility from those who pointed to factors such as trade union participation and communal or 'solidaristic' forms of working-class styles of life as containing ideals of brotherhood and humanity often missing from the alleged instrumentality of the middle-classes. Even more antagonistic were those who, mistakenly, saw Lipset as portraying 'inherent' authoritarian tendencies amongst the working-class. Many of these criticisms appear strange, given Lipset's clear insistence elsewhere that fascism could be viewed as the extremism of the middle-classes. Lipset was simply saying that under certain conditions the working-class, in comparison with other classes, is more likely to seek simple, rigid answers to social and political questions, and this may or may not involve support for extremist movements. For individuals with a long-standing, possibly unreflective commitment to the principles of trade unionism, this could find expression in anti-fascist, trade union sponsored movements.

Lipset also suggested that working-class groups are especially likely to be 'intolerant' on liberal or non-economic issues such as the rights and freedoms of minority groups, but that this depends on a number of situational factors, such as levels of unemployment. He remarked that:

> the authoritarianism of any social stratum or class is highly relative, of course, and often modified by organisational commitments to democracy and by individual cross-pressures.[14]

Lipset was claiming then that certain social or cultural conditions may modify

> the relatively greater predisposition of the working class to support extremist or intolerant movements. Important among these factors are 'norms of tolerance', which in a country like Britain . . . are well developed and widespread in every social stratum. Even the lowest class may be less authoritarian and more sophisticated than the most highly educated stratum in another country.[15]

More recently Lipset and others such as Shils[16] have tried to be more specific about these 'norms of tolerance' as characteristics which mark off the British working-class from its American counterpart. It appears that such norms spring from a highly developed sense of hierarchy, a 'respect for one's betters', and a feeling for civility and deference. Specifically these attitudes help to explain why movements of the far Right are more likely to attract popular support in the United States than in Britain. The explanation rests on the claim that deferential attitudes towards authority guarantee the comparative stability of British institutions and protect them from extremism of both the Left and the Right.

The Lipset–Shils argument runs as follows. Where challenges from the radical Right have gathered widespread popular support in the United States, their *mass* following has been drawn disproportionately from those of low socio-economic status. Individuals of low status are particularly vulnerable to the illiberal appeals of the far Right. In Britain, however, the widespread existence of deferential attitudes to authority, particularly amongst the working-class, curbs any tendency to support radical challenges from the Right. In the United States, on the other hand, for a number of historical reasons such deference is less common and the populism of American culture encourages the intolerant masses to intrude into the political arena. Deference, therefore, performs the function in Britain of insulating the political system from serious challenges posed by the radical Right.

Shils has suggested that in both the United States and Britain the mass of the population is generally highly intolerant, but in contrast to the United States this mass does not intrude into the political arena in Britain. This is because 'although democratic and pluralist . . . Great Britain is a hierarchical country'. Government is 'the object of deference' and participation 'does not express populist sentiments'. In Britain therefore 'the respect for one's betters' and mutual trust within the ruling classes combine to exclude the intolerant mass from political influence.[17]

Shils contrasts this situation with that existing in the United States where there exists no aristocratic tradition of closed government. The political elite is very open and vulnerable to pressure from below. These pressures are not slow to materialise, since there exists no widespread tendency to defer to elites. Unlike Britain, 'American culture is a populistic culture'.[18]

Similarly, Lipset has developed these themes explicitly with regard to the question of support for the radical Right:

> Many have argued that the more widespread deferential respect for elites in Britain . . . as compared to the anti-elitism . . . of the U.S.A., underlies the freedom of dissent and guaranteed civil liberties so characteristic of Britain . . . The emphasis on elitism and diffuseness is reflected in the ability of the more unified and influential elites to control the system so as to inhibit the emergence of populist movements that express political intolerance.[19]

In *The Politics of Unreason* Lipset and Raab place the burden of explanation for radical rightism on the status anxiety experienced by displaced social groups. There are many such groups in America as 'new areas, new industries, new migrant groups, new ethnic groups, have continually encroached upon the old as important and influential'.[20] One of the most crucial of disinherited American groups consists of those white, blue-collar city dwellers who have had to face the challenge of aspiring blacks.

This approach is quite compatible with the earlier stress on the absence of deference in American society. The problem of status displacement in the USA is a consequence of the fact 'that no group has enjoyed a status tenure in the style of the European ruling classes'. In America no firmly entrenched social group provides the focus point for a stable social hierarchy. Lipset and Raab then go on to stress the allegedly unique attachment to the values of egalitarianism and individualism held by Americans and the effect this attachment has in furthering the diminution of deferential orientations:

> . . . in this emphasis on equality and rugged individualism also inheres resistance to any generalised deference to elite groups, whether of intellect, wealth or political power . . . the type of respect for law and order, for legitimate authority which emerged in Britain did not develop to the same degree in the United States.[21]

Consequently, Britain's political culture has reduced to a minimum those intolerant challenges from the radical Right that are endemic in American society.

The extent to which this type of account has become part of the conventional wisdom of political science may be judged from the fact that the major study of the fascist movement in Britain accepts it without question. Benewick has written that one of the important reasons for the failure of the BUF to attract more popular support was that 'the Fascist political style, with its emphasis on revolution and counter-revolution, rather than continuity and evolution, and its search for order through political violence, was alien to the traditions of British political life'. He goes on to say that 'the establishment of legitimacy and the development of a distinctive national style – what Shils has called the politics of civility – interacts with and is dependent upon the beliefs and values held by most Englishmen'.[22]

Although claims that the British people are peculiarly deferential have been queried recently, particularly by Kavanagh and Sharpe,[23] no attempt has been made to question these accounts of the specific relationship between deference and the radical Right – that deference suppresses extremist right wing tendencies, especially amongst the British working-class. This can be done by an analysis of the evidence presented by those who advance the theory; by an examination of other relevant evidence; and finally by offering alternative suggestions as to the relationship between deferential attitudes and support for the far Right.

Evidence

Two conditions are necessary for a satisfactory test of the deference thesis. First, evidence must be comparative. Studies such as Kavanagh's which cast doubt on the notion that deference is widespread in Britain, whilst useful, are not as relevant to the present discussion as others, since even if the British are much less deferential than was supposed, Americans could be less deferential still. Secondly, the comparative data must compare the incidence of deference among those groups who help provide the mass support for the radical Right in the United States with comparable groups in Britain. If on this evidence these Americans are no less deferential then the deference thesis is not supported.

Lipset and Raab's analysis of a mass of survey evidence leads them to the conclusion that the *popular* success of Coughlin, McCarthy and Wallace at varying points in American political history is largely explained by the disproportionate backing given them by individuals of low socio-economic status. Analysis of Coughlin's support reveals that 'the lower the economic level, the greater the proportion of supporters to opponents'.[24] Similarly, whilst the support received by McCarthy (as indicated by survey data) included some individuals of high status, nonetheless McCarthy's support came

> disproportionately from Catholics, New Englanders, Republicans, the less educated, the lower class, manual workers, farmers, elderly people and the Irish . . . workers were more favourable to McCarthy than those in middle class occupations with the exception of independent businessmen.[25]

Wallace's support reveals a similar pattern. In 1964 he did 'extremely well in working class districts', while in 1968 the polls also showed that the 'poorer and less educated were more favourable to Wallace . . . Among the urban strata, manual workers were more likely than those in the non-manual middle classes to be pro-Wallace'. As Lipset and Raab remark, 'the pattern of support for George Wallace before the beginning of the 1968 campaign resembled that of Father Coughlin and Senator Joseph McCarthy'.[26]

What distinguishes the United States from Britain, therefore, is that in the former a number of radical right politicians have achieved a measure of popular success by mobilising support from those of low socio-economic status. If the deference thesis is to be maintained it must be shown not that Americans are less deferential than Britons, but that low status Americans are less so than their British counterparts. There are three sources of available evidence: survey data relating to social and political attitudes; figures on rates of political participation; and evidence concerning the characteristics of those institutions typically supported by those of low socio-economic status in the two countries.

Survey data   The only comparative survey data of relevance here is contained in Almond and Verba's *The Civic Culture*.[27] Their concern is with political deference and their main indicator is provided by answers to a question which asked respondents how far the ordinary citizen ought to participate in the affairs of the local community. The implication that deference and passivity go together is at least a plausible one. It could be suggested, and indeed is an important part of the case advanced by Shils, that deference insulates elites from the intolerant pressures of the population by reducing the extent to which people desire to participate in politics.

Certainly the figures indicate differences between the two countries: 51 per cent of Americans but only 39 per cent of Britons felt that the ordinary citizen ought to be active in local affairs. But on further examination it becomes clear that the thesis linking levels of deference with support for the radical Right is not supported by this evidence. If the deference thesis is to be supported, those with least education in Britain ought to be more deferential than their American counterparts. But if Almond and Verba's indicator is any guide this is emphatically not so; almost identical percentages in the lowest educational category in Britain and the United States felt that ordinary people ought to be active in the local community. The greater 'passivity' of the British is accounted for by those with higher levels of education. Furthermore, the *higher* the level of education, the greater the gap between the two countries. Thirty-five per cent of Americans and 37 per cent of Britons with 'primary education or less' believe that the ordinary man should be active in the local community; the corresponding figures for those with some higher education are 66 and 42 per cent respectively. The responses contradict the view that the weakness of the radical Right in Britain is explained by the peculiarly deferential character of the working-class. Those who appear to be especially deferential are the better educated.

Percentage who say the ordinary man should be active
in his local community

Nation	Total	Primary education or less	Some secondary education	Some higher education
US	51	35	56	66
GB	39	37	42	42

Source: Almond and Verba, *The Civic Culture* (1963), p. 176.

This view appears to be corroborated by other evidence in *The Civic Culture*, which concerns the patterns of socialisation in the two countries. Almond and Verba quite plausibly suggest that an individual's experiences in the family, the school or the work situation may affect such attitudes. For instance, 'if in most social situations the individual finds himself subservient to some authority figure, it is likely that he will expect such an authority relationship in the political sphere'.[31]

Whilst hardly an established proposition, this is at least a reasonable hypothesis. If the Shils–Lipset thesis is correct we might expect 'deference inducing' situations to be more common among those of low socio-economic status in Britain than among their American counterparts. But such evidence as is available in the study shows that this is not the case. Respondents were asked a number of questions about their experiences with authority outside the political sphere. One question asked respondents if they could recall ever actually protesting as children about family decisions. The only significant differences between the two countries occurred in the groups with some experience of higher education: 75 per cent of Americans but only 54 per cent of Britons with some higher education could remember voicing some protest, whilst the comparable figures for those with primary education or less were 50 per cent for the United States and 56 per cent for Great Britain. In other words, it is only among the group supposedly least vulnerable to the appeal of the radical Right – the most educated – that Britons reported a more 'deference inducing' family situation than Americans.

Percentage reporting actual protests about family decisions

Nation	Total	Primary education or less	Some secondary education	Some higher education
US	66	50	72	75
GB	62	56	72	54

Source: Almond and Verba (1963), p. 335.

This pattern is repeated when recollections of authority in the school are studied. Forty-six per cent of Americans as against 36 per cent of Britons said that they could recall actually voicing dissent and disagreement with teachers about unfair treatment during their schooldays. But hardly any of this difference is accounted for by those with the least education. Thirty-one per cent of Britons and 32 per cent of Americans with only primary education or less reported voicing such dissent.

Finally, Almond and Verba's respondents were asked to what extent they felt free to protest against decisions made at their place of work. This is useful since it refers to adult rather than childhood behaviour towards authority. The results do not support the Shils–Lipset thesis and indeed they contradict the view that levels of deference are higher in this country than in the United States. Substantially more Britons than Americans reported that they felt free to protest in the work situation. Furthermore, the differences are maintained at all occupational levels, from the unskilled worker to the manager.

Percentage saying they feel free to protest job decisions

Nation	Total	Unskilled	Skilled	White-collar	Professional/ managerial
US	82	71	85	81	87
GB	93	81	91	96	95

Source: Almond and Verba (1963), p. 336.

What conclusions can be drawn from this analysis of *The Civic Culture*? The chief implication seems to be that the data does not support the view that political deference can in some fashion account for the limited success of the radical Right in this country compared to the United States. A number of measures suggest that the level of deference may be higher in Britain but this is accounted for largely by differences between groups in the two countries allegedly least likely to support the radical Right – those with the most formal education.

Rates of participation   Let us now turn to the second source of evidence: rates of political participation. This may, at least indirectly, add credence to the deference thesis. If we discover, for instance, that low status groups in America participate more in political activity than do their British equivalents, then this will at least add substance to the suggestion that the latter are more deferential than the former. More specifically, if, as has been asserted, the British – and especially the British working-class – are peculiarly prone to deference, then surely this ought to be reflected in the sort of political leaders they support. Ought the British not to show a stronger tendency than do the Americans to select for political leadership individuals of high ascribed status?

This is not in fact the case. The American Congress contains a much smaller proportion of members drawn from the families of manual workers than is the case with the House of Commons.[29] Nor is Congress an atypical American political institution in this respect: Epstein's examination of the social composition of state legislatures, Newton's analysis of the evidence relating to city politics, and Sharpe's recent survey of a wide range of literature, all suggest the same general conclusion: ascriptive elitism is more important as a factor in political recruitment in the United States than in Britain.[30] There is a greater predilection for upper- and middle-class political leadership in the United States, a point which Epstein relates to the absence of a truly social democratic party as found in most European countries: 'The truth is that at no level can American political recruitment be found to resemble the working class leadership of a European style socialist party'[31] – parties which have normally provided at least a small avenue of recruitment for manual workers.

There is still an obvious retort to this argument and it has been provided by Shils: participation by those of low status may be higher in Britain, but this does not modify the view that the British are especially deferential since such participation, unlike the situation in America, 'does not express populist sentiments'.[32] This implies that while participation in Britain can be seen as an expression of support for authority, in the United States it is much more directly focused on ensuring popular control over political leaders. This contrast is illustrated, the argument runs, by the different theories of representation allegedly dominant in the two countries – the 'Burkean' model of elite representation in Britain and the 'mandated delegate' model in the United States.

These assertions can be tested, albeit in indirect fashion. Let us look at Britain first. There is substantial evidence that support for Burkean notions varies inversely with socio-economic position. Thus it is in the Conservative Party that this model of leadership is most influential. In working-class organisations it is strongly challenged. The 'mandated delegate' model prevails almost universally in the trade union movement and there is a long tradition in the Labour Party of vigorous attempts by constituencies to exercise tight control over parliamentary representatives. These have often been resisted but it would be incorrect to describe the turbulent history of the party in terms of deferential acquiescence to a parliamentary leadership.

The evidence for the United States indicates that the relationship between leaders and led is far more complex than is implied by the mandated delegate model. We might note at the outset that it is very unlikely that those most susceptible to the appeals of the radical Right – the poor and the badly educated – will actually attempt to exercise intolerant pressures on political leaders since these are the very groups which tend to participate least in political life. Furthermore, Miller and Stoke's well-known study of the relationship between Congressmen and their constituents reveals that the electorate does not scrutinise the behaviour of Congressmen and indicates that in general people neither know nor care about their representative's views on specific issues: 'Of detailed information about policy stands not more than a chemical trace was found'.[33] This hardly coincides with the picture of the non-deferential lower status Americans impelling their representatives towards extremism; nor does it support the view that participation is especially populist in character.

The 'character' of institutions Let us now turn to our final source of evidence which concerns the 'character' of those institutions based on groups of low socio-economic status in the two countries. It can be argued that the greater political representation of the working-class in Britain is of little account since this represents no fundamental challenge to the existing relations of power and authority. This is the point that Lipset appears to be making in *The First New Nation* when he remarks on the timidity of the labour movement in Britain.

The relative success of the Labour Party casts doubt on this suggestion. Labour's critique of prevailing values has been mild but it remains a more radical institution than the Democratic Party which is supported by the majority of the American working-class. In turn the working-class in Britain is usually more 'solid' than its American counterpart. If voting Republican is a form of American Toryism, then there are more 'working-class Tories' in the United States than in Britain.

A similar picture emerges when we compare trade union movements. American unions organise a smaller proportion of the workforce than do those in Britain, and they are almost totally a means of securing piecemeal economic concessions rather than of attacking the existing social order. While unions in this country have also been highly instrumental, those organising manual workers have frequently advanced fundamental critiques of established values and institutions. By contrast with the United States, British manual workers' unions have been politically radical.

In the American case there is evidence that the deference which characterises the labour movement is rooted in the general attitudes of people of low socio-economic status in American society. Drawing on a wide range of survey evidence, Hyman[34] has shown that there are strong class-related differences in job aspiration and achievement motivation in American society. The lower a person is in the social hierarchy, the less exalted are his aspirations. Such feelings develop early. In a study of adolescence, Macoby found that the lower a boy's class position, the less likely he was to aspire to a job involving the exercise of responsibility and authority.[35] Finally, in an extensive analysis of the literature on parent–child relationships in the United States, Kohn concluded that children reared in families of low socio-economic status are very likely to be more actively encouraged to develop strong feelings of deference towards authority generally than are children of non-manual workers:

> Working class parents want their children to conform to external authority because the parents themselves are willing to accord respect to authority in return for security and respectability. Their conservatism in child rearing is part of a more general conservatism and traditionalism.[36]

To sum up: we have been concerned to discover how far the available evidence supports the view that groups of low socio-economic status in Britain are more deferential than their American counterparts. The evidence of *The Civic Culture* seems to suggest that deference is not more widespread in Britain. Data on political participation and recruitment suggest that, if anything, the British may be considerably less deferential than Americans.

The thesis examined here assumes that deference inhibits support for the radical Right, but in the light of the above discussion there are grounds for believing that the *reverse* may be the case, that both radical rightism and deference are similar expressions of a common set of attitudes, namely those associated with nationalism and authoritarianism. The authoritarian, nationalist appeals of the radical Right may well attract the deferential: those with a developed sense of respect for traditional elites and their values of hierarchy and patriotism. Lipset and Raab themselves point out that the radical Right in the United States, despite attacking specific elites, has usually presented itself as a defender of traditional American values.[37]

Whilst it seems plausible to suggest that one reason for the popular success of certain radical right individuals and groups may derive from the attachment to such values felt by groups of Americans with low status, the traditionalism of American radical rightism is of course by no means confined to low social status groups. To attain popular support such attitudes must be attractive to such groups. But the more clearly higher status appeal of organisations such as the John Birch Society, the Christian Anti-Communist Crusade, and individuals such as Barry Goldwater testifies to middle-class rightist impulses in the United States.[38]

We might also note in this context the strong support given to figures of authority such as the police by George Wallace, and the fact that, in turn, the police have been among his staunchest supporters and admirers. It is not far fetched to suggest that much of Wallace's support springs from the backing he gives to defenders of law and order. Thus, far from being a revolt against authority, support for the radical Right may well derive from an exaggerated tendency to defer to at least some forms of authority.

The evidence available on British radical Right movements and attitudes is also suggestive. Benewick, for example, asserts that British Union of Fascist activists came disproportionately from groups (e.g. the public school educated, retired officers) who might be thought to have a stake in defending traditional values and institutions, whilst Mosley himself was a member of the British upper classes:

> . . . the B.U.F. attempted to project an image that was not based on class, yet it was popularly identified as a middle class movement . . . the Fascist elite, in terms of occupational breakdown, was distinctly middle class in character.[39]

Mandle's study of 103 BUF leaders similarly showed that they were well educated, 28 having been to university (and these were not necessarily amongst the most active), whilst of the 51 who had a secondary education 34 had attended public school.[40] Furthermore, 62 per cent of Mandle's sample had been in the armed services (58 per cent as officers), an impressively high figure when age is taken into account, given, as Benewick has pointed out,

211

that those under thirty-five in 1935 were unlikely to have seen service in the First World War.

In consequence it appears likely that deference and radical rightism in both Britain and the United States link a shared desire to defend traditional values. In Britain, however, this combination is more likely to be found amongst traditional elites and *higher* status groups, whilst the defence of traditional American values seems to be more widely dispersed amongst the social classes. Historically, the American working-classes have more in common with their class superiors, perhaps because of America's 'populist' culture, than do the British working-class with the British upper-class.

One reason why the positive association between deference and radical rightism amongst the British middle classes has generally been overlooked is because many studies have looked at deference as an explanation for working-class conservatism whilst ignoring middle-class deference. Kavanagh has written that studies of deference have generally failed to include middle-class respondents; this has meant

> that working class support for the Conservative Party and for elite and traditional symbols like the House of Lords and the monarchy has been sweepingly attributed to its social deference. . . . This is a serious ommision given that the research has been designed to prove that English workers are particularly deferential, presumably in comparison with the middle class or other national working classes.[41]

Kavanagh also points out that originally Bagehot 'observed that passivity and social deference were not confined to the lower classes; the distribution of social status was pyramidal and the middle class were quite willing to defer to the aristocracy. Thus, deference was not a property unique to the working class'.[42] That this remains the case is indicated by the discussion of Almond and Verba's survey material above and appears to be borne out by Butler and Stoke's study of British political attitudes. They found that if attitudes to the monarchy were taken as indicators of deferences then it is possible

> to see much of the Conservatives support in the middle class as well as the working class in terms of social deference. . . . If the Conservatives' appeal as a national party aligned with national institutions is to be styled in terms of deference, it is at least clear that this is not a deference that is peculiarly likely to be evoked among people within the lower social strata by reason of their humble station.[43]

Similarly, Jessop's recent study has found that whilst the proportion of deference was the lowest yet reported in a study concerned explicitly with deference, 'it was greater for the middle class or non-manual respondents

212

than for the manual working class'.[44] That respect for authority may provide a source of support for the radical Right is hardly a novel suggestion. For many years it has been part of the standard explanations offered regarding support for such ideologies. Indeed, both Lipset and Shils are also aware of the affinities between authoritarianism and the radical Right in the United States, but they neglect the possibility of a *positive* relationship between certain forms of deference and authoritarianism. In essence, the implication of their respective analyses is that the two are polar phenomena.

Yet most notions of authoritarianism incorporate the idea of deference: the authoritarian individual sees himself as part of an ordered hierarchy where there are certain clearly defined groups or individuals who can exercise authority over him and others who must defer to his authority. Lipset and Shils, like so many writers on the subject, forget that deference refers to or involves a two-sided process. Not only does deference 'typically involve the acquiescence of someone in the actual or imputed wishes of another person in return for acceptance',[45] but it may well involve the contempt or disdain by that someone of those he perceives to be *his* inferiors.

This is more likely to be true for middle-class deferentials fearful of groups below them. They may be more susceptible to what has been termed the 'bicycle phenomena' – head bowed but kicking furiously. Indeed Lipset himself has demonstrated the appeal of National Socialism to the middle-classes and pointed to their intermediate position between the two major classes. However, he does not link this form of authoritarianism to deference despite the commitment to nationalism and hierarchy in the movement.[46]

By seeing deference as primarily a working-class phenomenon, a way of exploring working-class conservatism, many writers have ignored the 'downward' social relationships held by deferentials with those below them and their concomitant authoritarian consequence. A deferential vote should not necessarily be treated as a non-class conscious vote, as it may well be symptomatic of the heightened class consciousness of those classes with a sinking economic and social base, fearful of working-class mobility and trade unionism: that is, classes especially prone to radical rightism. Deferential individuals may be those who openly accept the class stratified nature of society, welcome it, and are deferential for that reason, but who are therefore very conscious of their class position.

The argument that such individuals and groups may be prone to the authoritarianism of certain radical right ideologies appears to be given further weight by Jessop's findings that middle-class deferentials are disproportionately uncivil compared with deferentials from other classes: 'They distrust majority opinion and the rights of the ill-informed and the ill-educated to participate in elections'.[47]

The interpretation here which positively relates deference to authoritarianism, and links both to right wing attitudes, brings these issues and their possible explanations much closer to many well-established social psychological findings on the authoritarian personality, such as those of Fromm and Adorno, and is worthy of further study.

Conclusion – the British Right

The 'Lipset–Shils deference theory' too cavalierly accepts impressionistic accounts of the deferential propensity of the British working-class. General statements about national political cultures become hazardous in times of rapid social change. If deference ever existed amongst the British working-class, the growth of coloured immigration, Britain's declining economic performance, and persisting unemployment and inflation have changed social and political attitudes.

Explanations for the popular support of parties of the far Right must always take account of specific historical circumstances. This is particularly important when it comes to explaining why the extreme Right in Britain has been less successful than its foreign counterparts in tapping potential support. Mosley's BUF, middle-class in orientation and leadership, never attracted support from this class on the scale of continental fascism nor did it approach the appeal of Italian and German fascism to other social groups. Two sets of conditions, one political and the other economic, appear especially important.

Political conditions   A precondition for fascist success in the inter-war years was the weakness and instability of political systems. In Germany, the aftermath of Bismarck's conservative national revolution continually bedevilled the Weimar experiment in parliamentary democracy. The industrialisation and unification of Germany by the State with the acquiescence of the bourgeoisie culminated in a military–bureaucratic power state at the turn of the century that blocked the participation of the growing class of workers and their social democratic and trade union organisations. It severely hampered the development of a workable parliamentary system and responsible political parties.

Bracher points out that the very act of setting up parliamentary institutions to replace monarchical authoritarianism came about through defeat in war – by the last dictatorial act of the defeated Ludendorf.[48] This was hardly an auspicious start, nor was it helped by the 'stab-in-the-back' legend held to by the military who blamed defeat on the politicians.

214

Throughout Weimar, the country was governed either by unpopular minority cabinets, internally weak coalitions, or authoritarian, extra-parliamentary presidential cabinets. Most of the twenty cabinets of the Republic lasted only for brief periods (eight and a half months on average). It was an instability that enabled minority and extremist parties like the Nazis to achieve an influence out of proportion to their initial electoral appeal.

Similarly, Italian political life was characterised before 1922 by a lack of established national party structures and programmes, and regional, municipal and local interests predominated. Woolf suggests that this enabled the fascist movement to develop as a mass party on a local basis.[49] They were able to graft themselves on to local traditions, exploit local rivalries, and change their ideological colours according to the strength of local groupings.

In Britain, however, the political system was able to contain the extreme Right. As Benewick states:

> The BUF, unlike its Continental counterparts, attacked a political system the legitimacy of which had been established. The political forms were accepted, the political leaders respected, and the political process over time effective.[50]

Furthermore, a well-supported and relatively moderate Conservative party – absent in Germany and Italy – was able to assimilate much of the discontent on the far Right.

Poulantzas has argued that fascism was an offensive by the ruling classes against a demoralised working-class that was already 'on the run'. But in Britain radical grievances amongst the working-class were articulated and channelled by a powerful Labour Party and strong trade unions. Whilst a large well-organised working-class may fuel middle-class fears and resentments (as did attempted socialist insurrections in parts of Germany throughout Weimar), the experience of British working-class leaders and their comparative compliance, particularly during the General Strike of 1926, had diminished such a possibility. Traditional working-class loyalties proved a successful bulwark against the blandishments of the BUF. They made little progress in areas worst hit by unemployment. Scotland, South Wales and the North East were strong working-class and Labour strongholds, and the BUF 'was popularly identified as a middle-class movement'.[51]

Economic conditions   One of the essential requirements for fascist movements is economic crisis. There is a clear association between the depression of the 1920s and 1930s and the popular attractiveness of the extreme Right in many European countries. In Germany Hitler's National Socialist party attained its massive momentum between 1928 and 1932, the years of highest unemployment.

There is evidence, however, that the economic depression was never as severe in Britain as in other industrial countries, partly because of the absence of a comparative boom in the early 1920s. Glynn and Oxborrow have argued that popular impressions of economic gloom and depression in the inter-war years are somewhat misleading for Britain, and are hardly supported by economic analysis:

> The inter-war years present a paradox in British history. The popular image is of a period of depression and distress at home, with a gathering storm of fascism abroad. On the other hand, to set against that image is the record of economic growth. This record suggests that the inter-war years were a period of economic progress, with rising material standards.[52]

Between 1871 and 1901 per capita GDP in both Germany and the USA grew faster than in Britain, the USA at 2·5 per cent and Germany at 1·9 per cent. In the inter-war years the difference disappears and Britain's growth rate, relative to Germany and the USA, was higher than it had been in the nineteenth century:

> In Germany, the volume of total output did not recover its pre-war value until 1927, due to hyper-inflation, the French occupation of the Ruhr and other disturbances consequent upon the war . . . Between 1931 and 1933 German output had fallen again below the 1913 level.

Glynn and Oxborrow go on to conclude that 'it becomes clear that both historically and compared with other countries the British growth performance in the inter-war years was relatively good'.[53]

Other indices reveal a similar picture. Britain was relatively alone in guarding consumer expenditure against the depression. As a large importer of foodstuffs, and with a small agricultural sector, the fall in the price of primary goods proved quite beneficial and although overall world demand for industrial production fell, this harmed other countries more. By 1931 the annual wheat import into the United Kingdom was costing £60m less than in 1925, and £30m less than in 1929, whilst the price of a given basket of common foodstuffs fell between 1927 and 1933 by 25 per cent.[54]

This fall in food prices, which benefited poorer families most because they represented a larger than average proportion of expenditure, ensured a continuous rise in working-class living standards from 1924 onwards. Similarly, the middle-classes were relatively untouched by the depression compared with their European neighbours. Apart from escaping the worst of unemployment (the 1931 Census discovered a rate of 30 per cent for unskilled manual workers, and 5 per cent for clerks and higher office workers), the general level of salaries changed little in money terms throughout the period. Furthermore, there was a clear regional imbalance in levels of hardship. Whilst the national average for unemployment stood at 16 per cent in 1930, it reached 25 per cent in the North East, the North West and Wales; in London and the South East it stayed at 8 per cent.

Unemployment as a proportion of total labour force, 1931–33

	UK	Germany
1931	12·6	13·9
1932	13·1	17·2
1933	11·7	14·8

Source: A. Maddison, *Economic Growth in the West* (1964), reproduced in Glynn and Oxborrow, *Interwar Britain* (1976).

Regional unemployment rates, 1930

	Percentage of insured workforce unemployed
National average	16·1
London	8·1
South East	8·0
South West	10·4
Midlands	14·7
North East	20·2
North West	23·8
Scotland	18·5
Wales	25·9

Source: W. Beveridge, *Full Employment in a Free Society* (1944), reproduced in Glynn and Oxborrow.

Thus whilst in Germany, in the period up to Hitler's assumption of power in 1933, reparations and war debts made the depression much worse for all classes, all the political and economic indicators were against Mosley as he sought to build up fascism in Britain in the early 1930s.

217

Since 1945 extreme rightism in Britain has been operating in an altered context to that prevailing in the inter-war years. Racialism and resentment of coloured immigration and loss of Empire are characteristic features of those parties on the extreme Right portrayed by Nugent.[55] Whilst the BUF's activists were middle-class and professional, groups such as the National Front appear to reveal a larger working-class, frequently ex-Labour, composition. Hanna, Nugent and Scott all suggest that both the National Front and the National Party appear to be predominantly lower middle- or working-class as regards membership.[56] Butler and Kavanagh's breakdown of the background of National Front candidates at the October 1974 election shows that whilst the professional/business categories were over-represented (42 per cent), as in other parties, the proportion of workers (40 per cent) was second only to that in the Communist Party.[57]

Nevertheless, it would be wrong to argue from this that recent extreme rightism has little in common with classical fascism's attraction for middle-class authoritarians. It has been argued here that if deference does facilitate extreme rightism, it is more likely to be a middle-class phenomenon. This is not to suggest that all extreme rightists are necessarily middle-class and deferential/authoritarian, but rather that it is reasonable to predict that some are. Recent attention given to the undoubted appeal of parties like the National Front and the National Party to sections of the working-class may obscure the continuing role that the middle-class play in such organisations.

In his Fettlerbridge sample Scott clearly identifies amongst his core of about twenty regular NF activists a middle-class group of five or six persons who effectively controlled the branch. Significantly, too, the working-class group, those that carried out 'a substantial proportion of the work of the branch', came from 'above the lowest skill areas'. As Scott remarks, this part of the working-class is where one might expect 'social and economic tensions to be greatest'. One might also expect such a group to experience the same fears and worries about their class and status position as the middle-class elite who, says Scott, 'expressed a concern about their place in society and the differing ways in which they were being threatened'.[58]

Branches other than Fettlerbridge, 'a medium sized industrial town North of London', may have a larger middle-class component. Hanna has pointed to the predominantly middle-class membership of National Front branches in places such as the London boroughs of Camden and Brent and South Coast towns like Worthing.

Finally, as Nugent rightly suggests, it is easy to ignore the long term view in accounting for the electoral support of the extreme Right. The recent ability of the National Front to take votes away from Labour in local elections may have been exaggerated by the large Labour gains in previous elections. This situation may change. Richardson and Lethbridge's study of the vote for the British Campaign to Stop Immigration in 1971 showed that it came disproportionately from the Tories.[64] This was a period of Conservative government and at a time when they were defending huge gains from previous local polls.

The relationship between deference, authoritarianism and middle-class support for extreme rightism still seems worth exploring, particularly the role of middle-class activists in parties like the National Front, although with a different theoretical emphasis to that found in the works of Shils and Lipset. Economic crises and social change, declining living standards and the perceived threat from organised workers are likely to feed still further the authoritarian dreams of those individuals acutely conscious of their declining place in the ordered scheme of things.

Notes

[1] See the collection of essays edited by D. Bell, *The Radical Right*, Anchor Books, New York 1963.
[2] S. M. Lipset, *Political Man*, Heinemann, London 1960.
[3] Ibid., p. 133.
[4] Ibid., p. 137.
[5] Ibid., pp. 140–9.
[6] R. Benewick, *The Fascist Movement in Britain*, Penguin, London 1972, p. 13.
[7] E. Fromm, *The Fear of Freedom*, Routledge and Kegan Paul, London 1960.
[8] W. Kornhauser, *The Politics of Mass Society*, Routledge and Kegan Paul, London 1960.
[9] N. Poulantzas, *Fascism and Dictatorship*, New Left Books, London 1974.
[10] Ibid., p. 4.
[11] S. M. Lipset and E. Raab, *The Politics of Unreason: Right Wing Extremism in America 1790–1970*, Heinemann, London 1971.
[12] K. Newton, 'Community decision-making in Britain and the United States', in T. Clark (ed.), *Comparative Community Politics*, Sage Publications, California 1974.
[13] S. M. Lipset, 'Working class authoritarianism', in *Political Man*, op. cit.

[14] Ibid., p. 100.

[15] Ibid.

[16] S. M. Lipset, 'Anglo-American society', in David L. Sills (ed.), *International Encyclopaedia of the Social Sciences*, Macmillan and the Free Press, New York 1968; E. Shils, *The Torment of Secrecy*, Free Press, Glencoe 1956.

[17] Shils, pp. 48–9.

[18] Ibid., p. 41.

[19] S. M. Lipset, *The First New Nation*, Heinemann, London 1963, p. 297.

[20] Lipset and Raab, op. cit., p. 24.

[21] Ibid., p. 29.

[22] Ibid., p. 13.

[23] D. Kavanagh, 'The deferential English: a comparative perspective', *Government and Opposition*, vol. 6, 1971, pp. 333–60; L. Sharpe, 'American democracy reconsidered', *British Journal of Political Science*, vol. 3, Jan. and April 1973.

[24] Lipset and Raab, op. cit., p. 173.

[25] Ibid., pp. 224–5 and 227.

[26] Ibid., pp. 358–9 and 361.

[27] G. Almond and S. Verba, *The Civic Culture*, Princeton University Press, Princeton 1963.

[28] Ibid., p. 327

[29] R. Alford, *Party and Society*, Murray, London 1963, p. 98.

[30] L. Epstein, *Political Parties in Western Democracies*, Pall Mall Press, London 1967, p. 188; Newton, op. cit.; and Sharp, op. cit.

[31] Epstein, op. cit., p. 194.

[32] Shils, op. cit., p. 105.

[33] W. Miller and D. Stokes, 'Constituency influence in Congress', in A. Campbell et al., *Elections and the Political Order*, Wiley, New York 1966, p. 368.

[34] H. Hyman, 'The value systems of social classes', in R. Bendix and S. M. Lipset, *Class, Status and Power*, Free Press, Glencoe 1953, p. 427.

[35] E. Macoby, 'Class differences in boys' choice of authority roles', in R. Coser (ed.), *Life Cycle and Achievement in America*, Harper, New York 1969, p. 46.

[36] M. Kohn, 'Social class and parent–child relationships', in Coser, op. cit., p. 35.

[37] Lipset and Raab, op. cit., p. 30.

[38] See R. Wolfinger et al., 'America's radical right: politics and ideology', in D. Apter (ed.), *Ideology and Discontent*, Free Press, New York 1964.

[39] Benewick, op. cit., p. 112.

[40] W. F. Mandle, 'The leadership of the British Union of Fascists', *Australian Journal of Politics and History*, December 1966.

[41] Kavanagh, op. cit., pp. 348–9.

[42] Ibid., p. 334.

[43] D. Butler and D. Stokes, *Political Change in Britain*, Penguin, London 1971, pp. 148–9.

[44] R. Jessop, *Traditionalism, Conservatism and the British Political Culture*, Cambridge University Press, London 1974.

[45] E. Shils, 'Deference', in J. A. Jackson (ed.), *Social Stratification*, Cambridge University Press, London 1968.

[46] Lipset, *Political Man*, op. cit., pp. 140–52.

[47] Jessop, op. cit., p. 138.

[48] K. Bracher, *The German Dictatorship*, Penguin, London 1973.

[49] S. Woolf (ed.), *European Fascism*, Weidenfeld and Nicolson, London 1970.

[50] Benewick, op. cit., p. 13.

[51] Ibid., p. 112.

[52] S. Glynn and J. Oxborrow, *Interwar Britain: A Social and Economic History*, Allen and Unwin, London 1976, p. 13.

[53] Ibid., pp. 20–1.

[54] Glynn and Oxborrow, op. cit., p. 74.

[55] See ch. 7 of this book.

[56] M. Hanna, 'The rise of the National Front', *New Community*, vol. 3, nos. 1–2, 1974; Nugent, ch. 7 of this book; and D. Scott, 'The National Front in local politics: some interpretations', in I. Crewe (ed.), *British Political Sociology Yearbook*, vol. 2, Croom Helm, London 1975.

[57] D. Butler and D. Kavanagh, *The British General Election of October 1974*, Macmillan, London 1975, p. 216.

[58] Scott, op. cit., p. 226.

[59] C. Richardson and J. Lethbridge, 'The anti-immigrant vote in Bradford', *Race Today*, vol. 4, no. 4, 1972.

Bibliography

Ch. 1   The concept of the Right

Bell, D., *The Radical Right*, Doubleday, New York 1963.
Beer, S., *Modern British Politics*, Faber, London 1969.
Brittan, S., *Left or Right. The Bogus Dilemma*, Secker and Warburg, London 1968.
Caute, D., *The Left in Europe*, Weidenfeld and Nicolson, London 1966.
Hayes, P., *Fascism*, Allen and Unwin, London 1973.
Lipset, S., and Raab, E., *The Politics of Unreason; Right Wing Extremism in America 1790–1970*, Heinemann, London 1971.
McClelland, J. S., *The French Right*, Cape, London 1970. This book is part of the 'Roots of the Right' series. All these can be usefully consulted, especially the introductions by the editors of each volume.
Remond, R., *The Right Wing in France*, University of Pennsylvania Press, Philadelphia 1969.
Rogger, H., and Weber, E., *The European Right*, Weidenfeld and Nicolson, London 1965.
Smith, D., *Left and Right in Europe*, Longman, London.
Viereck, P., *Conservatism*, Van Nostrand, Toronto 1956.
Weber, E., *Varieties of Fascism*, Van Nostrand, Toronto 1964.

Ch. 2   Conservatism

A useful detailed bibliography can be found in G. D. M. Block, 'A source book of conservatism', Conservative Political Centre (CPC) 1964.
Blake, R., *The Conservative Party from Peel to Churchill*, Fontana, London 1972.
Buck, P. W. (ed.), *How Conservatives Think*, Penguin, London 1975.
Butler, Sir G., 'The Tory tradition', CPC 1957.
Cecil, Lord H., *Conservatism*, Home University Library, London 1912.
Epstein, L. D., 'The politics of British conservatism', *American Political Science Review*, March 1954.
Glickman, H., 'The Toryness of English conservatism', *Journal of British Studies*, November 1961.
Hailsham, Viscount, *The Conservative Case*, Penguin, London 1959.

Harris, N., *Competition and the Corporate Society*, University Paperback, London 1973.

Howell, D., 'Modern conservatism in search of its principles', *Crossbow*, July–Sept. 1963.

Huntington, S. P., 'Conservatism as an ideology', *American Political Science Review*, vol. 6, 1957.

Kirk, R., *The Conservative Mind*, Faber, London 1954.

Mannheim, K., 'Conservative thought', in *Essays on Sociology and Social Psychology*, Routledge and Kegan Paul, London 1953.

Oakeshott, M., *Rationalism in Politics*, University Paperback, London 1967.

Patterson, B., 'The character of conservatism', CPC 1973.

Rose, R., 'Tensions in Conservative philosophy', *Political Quarterly*, vol. 32, 1961.

Viereck, P., *Conservatism*, Van Nostrand Reinhold Ltd, Anvil Books, New York 1956.

White, R. J. (ed.), *The Conservative Tradition*, Black, London 1950.

The New Conservatism; An Anthology of Post-war Thought, CPC, 1955.

Ch. 3   The Conservative Party: from Macmillan to Thatcher

Bogdanor, V., and Skidelsky, R. (eds), *The Age of Affluence, 1951–1954*, Macmillan, London 1970.

Bruce-Gardyne, J., *Whatever Happened to the Quiet Revolution?*, Knight, London 1974.

Butler, D., and Pinto-Duschinsky, M., *The British General Election of 1970*, Macmillan, London 1971.

Gamble, A., *The Conservative Nation*, Routledge and Kegan Paul, London 1974.

Greenwood, J., 'The Conservative Party and the working class – the organisational response', University of Warwick, Department of Politics Working Paper no. 2, June 1974.

Harris, N., *Competition and the Corporate Society*, Methuen, London 1972.

King, A., 'The changing Tories', in J. D. Lees and R. Kimber, *Political Parties in Modern Britain*, Routledge and Kegan Paul, London 1972.

Leruez, J., *Economic Planning and Politics in Britain*, Martin Robertson, London 1975.

Macmillan, H., *Riding the Storm*, Macmillan, London 1971.

Macmillan, H., *Pointing the Way*, Macmillan, London 1972.

Macmillan, H., *At the End of the Day*, Macmillan, London 1973.

McKie, D., and Cook, C. (eds), *The Decade of Disillusion: British Politics in the Sixties*, Macmillan, London 1972.

Moran, M., *The Politics of Industrial Relations*, Macmillan (forthcoming).

National Union of Conservative and Unionist Associations, *Handbooks* and *Verbatim Reports*, 1957–75.

Pahl, R. E., and Winkler, J. T., 'The coming corporatism', *New Society*, 10 October 1974.

Peston, M., 'Conservative economic policy and philosophy', *Political Quarterly*, vol. 44, 1973, pp. 411–24.

Pinto-Duschinsky, M., 'Central office and "power" in the Conservative Party', *Political Studies*, vol. 20, no. 1, 1972, pp. 1–16.

Rose, R., 'The Bow Group's role in British politics', *Western Political Quarterly*, vol. 14, no. 4, 1961, pp. 865–78.

Sampson, A., *Macmillan: A Study of Ambiguity*, Allen Lane, London 1967.

Seyd, P., 'Democracy within the Conservative Party?', *Government and Opposition*, vol. 10, no. 2, Spring 1975, pp. 219–39.

Seyd, P., 'Factionalism within the Conservative Party: the Monday Club', *Government and Opposition*, vol. 7, no. 4, Autumn 1972, pp. 464–87.

Wilson, D. J., and Pinto-Duschinsky, M., 'Conservative city machines: the end of an era', *British Journal of Political Science*, vol. 6, part 2, April 1976, pp. 239–44.

Young, S., and Lowe, A. V., *Intervention in the Mixed Economy*, Croom Helm, London 1974.

Ch. 4   Grass roots conservatism

Because of the paucity of material this bibliography appears in note form.

The major sources of information are the National Union of Conservative and Unionist Associations' Handbooks and *Verbatim Reports*, 1945–73. Of other material on this particular aspect of grass roots conservatism Richard Rose's writings are virtually unique: 'Who are the Tory militants?', *Crossbow*, vol. 5, no. 17, 1961, pp. 35–9; and 'The political ideas of English party activists', *American Political Science Review*, vol. 56, no. 2, June 1962, pp. 360–71; see also his *The Problem of Party Government*, Macmillan, London 1974.

Other publications which are marginally useful are J. Critchley, 'Stresses and strains in the Conservative Party', *Political Quarterly*, vol. 44, 1973, pp. 401–10; W. Deedes, 'Conflicts within the Conservative Party', *Political Quarterly*, vol. 44, 1973; R. Hornby, 'Conservative principles', *Political Quarterly*, vol. 32, 1961, pp. 229–37; R. Rose, 'Tensions in Conservative philosophy', *Political Quarterly*, vol. 32, 1961, pp. 275–83; P. Seyd, 'Case study – democracy within the Conservative Party', *Government and Opposition*, vol. 10, 1975, pp. 219–37; and 'Factionalism within the Conservative Party:

the Monday Club', *Government and Opposition*, vol. 7, 1972, pp. 464–87.

The major bibliographical source for marginally relevant publications, written either by commentators or Conservatives themselves, is A. Gamble, *The Conservative Nation*, Routledge and Kegan Paul, London 1974.

On the issue of Conservative ideology – particularly libertarianism – Gamble's book is of course useful, as are S. H. Beer, *Modern British Politics*, Faber, London 1975; and N. Harris, *Competition and the Corporate Society*, Methuen, London 1972. But especially important is W. H. Greenleaf, 'The character of modern British conservatism', in R. Benewick, R. N. Berki and B. Parekh (eds), *Knowledge and Belief in Politics*, Allen and Unwin, London 1973, p. 178. Interesting insights are also provided by M. Peston, 'Conservative economic policy and philosophy', *Political Quarterly*, vol. 44, 1973, pp. 411–24, and by the numerous contemporary articles by Conservatives in various journals and newspapers, particularly those in *The Times*, *Sunday Times*, *Daily Telegraph* and *The Spectator*.

Ch. 5   Powellism

Published works of Enoch Powell and edited collections of his speeches and writings (listed chronologically).

Powell, J. E., 'Conservatives and the social services', *Political Quarterly*, vol. 24, no. 2, April–June 1953, pp. 156–66.

Powell, J. E., and Macleod, I., 'Social Services: Needs and Means', CPC pamphlet no. 115, 2nd revised ed., 1954.

Maude, A., and Powell, J. E., *Biography of a Nation*, Berker, London 1955.

Powell, J. E., '1951–9. Labour in opposition', *Political Quarterly*, vol. 30, no. 1, Jan.–Mar. 1959, pp. 336–43.

Powell, J. E., 'The limits of laissez-faire', *Crossbow*, vol. 11, 1960.

Powell, J. E., *Great Parliamentary Occasions*, Jenkins, London 1960.

Powell, J. E., 'The Welfare State', CPC pamphlet no. 245, 1961.

Powell, J. E., 'The social services', *The Spectator*, 12 June 1964, pp. 783–5.

Powell, J. E., 'Is it politically practicable', in A. Seldon (ed.), *Rebirth of Britain*, Pan, London 1964.

Powell, J. E., and Ridley, N., 'One Europe', CPC pamphlet, 1965.

Wood, J. (ed.), *A Nation Not Afraid*, Batsford, London 1965.

Powell, J. E., 'Savings in a free society', Institute of Economic Affairs, London 1966.

Powell, J. E., *A New Look at Medicine and Politics*, Pitman Medical, London 1966. 'Exchange rates and liquidity', Institute of Economic Affairs, London 1967.

Powell, J. E., and Wallis, K., *The House of Lords in the Middle Ages*, Weidenfeld and Nicolson, London 1968.

Wood, J. (ed.), *Freedom and Reality*, Batsford, London 1969.

Wood, J. (ed.), *Powell and the 1970 Election*, Elliot Rightway, London 1970.

Stacey, T. (ed.), *Immigration and Enoch Powell*, Stacey, London 1970.

Lejeune, A. (ed.), *Income Tax at 4/3 in the £*, Stacey, London 1970.

Powell, J. E., *The Common Market. The Case Against*, Elliot Rightway, London 1971.

Wood, J. (ed.), *Still to Decide*, Batsford, London 1972.

Powell, J. E., *No Easy Answers*, Sheldon, London 1973.

Powell, J. E., *The Common Market. Renegotiate or Come Out*, Elliot Rightway, London 1973.

Major studies and commentaries on Enoch Powell.

Foot, P., *The Rise of Enoch Powell*, Penguin, London 1969.

Johnson, R. W., and Schoen, D., 'The "Powell Effect": or how one man can win', *New Society*, 22 July 1976.

King, R., and Wood, M., 'The Support for Enoch Powell', in I. Crewe (ed.), *British Political Sociology Yearbook 1975*, Croom Helm, London 1975.

Nairn, T., 'Enoch Powell. The New Right', *New Left Review*, vol. 61, 1971, pp. 3–27.

Roth, A., *Enoch Powell. Tory Tribune*, Macdonald, London 1972.

Smithies, B., and Fiddick, P., *Enoch Powell and Immigration*, Sphere, London 1969.

Spearman, D., 'Enoch Powell's postbag', *New Society*, 9 May 1968.

Studler, D., 'British public opinion, colour issue and Enoch Powell. A longitudinal analysis', *British Journal of Political Science*, June 1974, p. 379.

Utley, T., *Enoch Powell. The Man and His Thinking*, Kimber, London 1968.

Ch. 6   The British Union of Fascists

Primary sources:

Action, February 1936 – June 1940.

Blackshirt, February 1933 – May 1939.

British Union of Fascists, *Britain and Jewry*, Abbey Supplies, London, n.d.

BUF, *British Union Quarterly*, 1937–40 (a number of important articles).

BUF, 'The Empire and the British Union', 1937.

BUF, 'Fascism and agriculture', n.d.

BUF, 'The miners' only hope', n.d.

Chesteron, A. K., *Oswald Mosley: Portrait of a Leader*, Action Press, London 1937.

Drennan, J., *B.U.F., Oswald Mosley and British Fascism*, Murray, London 1934.

Fascist Week, November 1933 – May 1934.

Fascist Quarterly, January 1935 – October 1936 (a number of important articles).

Joyce, W., *Dictatorship*, BUF Publications, London 1933.

Joyce, W., *Fascism and Jewry*, BUF publications, London 1936

Joyce, W., *Fascism and India*, BUF Publications, London 1933.

Mosley, Sir Oswald, *Blackshirt Policy*, BUF Publications, London (no date but almost certainly 1933).

Mosley, Sir Oswald, *The British Peace – How to Get It*, Greater Britain Publications (no date but definitely late 1939).

Mosley, Sir Oswald, *Fascism: 100 Questions Asked and Answered*, BUF Publications, London 1936.

Mosley, Sir Oswald, *Fascism Explained: Ten Points of Fascist Policy*, 1933.

Mosley, Sir Oswald, *Fascism in Britain* (no date but almost certainly 1933).

Mosley, Sir Oswald, *The Greater Britain*, BUF Publications, London 1932 and 1934 eds.

Mosley, Sir Oswald, *Mosley's Message to British Union Members and Supporters*, BUF Publications, London 1939.

Mosley, Sir Oswald, 'Revolution by reason', Birmingham Labour Party 1925.

Mosley, Sir Oswald, *Tomorrow We Live*, Greater Britain Publications, London 1936 and 1938 eds.

Raven Thomson, A., *The Coming Corporate State*, Greater Britain Publications, London 1937.

House of Commons Debates, 5th series, vols. 167–259 (1923–30).

The Times, 1932–40.

Secondary sources:

An extensive bibliography appears in Benewick. Included here are only those sources which are of particular relevance to the study of the ideas.

Benewick, R., *Political Violence and Public Order*, Penguin, London 1969.

Benewick, R., 'Interpretations of British Fascism', *Political Studies*, September 1976.

Bogdanor, V., 'A deeply flawed hero', *Encounter*, June 1975.

Cross, C., *The Fascists in Britain*, Barrie and Rockliff, London 1961.

Greiger, D. M., 'British Fascism as revealed in the British Union of Fascists' press', unpublished PhD thesis, New York University 1965.

Mandle, W. F., *Anti-Semitism and the British Union of Fascists*, Longman, London 1968.

Mandle, W. F., 'The leadership of the British Union of Fascists', *Australian Journal of Politics and History*, December 1966.

Mosley, Sir Oswald, *Mosley: The Facts*, Euphorion Distribution, London 1957.

Mosley, Sir Oswald, *My Answer*, Mosley Publications, London 1946.

Mosley, Sir Oswald, *My Life*, Nelson, London 1968.

Mullaby, F., *Fascism Inside England*, Claude Morris Books, London 1946.

Semmel, B., *Imperialism and Social Reform*, Allen and Unwin, London 1960.

Skidelsky, R., 'Great Britain', in S. J. Woolf (ed.), *European Fascism*, Weidenfeld and Nicolson, London 1968.

Skidelsky, R., *Oswald Mosley*, Macmillan, London 1975.

Weber, E., *Varieties of Fascism*, Van Nostrand, London 1964.

Ch. 7   The political parties of the extreme Right

Primary sources:

The journals of the organisations themselves include:

British Movement, *British Patriot* (monthly).
National Front, *Spearhead* (monthly), and *National Front News* (monthly).
National Party, *Britain First* (monthly).
Union Movement, *Action* (fortnightly).

Secondary sources:

Barker, D., 'On the patriotic frontier', *The Guardian*, 2 June 1972.

Cockerell, M., 'Inside the National Front', *The Listener*, 28 December 1972.

Cross, C., 'Britain's racialists', *New Society*, 3 June 1965.

Deakin, N. (ed.), *Colour and the British Electorate*, Pall Mall Press, London 1965.

Eisenberg, D., *The Re-emergence of Fascism*, MacGibbon and Kee, London 1967.

Foot, P., *Immigration and Race in British Politics*, Penguin, London 1965.

Glass, R., *Newcomers*, Centre for Urban Studies, and Allen and Unwin, London 1960.

Hanna, M., 'The National Front and other right wing organisations', *New Community*, vol. 3, Winter–Spring 1974.

Husbands, C. T., 'The National Front: a response to crisis?', *New Society*, 15 May 1975.

Richardson, C. T., and Lethbridge, J., 'The anti-immigrant vote in Bradford', *Race Today*, April 1972.

Rogger, H., and Weber, E., *The European Right*, Weidenfeld and Nicolson, London 1965.

Rose, E. J. B., et al., *Colour and Citizenship*, Oxford University Press, Oxford 1969.

Scott, D., 'The National Front in local politics', in I. Crewe (ed.), *British Political Sociology Yearbook*, vol. 2, Croom Helm, London 1975.

Skidelsky, R., *Oswald Mosley*, Macmillan, London 1975.

Thayer, G., *The British Political Fringe*, Blond, London 1965.

'The British Campaign to Stop Immigration: A pressure group at the polls', *Race Today*, June 1972.

General election results appear in the Nuffield Studies.

In addition to the above, articles frequently appear in *Private Eye* and the left wing anti-fascist press; much of it, however, is little more than uninformed polemics. *Searchlight*, published by A.F. and R. Publications of Birmingham, is concerned almost solely with 'exposing' the activities of the ultra Right.

Ch. 8 Support for fascism and the radical Right

Adorno, T., et al., *The Authoritarian Personality*, Harper, New York, 1950.

Alford, R., *Party and Society*, Murray, London 1963.

Allardyce, G. (ed.), *The Place of Fascism in European History*, Prentice Hall, New Jersey 1971.

Almond, G., and Verba, S., *The Civic Culture*, Princeton University Press, Princeton 1963.

Apter, D. (ed.), *Ideology and Discontent*, Free Press, New York 1964.

Bell, D. (ed.), *The Radical Right*, Anchor Books, New York 1963.

Benewick, R., *The Fascist Movement in Britain*, Penguin, London 1972.

Bracher, K., *The German Dictatorship*, Penguin, London 1973.

Butler, D., and Stokes, D., *Political Change in Britain*, Penguin, London 1971.

Cammet, J., 'Communist theories of fascism, 1920–1935' in *Science and Society*, vol. 2, no. 1, 1967, pp. 149–63.

Campbell, A., et al., *Elections and the Political Order*, Wiley, New York 1966.

Christie, R., and Jahoda, M. (eds), Studies in the Scope and Method of *'The Authoritarian Personality'*, Free Press, New York 1954.

Clark, T. (ed.), *Comparative Community Politics*, Sage Publications, California 1974.

Cross, C., *The Fascists in Britain*, Barrie and Rockcliff, London 1961.

Epstein, L., *Political Parties in Western Democracies*, Pall Mall Press, London 1967.

Fromm, E., *The Fear of Freedom*, Routledge and Kegan Paul, London 1960.

Glynn, S., and Oxborrow, J., *Interwar Britain: A Social and Economic History*, Allen and Unwin, London 1976.

Jessop, R., *Traditionalism, Conservatism and the British Political Culture*, Cambridge University Press, London 1974.

Kavanagh, D., 'The deferential English: a comparative perspective', *Government and Opposition*, vol. 6, 1971.

Kitchen, M., *Fascism*, Macmillan, London 1976.

Kohn, M., 'Social class and parent–child relationships', in R. Coser (ed.), *Life Cycle and Achievement in America*, Harper, New York 1969.

Kornhauser, W., *The Politics of Mass Society*, Routledge and Kegan Paul, London 1960.

Lane, R., *Political Ideology*, Free Press, Glencoe 1962.

Lipset, S. M., *Political Man*, Heinemann, London 1960.

Lipset, S. M., *The First New Nation*, Heinemann, London 1963.

Lipset, S. M., 'Anglo-American society', in David L. Sills (ed.), *International Encyclopaedia of the Social Sciences*, Macmillan and the Free Press, New York 1968.

Lipset, S. M., and Raab, E., *The Politics of Unreason: Right-Wing Extremism in America 1790–1970*, Heinemann, London 1971.

Maccoby, E., 'Class differences in boys' choice of authority roles', in R. Coser (ed.), *Life Cycle and Achievement in America*, Harper, New York 1969, p. 46.

Mandle, W. F., *Anti-Semitism and the British Union of Fascists*, Longman, London 1968.

Mandle, W. F., 'The leadership of the British Union of Fascists', *Australian Journal of Politics and History*, December 1966.

Moore, B., *Social Origins of Dictatorship and Democracy*, Penguin, London 1967.

Neumann, F., *Behemoth: The Structure and Practice of National Socialism*, Gollancz, London 1942.

Poulantzas, N., *Fascism and Dictatorship*, New Left Books, London 1974.

Richardson, C., and Lethbridge, J., 'The anti-immigrant vote in Bradford', *Race Today*, vol. 4, no. 4, 1972.

Rose, R., *Governing Without Consensus: An Irish Perspective*, Faber, London 1971.

Scott, D., 'The National Front in local politics: some interpretations', in I. Crewe (ed.), *British Political Sociology Yearbook*, vol. 2, Croom Helm, London 1975.

Sharpe, L., 'American democracy reconsidered', *British Journal of Political Science*, vol. 3, Jan. and April 1973.

Shils, E., *The Torment of Secrecy*, Free Press, Glencoe 1956.

The editors

Roger King is Principal Lecturer in Sociology at Huddersfield Polytechnic
Neill Nugent is Senior Lecturer in Politics at Manchester Polytechnic

The contributors

Rab Bennett is Lecturer in Politics at Manchester Polytechnic
Ken Phillips is Senior Lecturer in Politics at Preston Polytechnic
Mike Wilson is Senior Lecturer in Politics at Preston Polytechnic